Immanence – Deleuze and Philosophy

Plateaus – New Directions in Deleuze Studies

'It's not a matter of bringing all sorts of things together under a single concept but rather of relating each concept to variables that explain its mutations.'
Gilles Deleuze, *Negotiations*

Series Editors
Ian Buchanan, University of Wollongong
Claire Colebrook, Penn State University

Editorial Advisory Board
Keith Ansell Pearson
Ronald Bogue
Constantin V. Boundas
Rosi Braidotti
Eugene Holland
Gregg Lambert
Dorothea Olkowski
Paul Patton
Daniel Smith
James Williams

Titles available in the series

Dorothea Olkowski, *The Universal (In the Realm of the Sensible): Beyond Continental Philosophy*
Christian Kerslake, *Immanence and the Vertigo of Philosophy: From Kant to Deleuze*
Jean-Clet Martin, *Variations: The Philosophy of Gilles Deleuze*, translated by Constantin V. Boundas and Susan Dyrkton
Simone Bignall, *Postcolonial Agency: Critique and Constructivism*
Miguel de Beistegui, *Immanence – Deleuze and Philosophy*
Jean-Jacques Lecercle, *Badiou and Deleuze Read Literature*
Ronald Bogue, *Deleuzian Fabulation and the Scars of History*
Sean Bowden, *The Priority of Events: Deleuze's Logic of Sense*
Craig Lundy, *History and Becoming: Deleuze's Philosophy of Creativity*
Aidan Tynan, *Deleuze's Literary Clinic: Criticism and the Politics of Symptoms*

Visit the Plateaus website at www.euppublishing.com/series/plat

IMMANENCE –
DELEUZE AND PHILOSOPHY

Miguel de Beistegui

EDINBURGH UNIVERSITY PRESS

© Miguel de Beistegui, 2010, 2012

First published in hardback by Edinburgh University Press 2010

Edinburgh University Press Ltd
22 George Square, Edinburgh EH8 9LF

www.euppublishing.com

Typeset in Sabon
by Servis Filmsetting Ltd, Stockport, Cheshire

A CIP record for this book is available from the British Library

ISBN 978 0 7486 3830 7 (hardback)
ISBN 978 0 7486 4906 8 (paperback)

The right of Miguel de Beistegui
to be identified as author of this work
has been asserted in accordance with
the Copyright, Designs and Patents Act 1988.

Contents

List of Abbreviations	vi
Preface	ix
Introduction	1
1　Noology	5
2　Ontology I: Genesis	24
3　Ontology II: Cartography	47
4　Logic	77
5　Ethics	107
6　Aesthetics	160
Conclusion	192
Bibliography	196
Index	203

List of Abbreviations

Works by Gilles Deleuze

C-1   *Cinéma-1: L'Image-mouvement* (Paris: Les Éditions de Minuit, 1983). Trans. H. Tomlinson and B. Habberjam, *Cinema-1: The Movement-Image* (London: The Athlone Press, 1986).

C-2   *Cinéma-2: L'Image-temps* (Paris: Les Éditions de Minuit, 1986). Trans. H. Tomlinson and R. Galeta, *Cinema-2: The Time-Image* (London: The Athlone Press, 1989).

DI   *L'Île déserte et autres texts, textes et entretiens 1953–1974* (Paris: Les Éditions de Minuit, 2002). Trans. M. Taormina, *Desert Islands and Other Texts* (New York: Semiotext(e), 2003).

DR   *Différence et répétition* (Paris: Presses Universitaires de France, 1968). Trans. P. Patton, *Difference and Repetition* (New York: Columbia University Press, 1994).

EPS   *Spinoza et le problème de l'expression* (Paris: Les Éditions de Minuit, 1969). Trans. M. Joughin, *Expressionism in Philosophy: Spinoza* (New York: Zone Books, 1990).

FB   *Francis Bacon: Logique de la sensation* (Paris: Éditions de la différence, 1981). Trans. D. Smith, *Francis Bacon: the Logic of Sensation* (London: Continuum, 2003).

KCP   *La Philosophie critique de Kant* (Paris: Presses Universitaires de France, 1963). Trans. H. Tomlinson and B. Habberjam, *Kant's Critical Philosophy* (Minneapolis: University of Minnesota Press, 1984).

LS   *Logique du Sens* (Paris: Éditions de Minuit, 1969). Trans. M. Lester with C. Stivale, *The Logic of Sense* (London: The Athlone Press, 1990).

List of Abbreviations

N	*Pourparlers 1972–1990* (Paris: Les Éditions de Minuit, 1990). Trans. M. Joughin, *Negotiations 1972–1990* (New York: Columbia University Press, 1995).
NP	*Nietzsche et la philosophie* (Paris: Presses Universitaires de France, 1962). Trans. H. Tomlinson, *Nietzsche and Philosophy* (New York: Columbia University Press, 1983).
PS	*Proust et les signes* (Paris: Presses Universitaires de France, 1970). Trans. R. Howard, *Proust and Signs* (London: The Athlone Press, 2000).
SPP	*Spinoza: Philosophie pratique* (Paris: Minuit, 1981). Trans. R. Hurley, *Spinoza: Practical Philosophy* (San Francisco: City Lights, 1988).
TRM	*Deux Régimes de fous, textes et entretiens 1975–1995* (Paris: Les Éditions de Minuit, 2003). Trans. A. Hodges and M. Taormina, *Two Regimes of Madness* (New York: Semiotext(e), 2006).

Works by Gilles Deleuze and Félix Guattari

AO	*Capitalisme et schizophrénie tome 1: l'Anti-Œdipe* (Paris: Les Éditions de Minuit, 1972). Trans. R. Hurley, M. Seem and H. Lane, *Anti-Oedipus: Capitalism and Schizophrenia* (London: The Athlone Press, 1984).
ATP	*Capitalisme et schizophrénie tome 2: Mille Plateaux* (Paris: Les Éditions de Minuit, 1980). Trans. B. Massumi, *A Thousand Plateaus: Capitalism and Schizophrenia* (London: The Athlone Press, 1988).
K	*Kafka: Pour une littérature mineure* (Paris: Les Éditions de Minuit, 1975). Trans. D. Polan, *Kafka: Toward a Minor Literature* (Minneapolis, MN: University of Minnesota Press, 1987).
WP	*Qu'est-ce que la philosophie?* (Paris: Minuit, 1991). Trans. G. Burchell and H. Tomlinson, *What is Philosophy?* (London: Verso, 1994).

Work by Gilles Deleuze and Claire Parnet

Dialogues	*Dialogues* (Paris: Flammarion, 1977). Trans. H. Tomlinson and B. Habberjam, *Dialogues* (New York: Columbia University Press, 1987).

Works by Jacques Lacan

Écrits *Écrits* (Paris: Éditions du Seuil, 1966). Trans. A. Sheridan, *Écrits: A Selection* (London: Tavistock, 1977).

Seminar I J. A. Miller, editor. *Le Séminaire de Jacques Lacan, Livre I : Les écrits techniques de Freud 1953–1954* (Paris: Éditions du Seuil, 1975).

Seminar II J. A. Miller, editor. *Le Séminaire de Jacques Lacan, Livre II: Le moi dans la théorie de Freud et dans la technique de la psychanalyse 1954–1955* (Paris: Éditions du Seuil, 1978). Trans. S. Tomaselli, with notes by J. Forrester, *The Seminar of Jacques Lacan, Book II: The Ego in Freud's Theory and in the Technique of Psychoanalysis, 1954–55* (New York & London: Norton, 1991).

Seminar III J. A. Miller, editor. *Le Séminaire de Jacques Lacan, Livre III: Les psychoses 1955–1956* (Paris: Éditions du Seuil, 1981). Trans. and notes R. Grigg, *The Seminar of Jacques Lacan, Book III: The Psychoses, 1955–56* (London: Routledge, 1993).

Seminar IV J. A. Miller, editor. *Le Séminaire de Jacques Lacan, Livre IV: La relation d'objet: Les psychoses 1956–1957* (Paris: Éditions du Seuil, 1994).

Seminar V J. A. Miller, editor. *Le Séminaire de Jacques Lacan, Livre V: Les formations de l'inconscient 1957–1958* (Paris: Éditions du Seuil, 1998).

Seminar VII J. A. Miller, editor. *Le Séminaire de Jacques Lacan, Livre VII: L'Éthique de la psychanalyse* (Paris: Éditions du Seuil, 1986). Trans. and notes D. Porter, *The Seminar of Jacques Lacan. Book VII: The Ethics of Psychoanalysis, 1959–1960* (London: Routledge: 1992).

Seminar XI J. A. Miller, editor. *Le Séminaire de Jacques Lacan, Livre XI: Les quatre concepts fondamentaux de la psychanalyse* (Paris: Éditions du Seuil, 1975). Trans. A. Sheridan, *The Four Fundamentals of Psychoanalysis* (New York: Norton, 1981).

All abbreviations will be followed by the French and English pagination.

Preface

This book follows from another, *Truth and Genesis*,[1] which identified the Deleuzian enterprise, as it is formulated in *Difference and Repetition*, with ontogenesis. Genesis, I argued, especially as exemplified in contemporary science, is precisely the aspect of being that Heidegger, in whose thought of the ontological difference the book as a whole is anchored, failed to thematise. Genesis signals the possibility of a genuine compatibility between ontology and science. The other key concept, truth, signalled the side or aspect of being that is irreducible to genesis, the Open (or difference) as such, to which philosophical thought, but also literature and art, respond. *Truth and Genesis* ends with a claim regarding the compatibility, and even the necessary link, between the two concepts, the two 'ways' of being, or nature. With respect to Deleuze himself, and to the extent that, from his thought as a whole, I had extracted only one of the ways of being, I needed to find out whether his ontology also contains elements that could relate to what, following Heidegger, I have called truth, or whether such an ontology is entirely confined to the project of ontogenesis. This book is the result of such a question. It claims that Deleuze's ontology indeed exceeds the boundaries of ontogenesis, and so confirms the intuition that governed *Truth and Genesis*, albeit with a different vocabulary. If I were to retain one concept to designate that other way – a way that can give the appearance of an absolute proximity with that of ontogenesis, yet one that involves a different orientation, and a different temporality – it would be that of *becoming*. At stake in such a concept is the possibility of experiencing the transcendental field of nature, being, or *matter*, itself, that is, in its raw, pre-individual state, and not, as in ontogenesis, of identifying the real conditions of experience, or the phenomenality of phenomena. In this book, then, the distinction shifts, from genesis and truth, to genesis and becoming, in what amounts to an intra-Deleuzian operation, and a further move into materialism, or, better said perhaps, a further move away from any opposition between idealism and materialism, or thought and being. To avoid the possible objection of a dualism of his thought, and to address the question of the impetus, or the intuition, behind genesis *and* becoming, this book takes the form of an investigation into *immanence* as the unsurpassable horizon of thought. Beneath genesis and becoming, and beneath the difference that relates them to one another, there is what Deleuze calls the plane of immanence, without which thought would be nothing.

Note

1. Miguel de Beistegui, *Truth and Genesis: Philosophy as Differential Ontology* (Bloomington & Indianapolis: Indiana University Press, 2004).

Introduction

Given the relatively recent nature of Deleuzian scholarship, and despite its impressive, almost exponential growth, we still lack a unified understanding of the significance of Deleuze's thought.[1] We still don't quite know what the name 'Deleuze' stands for, or the place we ought to give it in the history of thought. His is a thought that is in the process of being canonised, yet there seems to be little agreement as to what exactly is entering the canon. Of Deleuze, we could say what he himself said of Spinoza, to whom he devoted two books and many lecture courses: 'We have not yet begun to understand Spinoza, and I myself no more than others.'[2] In a way, the recent explosion of publications on Deleuze bears witness to this confusion, and this lack of agreement. At the same time, and almost paradoxically, Deleuze's thought seems to be facing a twofold danger. First, to the extent that its conceptuality underwent a series of (often abrupt) changes – the necessity of which Deleuze rarely felt the need or the desire to justify or clarify – we can easily have the impression of a thought that lacks coherence and unity. Second – and this only aggravates the first danger – because Deleuze writes about science, cinema, literature, the visual arts, economics, ethics and politics, as well as the history of philosophy, his thought runs the risk of being fragmented and distributed across those various fields, chopped into bits as it were. Here again, the literature bears witness to the extraordinary interest, and at times the fascination, which Deleuze's thought continues to generate in the humanities and the social sciences, comparable to that which Derrida generated between the 1970s and the 1990s. Now this wouldn't be a problem, were it not for the fact that Deleuze's commitment to philosophy as 'univocal ontology' aims to overcome the fragmented nature of today's epistemological field, and of philosophy itself. That being said, it cannot be a question of minimising the significance of the changes this thought undergoes: after all, how compatible are Deleuze's early insistence, say, in relation to Proust (1964), that thinking is interpretation, or a decoding of signs, and the later insistence, say, in *Capitalism and Schizophrenia*, and even in the later edition of

1

Proust and Signs (1970), that thought has nothing to do with interpretation, but is essentially a process of production and creation? Can we reconcile the image of the professor at the Sorbonne with that of the professor at Vincennes, the historian of philosophy of the early years with the *anarcho-désirant* of the 1970s? The greatest danger, then, in the context of the fragmentation and division of Deleuze's thought, is one of finding oneself in the situation of having to adopt one aspect or moment of his thought, before having had a chance to grasp it in its unity and inner consistency. This is the possibility I wish to explore. No doubt, it is a delicate task – extracting the consistency of a thought always is – made more complex by the extraordinary diversity and versatility of the thought we are confronted with.

In the course of this book, I shall try to understand something like the necessity of Deleuze's thought, something like that which, at the most fundamental level, a level that can only remain partially clarified by the thinker himself, motivates that thought, sets it in motion. I shall try to identify something like the original impetus or the driving force behind his philosophy as a whole, behind, that is, even its most abrupt and radical changes, and its boldest innovations. I am seeking to find a way through a philosophy in its entirety. Needless to say, this has nothing to do with an attempt to summarise or synthesise that thought, or to review all of Deleuze's published work. It has everything to do, however, with the possibility of extracting the inner *consistency* of his thought. To ask about the consistency of that thought, however, is tantamount to asking about the meaning of thought itself for Deleuze, and it is with this question that the book begins: What, exactly, does *thinking* mean for Deleuze? What – to use his own vocabulary – is the 'image' of his thought?

Let me be more specific. My aim is to return to the *source* of Deleuze's thought. The source in question, however, does not coincide with Deleuze's philosophical beginnings, with his first attempts at writing philosophy. The method I shall adopt will not consist in following the development of such beginnings, from the early work on. In fact, the source in question will be identified in the later work, and used as a guiding thread through Deleuze's thought as a whole, illuminating it only retrospectively. To follow that thread is not tantamount to carrying out a historical, genealogical approach – an entirely valid approach, I might add. It is not an effort to follow the progressive emergence of a philosophy, to trace its influences and its development. 'What History grasps of the event', Deleuze writes, 'is its effectuation in states of affairs or in lived experience, but the

Introduction

event in its becoming, in its specific consistency, its self-positing as a concept, escapes History.'[3] Another way of describing my goal, then, and using Deleuze's own vocabulary, would be to say that what I am seeking to identify is the *event* of that thought. And if Deleuze himself is indeed, at times and in certain ways, a historian of philosophy, it is precisely in the sense of being engaged in extracting the event or the becoming that belongs to a given thought. My concern, then, will not be that of the historian of philosophy. In many ways, it will be more tentative, and less secure. Potentially, it is philosophically more fruitful. Taking my clue in Deleuze's later work, I will look back at his thought in its entirety, and formulate a hypothesis regarding its trajectory. Naturally, the hypothesis in question needs to be put to the test of a series of close readings of Deleuze's most significant texts – something that I shall be able to accomplish only to an extent. Ultimately, though, it will be a question of asking whether there is something like a singular philosophical intuition, a single problematical horizon, *behind* the proliferation of concepts with which we have come to associate his thought. In order to identify the source of a thought, it is not enough to analyse its concepts. It requires that we identify its consistency. And that, we can hope to do by looking at that aspect of a thought that always remains concealed to it (at least in part), by looking at what we could call its *unthought*. The unthought is the true source, or the horizon, from which the thinker's thought unfolds. The source of a thought, then, is not to be mistaken for where (or when) that thought actually begins. Rather, it indicates the virtual place from which it flows. It is, as such, always difficult to locate, and especially so in the case of Deleuze, for reasons that will become apparent. What I wish to do, then, is to ask about what, exactly, orients Deleuzian thought. It is a question of direction. And if, as we shall see in some detail, following Deleuze's own conceptuality, I choose to refer to it as a 'plane', it is precisely insofar as a plane defines neither a surface nor a volume, but a direction, or a manifold of directions. That which orients and guides a thought does not lie only behind it. It is also ahead of it. For reasons that will also become apparent, it is most difficult, if not altogether impossible, to produce the concept of that source, that is, to *grasp* it fully.

Notes

1. I began writing this book a few years ago. A first version, which differs significantly from this expanded, modified and (hopefully) improved

version, was published in Italian in 2006. Since completing that first, in many ways unsatisfactory, version, the following monographs were published: Fadi Abou-Rihan, *Deleuze and Guattari* (London and New York: Continuum, 2009); Levi R. Bryant, *Difference and Givenness: Deleuze's Transcendental Empiricism and the Ontology of Immanence* (Evanston: Northwestern University Press, 2008); Pierre Montebello, *Deleuze* (Paris: Vrin, 2008); James Williams, *Gilles Deleuze's Logic of Sense. A Critical Introduction and Guide* (Edinburgh: Edinburgh University Press, 2008); Arnaud Bouaniche, *Gilles Deleuze, une introduction* (Paris: Pocket, 2007); François Dosse, *Gilles Deleuze et Félix Guattari, bibliographie croisée* (Paris: Éditions La Découverte, 2007); Reidar Andres Due, *Deleuze* (Cambridge: Polity, 2007); Christian Kerslake, *Deleuze and the Unconscious* (London: Continuum, 2007); Jeffrey Bell, *Philosophy at the Edge of Chaos: Gilles Deleuze and the Philosophy of Difference* (Toronto: Toronto University Press, 2006); Constantin Boundas (ed.), *Deleuze and Philosophy* (Edinburgh: Edinburgh University Press, 2006); Claire Colebrook, *Deleuze: A Guide for the Perplexed* (London: Continuum, 2006); Peter Hallward, *Out of this World: Deleuze and the Philosophy of Creation* (London: Verso, 2006); Gregg Lambert, *Who's Afraid of Deleuze and Guattari* (London & New York: Continuum, 2006); Albert Toscano, *The Theatre of Production: Philosophy and Individuation between Kant and Deleuze* (Basingstoke: Palgrave Macmillan, 2006). The reader has every right to be perplexed before this ever expanding list, and wonder how, if at all, my own book differs from previous monographs devoted to Deleuze. The brief Preface and the Introduction attempt to justify my own approach, which doesn't so much seek to dismiss other approaches as to complement them.
2. *Dialogues*, 22/15.
3. WP, 106/110.

1

Noology

In his last book, written with Félix Guattari, Deleuze looks back at his thought as a whole and wonders about its driving force, its source.[1] This is a text of maturity, in the strongest and best sense of the word, that is, a crucial testimony – a philosophical testament, almost – in which, among other things, Deleuze is concerned to identify the nature and ultimate significance of his philosophical trajectory as a whole. Besides the general tone of the text (jolly and humorous, as usual), and its (still) experimental nature, there is a kind of serenity, I would not be afraid to say of wisdom, which prevails. Most of all, though, the book has the virtue of isolating the thread which, I believe, runs through Deleuze's work as a whole – a thread best summarised in the concept of 'immanence'. This concept, however, is as complex as it is problematic. In fact, I shall ask whether it is a concept at all. I shall ask whether immanence can itself become an object of thought, can be turned into something which, from its position of withdrawal and presupposition, thought could hold up before itself, and clarify completely. In a way, all I shall be doing in this book is probe the ambiguous and problematic nature of immanence as the very project of philosophy itself, and for which Deleuze's own thought stands.

1. *Concepts*

What is Philosophy? famously defines philosophy as the creation of concepts.[2] Philosophy, Deleuze and Guattari tell us, begins with the creation of concepts. And concepts, we are told, exist only in so far as they attempt to solve specific problems. Philosophy is the art of posing the right problems and developing the concepts by means of which such problems can be solved. In this respect, concepts are valuable only to the extent that they allow us to designate specific problems and not mere generalities, events and not universal rules or essences. They must allow us to delimit and define situations that are themselves singular. Thus, Deleuze claims, the concept of a bird designates neither a genus, nor a species, but a composition of postures, colours and songs. Nothing is – or should be – more concrete and precise than a concept. This, perhaps, is the most significant lesson that Deleuze draws from Bergson, and one that he tries to apply systematically. Leaving aside for the moment the question of how Deleuze understands the 'creation' in question, I wish simply to emphasise the fact that it is not a creation *ex nihilo*, but an effort to extract from the sensible the singular points at which the constitution of a phenomenon, whatever its nature, is being decided. In that respect, whilst created, concepts are the concepts of the sensible itself, and not, as idealism believes, the *a priori* categories of a faculty of understanding that, when used in connection with a faculty of intuition, produces knowledge. Concepts are neither given nor generated spontaneously, from within as it were. Rather, they are produced in response to specific events that take place in the empirical world. Now if this understanding of concepts as originating in the sensible itself amounts to a form of empiricism, Deleuze immediately goes on to characterise it as a 'superior' form of empiricism, or as a *transcendental* empiricism, thus doing away with the very opposition between empiricism and idealism, and running the risk of not saying very much. In itself, he remarks lucidly in *Two Regimes of Madness*, and until the conditions of this term are precisely defined, 'transcendental empiricism' means nothing. It is, for example, absolutely crucial not to model (*décalquer*) the transcendental after the empirical, as Kant does. Equally though, the transcendental must be explored for its own sake, and thus experimented with. Philosophy is concerned with experiencing, and experimenting with, the transcendental itself, thus indicating the sort of work involved in the creation of concepts.[3] For the time being, let me simply mention that if Deleuze insists that concepts be created or invented, it is to emphasise the fact that they do not exist already constituted, like Platonic Ideas, waiting to be un- or discovered. Concepts, Deleuze writes, 'are not waiting for us ready-made, like heavenly bodies'.[4] To think of concepts as pre-existing thought, as objects of recollection or contemplation, is already tantamount to inscribing thought within a horizon of transcendence. Concepts are neither realities in themselves, Ideas existing in a world apart, nor categories of a transcendental subjectivity, given in advance, and simply applied to a synthesised manifold of intuition. This means that, whilst not engaged in a process of contemplation, thought is not engaged in one of reflection either. In other words, to think, for Deleuze, is not to direct one's gaze towards oneself, to delve into the wealth of innate ideas. Nor is thinking philosophically (or immanently) tantamount to reflecting on the various fields of knowledge already constituted. Scientists and artists, for example, do not need the help of philosophers to 'reflect' on their respective field: the only ones who can adequately reflect on mathematics are the mathematicians themselves, on film the filmmakers, etc. If the goal of philosophy were to reflect on something, Deleuze once said in a talk, it would have no reason to exist.[5] Philosophy is even less a theory of communication, whether in Habermas' or Rorty's sense. Unlike the theories of contemplation and reflection – which gave way to extraordinarily powerful works and concepts (one need think only of Plotinus and Kant, for example), and which Deleuze himself does not hesitate to draw on at times, if only to transform them – the so-called theory of communication lacks a rigorous and critical concept of its own. In fact, it is nothing more than the celebration of opinion (*doxa*), and the defence of democracy as the space in which it circulates freely. But if that's democracy, philosophy wants to have nothing to do with it. If it's going to have anything to do with democracy, it will be as a result of the heterodoxy for which it stands. Communication is itself not a concept, and should be left to marketing and advertising experts (which, it is true, now claim to be creating concepts).[6] In the end, philosophical concepts are neither objects of contemplation, nor acts of reflection, nor innate or *a priori* structures, nor even protocols of communication. Rather, they are processes of *creation*. I shall return to this characterisation of the philosophical concept later on.

To the concepts of philosophy belong also what Deleuze calls their 'conceptual characters' (*personnages conceptuels*). One such character, indeed a founding and decisive one for the entire history of western thought, is that of the Friend. It is a Greek invention. It is indeed Greek philosophy that first presents the image of the philosopher as the 'friend' of the concept. The philosopher is he who, with respect to truth, is in the position of the claimant, and even the lover. As such, he is the condition for the exercise of thought: in order to be 'wise', one must be a friend, and even a lover, of wisdom. But in this love of wisdom and knowledge, the friend has many rivals, other men and women who also claim to be the friends and lovers of truth. Thus, the history of philosophy can be seen as a history of friendship and love, but also of rivalry and dispute. The creation of the philosophical or conceptual character of the friend reveals a feature – what Deleuze calls an 'image' – that will remain for the most part unquestioned: if we have the ability to 'love' truth, it is because of a natural predisposition towards truth; and if we are so naturally inclined to love and seek truth, it is because truth itself is somehow already given to us, or at least directed towards us from the start. Between the philosopher and truth, there would be something like a natural affinity, or a reciprocal disposition, which Deleuze rejects. We are not naturally inclined to think, Deleuze insists. Thinking is not something that comes from within, or indeed spontaneously. The philosopher is not the friend of truth. He is perhaps the lover of truth, but love and friendship are two very different types of affects and dispositions for Deleuze. Love, as Proust so convincingly argued, is based on a certain opacity and impenetrability between the lover and the beloved, one that forces the lover into an endless deciphering of the signs produced by the beloved. Far from requiring friendship and benevolence, then, genuine thought presupposes something like a bad will (a *mauvaise volonté*, which is not to be mistaken for a *volonté méchante*) and a certain discord. In so far as the Deleuzian 'image' of thought rejects the figure of the friend, it can no longer be said to be 'Greek'. Naturally, this rejection would also have political consequences, given the Greek, and especially Aristotelian, characterisation of *philia* as the ethical and political virtue *par excellence*. If the philosopher still has a place and a role to play within the *polis*, it will no longer be that of the friend (of truth).

Finally, the creation of concepts always presupposes a proper name, or a signature. The philosopher, Deleuze and Guattari claim, distrusts the concepts inherited from other philosophers, and tries to create his or her own. As I will try to show, the notions of signature and proper name are in fact more complex than they seem, and reveal a reality different from the one we would be inclined to grant them with. With the proper name, we complete the configuration of what we could call the creative pole of the question regarding the being of philosophy, or the meaning of thought. The pole in question comprises three elements: concepts, conceptual characters, and the proper name.

2. *The Image, the Plane*

The question, now, is one of knowing whether the creative pole exhausts the question regarding the origin or meaning of thought. The answer Deleuze and Guattari provide is quite clear, and amounts to a resounding 'no'. For every creation of thought presupposes the constitution of what Deleuze calls an 'image' or a 'plane', which cannot be confused with the concepts that are produced as a result of it. This is the second pole or the second aspect of the response to the question: 'What is Philosophy?' Of a philosopher and his concepts, we must always ask: 'What is the plane on which his concepts move? To what plane do such concepts correspond?' A concept, Deleuze claims, always has the truth that befalls it, according to the conditions of its own creation. We always have the concepts we deserve. For they always emerge from a definite plane. It is utterly useless, Deleuze argues, to want to judge a thought, to ask if this or that philosopher is right or wrong. All we can do is delineate his or her plane, adopt it ourselves, or draw a different one.

I now wish to examine closely this second major thesis of *What is Philosophy?* introduced immediately after that concerning the creation of concepts. This second thesis stipulates that, behind or beneath every set of concepts constituting a thought, there is something like an intuition, or a pre-conceptual, pre-philosophical understanding that orients that thought. Following Deleuze, let me consider the example of Descartes' *cogito*, which is often, and correctly, understood as the first or founding concept of his thought. That concept, along with its various components (doubting, thinking, being), is nonetheless created only with a view to making possible what is announced as the ultimate project or plan of that thought, namely, to establish truth as absolute certainty, and to secure this new conception of truth and this new point of departure for philosophy. An integral and crucial part of this process involves the neutralisation of all explicit *objective* presuppositions, which philosophy had taken for granted up until that point, such as the definition of man as rational animal.[7] But even this plan or fundamental aim, this project that can be singled out as distinctly Cartesian, and which involves the elimination of all presuppositions, presupposes something. Even this project of objective presuppositionlessness, which so much of modern philosophy, up until Hegel at least, was concerned to carry out, involves something like a *subjective* presupposition, a pre-philosophical understanding of what it means to think.[8] In the case of Descartes, the presupposition that is at stake is the one according to which everyone knows what thinking, being, 'I', mean, and the fact that we, as thinking things, are *naturally* disposed or inclined towards truth (*lumen naturale*). In fact, this presupposition turns out to be not just that of Descartes, but also that of the history of philosophy in its quasi-entirety. And such is the reason why, in wanting to produce a thought without image, *Difference and Repetition* insists on the 'bad will' of the philosopher, that is, on his opposition to the 'good' and the 'common' sense that lie at the heart of the image that governs much of western thought.[9] As far as the example of Descartes is concerned, we should say that the *cogito* is at once the first *concept* on the plane of *objective* presuppositionlessness, the absolute and unquestionable point of departure for thought, and, at the same time, the result of a *subjective* presupposition regarding the *image* of thought. This image is what indicates, always indirectly, obliquely, what it *means* to think, to use thought, to orient oneself in thought.

We began by saying that philosophy is the activity of creation of concepts, and that philosophical thought *begins* with that activity. We now need to refine and nuance that statement, in so far as there always seems to be something that precedes that activity, something of the order of an image of thought, a pre-conceptual understanding of what it means to think. In other words, there seems to always be something pre-philosophical at the heart of philosophy, and something, which, furthermore, signals the internal conditions of philosophy. If philosophy indeed *begins* with the creation of concepts, the image of thought is where that thought really *originates*. The image is what institutes that thought as the thought that it is, with its concepts and notions. It designates the horizon from which it thinks, and so something like its unthought. In *What is Philosophy?* Deleuze and Guattari refer to it indifferently as a plane (*plan*) or an image (and to the plane of transcendence that tends to dominate western philosophy Deleuze will oppose a plane of immanence, through which philosophy would be genuinely completed). In that respect, *What is Philosophy?* seems to mark a shift from a fundamental aspect of *Difference and Repetition*, in so far as Deleuze and Guattari are now claiming that philosophy – including their own – can never quite shake off or determine entirely its own image: a purely imageless thought is but an illusion, or perhaps a regulative idea for thought.[10] Contrary to what Deleuze once thought, then, it would seem that thought cannot operate without a certain image, an image that, furthermore, it cannot quite turn into a concept. If philosophy proceeds by way of concepts, yet in such a way that the horizon from which it proceeds is itself not a concept, but indeed something like an image, does that not mean that non-philosophy figures (quite literally) at the heart of philosophy? That the 'purest' of philosophers is always he whose thought is born of a non-philosophical – or at least a pre-philosophical – origin, and that philosophy is, structurally, originally, irreducibly open to, and bound up with, something that is non-philosophical? This, in turn, would suggest that philosophy can never quite conceptualise its own image, or appropriate that which, in a way, belongs to it most properly. It would suggest that the dimension that shapes thought most decisively is also the dimension that escapes thought, that thought is never quite able to bend backwards towards its own presupposition, and make its own image transparent to itself. All that thought could ever hope to do would be to intimate its own image, to approach it, asymptotically as it were. What thought could not hope to do, however, would be to produce the concept of its own image. Concepts flow and follow from their own image or plane, of which there is no concept. Were this to be true, it is the classical, rationalist ideal of philosophy as grounding and self-grounding, as the science of foundations and the foundation of science itself, in short, as metaphysics, that would begin to collapse. It would mean that, with respect to its origin, philosophy could no longer be considered as involved in a relation of grounding.

What have we established thus far? That philosophy is the creation of concepts, but against the background of an intuition, or an image, of what it means to think. In other words: that philosophy begins with concepts, but finds itself instituted or established through a plane, which it draws, intuitively as it were, and which is itself pre-conceptual.

Before I turn to the notion of immanence, I need to say a few words about the notion of plane, to which it is attached. The French word *plan* can be heard in many ways – ways that Deleuze mobilises more or less explicitly, and which I'll draw on and clarify as we go along. At this early stage, and in a preliminary, preparatory way, let me simply say that it can suggest something like a background, an *arrière-plan*, as in photography or in painting, in the case of a visual object, or as in story-telling: it is on the basis of, or, more adequately perhaps, *from* a given background that the foreground of a picture becomes visible, that the characters of a story unfold. Likewise, it is on the basis of a distinct plane that philosophical concepts come to life. Yet the *plan*, as we shall see, also suggests something that is not so much behind, in the background, as it is ahead, orienting and shaping whatever it is the *plan* of. In that respect, it is a plan, a design, something that is drawn in advance and points forward. The image of thought is a plan in that sense: it provides a thought with its fundamental direction and its general climate; it orients and channels it. So, at this early stage, let me simply note the fact that the *plan* is both behind and ahead, both a background and a plan, and that thought, as creation of concepts, unfolds on a stage that it does not quite create. It creates concepts, yet against a background that it institutes more than creates, and through which, in any case, it finds itself instituted. One creates concepts, but one does not create the stage on which they unfold.

Let me now turn to the further characterisation of this plane as one of *immanence*. Deleuze and Guattari also call it a plane of *consistency*. Here again, the matter can be dealt with only tentatively. Only at the end of our journey, in Chapters 4 and 5 in particular, will this idea of a plane of immanence, or consistency, become clear. Consistency is not mere coherence: whereas the latter, I would argue, has to do with the relation between concepts, the former is concerned with the place or space from which a given thought unfolds. The (quasi) concept of immanence is far more delicate to grasp. It is one with which Deleuzian thought as a whole is often identified, however. Its difficulty and complexity, I believe, is a function of its ontological and epistemological status. It is difficult to know the sort of thing that it is, and how it can be turned into an object of philosophical investigation. How could it, indeed, if it is the condition of thought itself, or the pre-philosophical, pre-conceptual plane from which concepts themselves emerge? How can we even begin to talk about such a plane, and about 'immanence', if they are really the horizon from which philosophical discourse itself unfolds? The plane of immanence, Deleuze and Guattari state very clearly in *What is Philosophy?*, 'is not a concept that is or can be thought'.[11] Why? Because it is simply not a concept. Or if it is a concept, it is a concept of a kind that is radically different from the concepts that make up the fabric and the distinct colour of a given thought. But what is it, then? It is an image, precisely: the plane of immanence is 'the image of thought, the image thought gives itself of what it means to think, to make use of thought, to find one's bearings in thought [*s'orienter dans la pensée*]'.[12] From the start, and irreducibly, concepts find themselves indebted to something that is itself not conceptual, to a horizon from which they emerge, and which determines the meaning of thought. This horizon, this plane, is precisely the one that Deleuze's concepts attempt to make room for, to intimate, without there ever being a question of turning it into a concept. His own concepts, then, can be seen as an attempt to draw a plane, but one that would have no other goal than to bring out its own image, to bring to the surface the image that simmers beneath all concepts, and that makes such concepts possible in the first place. This is perhaps the greatest difficulty Deleuze is faced with: for isn't there something intrinsically problematic, if not paradoxical, in wanting to extract the pre-conceptual conditions of thought by way of *concepts* (thus resisting the temptation to locate the conditions of philosophy outside philosophy, in history, for example, or anthropology), in wanting to bring out the horizon or the plane on the basis of which philosophy unfolds, but which it itself does not institute? Isn't there an intrinsic difficulty, possibly a necessary incompleteness, built into the attempt to name, to conceptualise that on the basis of which concepts are generated, when the two most influential ways of addressing that problem – the Cartesian way, which stipulates that concepts or ideas are not generated, but innate, and the Hegelian way, which stipulates that concepts are indeed generated, yet from within, from the most immediate and abstract, to the most mediated and concrete – have been explicitly rejected? What remains, when both subjective and objective idealism have been rejected?

Deleuze's own image of thought is characterised by a twofold trait. First, as I've already suggested, Deleuze believes that thought is external to what it thinks: its ideas, its concepts are not generated from within, but from without, as a result of an encounter that comes from the sensible. Thought is set in motion, or generated, not as a result of some natural inclination and good will, then, not in the excitement of a taste for thinking, but under the impulse of a shock.[13] In other words, thought needs to be provoked. This, we recall, was what Deleuze described as the new image of thought in Nietzsche and Proust. Thought happens as a result of an *encounter* with the outside. It is a response – a creative response – to something that has taken hold of us. What does this mean? It means, once again, that we do not think naturally, that we are not naturally disposed towards thought and truth; it means that our ideas are not innate, and so are precisely not ours (all so-called 'good' and 'original' ideas are precisely not our own), that the conditions of thought are not within thought itself, that thought is not its own ground, and so certainly not that of the intelligibility of the real.[14] This is the extent to which Deleuze is an empiricist: our concepts are generated from our encounter with the external world; the external, sensible reality is where they originate. Thought, Deleuze claims, is essentially 'exogenetic'. At the same time, he claims that thought is entirely *immanent* to what it thinks, immanent, that is, to the real that provokes it. For idealism, on the other hand, it is the real that is immanent to thought. But to claim that the world, in so far as it is *thought*, can be immanent only to some instance or principle that is itself not worldly, not empirical, is tantamount to elevating such an instance or principle to the status of a transcendent authority. As such, Deleuze claims, it is unacceptable: there is no origin of the world, and of thought, other than the world itself. In that respect, Deleuzian empiricism opposes the two traditions of transcendental idealism represented by Kant and Husserl. At the same time, however, and as we've already suggested, Deleuze retains or reformulates a version of transcendentalism, one that would not equate it with a form of transcendence: in the absence of consciousness, as the classical site of the transcendental, which Deleuze seeks to neutralise, 'the transcendental field could be defined as a pure plane of immanence, because it escapes all transcendence, both of the subject and of the object'.[15] Absolute immanence, he adds, 'is in itself: it is not in anything, nor can it be attributed *to* something; it does not depend on an object or belong to a subject'.[16] This, according to Agamben, is what defines Deleuzian immanence.[17] Immanence is characterised by the fact that is immanent only to it.[18]

This is also the sense in which it is a 'transcendental field'. The transcendental is here opposed to the transcendent in so far as it does not presuppose a consciousness, but escapes all determinations of the subject. The notion of a transcendental field refers back to Sartre's essay from 1937, 'Transcendence of the Ego'.[19] In his essay, Sartre speaks of a 'transcendental impersonal field that has neither the form of a synthetic consciousness nor that of a subjective identity'.[20] The field, which Sartre did not manage to free entirely from the plane of consciousness, is taken one step further by Deleuze; now it is a matter of reaching a pre-individual and totally impersonal zone beyond (or perhaps prior to) consciousness itself. According to Deleuze, not only is it impossible to understand the transcendental in the way that Kant does, that is, 'in the personal form of an I', but it is equally impossible – and in this instance, it is Sartrean phenomenology that is being targeted – to preserve it in the form of an impersonal consciousness, 'even if we define this impersonal consciousness by means of pure intentionalities and retentions, which still presuppose centres of individuation'. Why? Because 'the error of all efforts to determine the transcendental as consciousness is that they think of the transcendental in the image of and in resemblance to that which it is supposed to ground'.[21] And if that is the case, it is because the transcendental field in question only uncovers the conditions of *possibility* of knowledge, and of experience, and not, as Deleuze wants, the conditions under which phenomena are actually *generated*. In so far as the 'condition' that classical transcendental thought seeks to identify is nothing more than the *form of possibility* of the conditioned, and this regardless of whether it is the form of logical, mathematical, physical, transcendental or moral possibility, it is altogether incapable of *generating* what it is actually supposed to 'found'. As a result, the conditioned is in no way 'affected' by the condition: the condition is merely an abstract doubling of the conditioned, and one to which it remains indifferent:

> But however we define form, it is an odd procedure, since it involves rising from the conditioned to the condition, in order to think of the condition as the simple possibility of the conditioned. Here we rise to a foundation, but what is founded remains what it was, independently of the operation that founded it, unaffected by it . . .[22]

And so, the very goal of the transcendental enterprise coincides with the attempt to purge the transcendental field of any trace of resemblance: 'We cannot think of the condition in the image of the conditioned. The task of a philosophy that wants to avoid the traps of consciousness and the cogito is to purge the transcendental field of all resemblance.'[23]

So long as we do not move beyond the point of view of consciousness, we remain trapped in the problematic of resemblance between the foundation and whatever it is that is being founded. The *cogito*, from Descartes to Husserl, grounds the possibility of treating the transcendental as a field of consciousness. But unlike Kant, for whom this field takes the form of a pure consciousness without experience, Deleuze definitively frees the transcendental from the very idea of consciousness (even in its Sartrean, impersonal mode). As such, it appears as an experience without consciousness or subject. The transcendental in Deleuze's sense amounts to a double twisting free, therefore: first, of *transcendence*, whether as God, being, or consciousness; second, of the problematic regarding the conditions of *possibility* of experience and knowledge in general, irreducibly complicit with the logic of resemblance. Instead, Deleuze privileges the standpoint of immanence and the problematic of genesis: transcendental empiricism is concerned with isolating the genetic and immanent conditions of existence of the real. Deleuzian empiricism, then, aims to do away with its classical opposition to transcendental philosophy, and to overcome the dualism between subject and object. It amounts to a monism of substance, or to an ontology, which renders the very distinction between subject and object, or thought and being, null and void.

The singularity and difficulty of Deleuzian thought lies in the double axiom constitutive of its image: exteriority *and* immanence, or 'exogenesis' and 'endoconsistency'. Immanence preserves the world, and the possibility of its meaningfulness, from being assigned to an origin that is not inner worldly. It turns thought itself into a worldly event. Exteriority, on the other hand, is what preserves thought from what Deleuze calls the image, or the model, of *recognition*, and the form of *doxa* (founded in the double presupposition of 'good sense' and 'common sense', of *Eudoxus* and orthodoxy): to assume that thought identifies and recognises its object, and so is in a state of natural affinity with the world, is to assume the exact opposite of what it means to think for Deleuze. This image of recognition, or this conception of thought as a disposition shared by all, produced by the concordance of all the faculties, and naturally disposed towards its object (truth), is the most stubborn of all, and one that Deleuze associates with virtually the whole of philosophy. Such is the reason why, in *Difference and Repetition*, he does not hesitate to speak of *the* Image of thought, as constituting the 'subjective presupposition of philosophy as a whole'.[24] Such, also, is the reason why *Difference and Repetition* calls for a thought *without* image. Thinking without image means understanding thought as having nothing to do with representation (and therefore idealism). But this, as I have already argued, and still need to show in detail, does not mean that non-representational thought doesn't have a plane of its own, an image of a radically different kind. We need to be careful to distinguish between two types of images of thought: one refers to the 'dogmatic' image of thought that dominates the history of philosophy, whilst the other refers to the image of thought without representation, or to what Deleuze calls the plane of immanence *stricto sensu*.

Ultimately, I wish to show that Deleuze's work after *Difference and Repetition* was a direct effect of the need to go further in the direction of a thought without image, further in the direction of immanence. At the same time, I wish to show how immanence itself, by virtue of not being a concept, proves to be a singularly elusive and highly problematic theme. Because immanence is not just of the order of the concept, thought cannot be grounded in the concept, but, to use Deleuze's own terminology, only 'ungrounded' in the image of thought. Any attempt to ground thought, and establish thought as its own ground, will be tantamount to reintroducing transcendence, to making immanence immanent to thought. What the recognition of the difference between image and thought, between plane and concept, requires is the relentless and always renewed creation of concepts that testify to the horizon of immanence of thought. Immanence is the plane or horizon of thought that effaces itself before other concepts, which all converge to establish it. At the same time, the plane of immanence can never be reduced to a single concept, and not even to a conceptual field. The conceptual order is one that it has exceeded form the start. Such is the reason why immanence does not figure as prominently as do other concepts in Deleuze's thought, why he does not analyse it as thoroughly as other concepts. Such, also, is the reason why he is able to associate his own thought with that quasi- or non-concept only retrospectively, at a meta-level as it were, when he is finally able to ask himself: 'What is it I have been doing all my life?'[25] What, in other words, has been insisting and persisting all along, trying to find its way through this series of texts and this creation of concepts? Could it have been this desire to bend philosophy backwards as it were, in the direction of its absolute presupposition, and, in so doing, to establish it as pure immanence?

So far, three different types or levels of presuppositions have emerged. First, we can question a given thought with respect to its *beginning*, that is, its desire to do away with what Deleuze calls all *objective* presuppositions, such as Descartes' implicit rejection of the definition of the human as the rational animal. Then, we can identify the remaining *subjective* presuppositions of the thought in question. According to Deleuze, these determine the objective presuppositions themselves, and run through the whole of modern philosophy. Together, they constitute what Deleuze calls the Image of thought, that is, the plane from which a given set of concepts unfolds. I referred to such an image, or plane, as the *origin* of thought. Finally, a third level of presupposition has emerged, the level that would designate philosophy as such and as a whole, and which Deleuze would have set out to extract, thus making philosophy *absolutely* presuppositionless. This is the plane of immanence proper. Beyond the critique of the old, dogmatic image of thought, and even beyond the extraction of a new image of thought in Nietzsche or Proust, the task of philosophy now consists of appropriating the plane or the soil of philosophy itself, of bringing it to the fore and making it the true object of philosophy. Yet because of the pre-philosophical and pre-conceptual nature of the plane of immanence, the task of philosophy remains an endless one, of which we can never know whether it has been entirely successful. 'Perhaps', Deleuze and Guattari write, 'this is the supreme act of philosophy: not so much to think THE plane of immanence as to show that it is there, unthought in every plane, and to think it in this way as the outside and inside of thought, as the not-external outside and the non-internal inside – that which cannot be thought and yet must be thought'.[26]

3. The Greeks, the Moderns

So far, in speaking of the beginning of philosophy (as the creation of concepts), of its origin (as the 'image' of a given thought), and even of its plane, I have not taken into account its history or, better said perhaps, its historicity. Following Deleuze, I even distinguished quite clearly the event of a given thought from its historical genesis. This, however, does not mean that Deleuze rejects all forms of historicism, or refuses to recognise the historical dimension of philosophy. Evidently, Deleuze and Guattari claim in *What is Philosophy?*, the Greek, the modern, and the contemporary planes of thought are not identical. It cannot be a question of ignoring their essential differences. Nor can it be a question of denying the historical (and geographical) point of departure of philosophy in Ancient Greece, which we could call its *birth*, thus adding another sense of beginning to our list. The question, however, is one of knowing whether the recognition of such a birth, and of the various key stages that followed it, require the elaboration of something like a rigorous history of philosophy or, more decisively still, a philosophy of history. Deleuze's answer to this question is clearly negative: the historical beginning in question is an entirely contingent event. There is nothing intrinsically 'Greek' about philosophy (most 'Greek' philosophers were in fact foreigners and émigrés). That being said, something decisive took place in Greece in the sixth century BCE; a number of elements came together and crystallised into what turned out to be a very significant event. A new modality of thought, if not thought itself, emerged in the context of the newly created Greek *polis*. Two decisive traits can be highlighted. First, by contrast with the highly ordered, vertical and hierarchical societies of the Mycenaean kingdom and the civilisations of the Middle East, the Greek city-state emerged as a society of friends, that is, as a society of free (*Homoioi*) and equal (*Isoi*) beings. In other words, something like a phenomenon of social and political *aplanissement*, or flattening, occurred: men were all on the same plane.²⁷ Despite his criticism of the philosopher as the 'friend' of truth and wisdom, to which I've already alluded, it seems that Deleuze wishes to retain a socio-political conception of friendship as a condition of philosophy itself, that is, as a condition for the emergence of a plane of immanence. Second, and following Vernant's analysis, we can identify the following two decisive traits that determined the emergence of philosophy in Greece: the constitution of a domain of thought external and foreign to religion, under the influence of the physicists from Ionia; the idea of a cosmic order that no longer relied (as was the case in traditional theogonies) on the power of a sovereign god, on its *monarchia* and its *basileia*, but on a law that was immanent to the universe. The law in question amounted to a rule of distribution (*nomos*), which imposed an egalitarian order on all the constitutive elements of nature, so that no one element could exercise its domination (*kratos*) over the others. For the first time, nature was envisaged without having recourse to the dramatic imagery of the ancient theogonies and cosmogonies, without the great figures of the primordial and supernatural Powers. With the physicists of Milet of Ionia (Thales, Anaximander, Anaximenes), positivity penetrated beings as a whole, and nothing was seen to exist outside nature. Human beings, the divine, the world as such and as a whole constituted a unified and homogeneous universe that co-existed on a single plane.²⁸ What was common to both the socio-political order and the cosmic order was the principle of equality (*ison*), the idea of an order ruled by equality (*isonomia*). The two aspects are of course linked, Deleuze stresses, in so far as only a society of friends (in the sense of equals) could draw such a plane of immanence (*tendre un plan d'immanence*), from which idols have been eliminated. The birth of philosophy thus coincided with the substitution of a plane of transcendence for a plane of immanence. The figure of the Philosopher challenged that of the Priest, or the Wise: 'Whenever there is transcendence, vertical Being, imperial State in the sky or on earth, there is religion; and there is philosophy whenever there is immanence, even if it functions as an arena for the *agon* and rivalry.'²⁹ From an historical perspective, and inasmuch as it amounts to an event that crystallised in Ancient Greece, immanence is best described as a 'milieu'. As such, it is precisely not an historical determination, but a geographical one: it designates a set of geographical contingencies, a place and a source, and not a destiny. It signals at once the plane of matter (or physical nature), the social and political organisation that makes its questioning possible (democracy), and the questioning itself (philosophy).

Immanence turns out to be what distinguishes philosophy from mythology, religion and various forms and practices of wisdom. It is the 'cornerstone' of philosophy. At the same time, we should note that, for a number of reasons, which will turn out to be very complex indeed, philosophy always falls short of total immanence. It is always somewhat tainted with transcendence, especially (but not exclusively) with Judeo-Christian theology. Time and again, instead of remaining faithful to immanence (or univocity), ontology becomes onto-theology (and analogy). As an event and a task, philosophy does not quite coincide with its history. Yet, to use the words of one commentator, the history of philosophy is 'the hypertext where the affirmation of immanence and the illusion of transcendence ceaselessly oppose one another'[30] – and, I would argue, where philosophy ceaselessly compromises with transcendence. Speaking of the difference between the Greeks and the Moderns, and with direct reference to Hölderlin's famous letter to Böhlendorf dated 4 December 1801, which contrasts the 'clarity of exposition' of the Moderns with the 'fire of heaven' of the Greeks, Deleuze and Guattari write:

> [T]he Greeks kept the plane of immanence that they constructed in enthusiasm and drunkenness, but they had to search for the concepts with which to fill it so as to avoid falling back into the figures of the East. As for us, we possess concepts – after so many centuries of Western thought we think we possess them – but we hardly know where to put them because we lack a genuine plane, misled as we are by Christian transcendence. In short, in its past form the concept is that which is not yet. We today possess concepts, but the Greeks did not yet possess them; they possessed the plane that we no longer possess.[31]

And so, today, we must strive to regain the plane of immanence, which we have lost. In the light of such a task, however, we must learn to use our concepts differently, and reinvent them so as to free them from their onto-theological heritage.

Notes

1. *WP*, 7/1.
2. *WP*, 8/2.
3. *TRM*, 339/362. This dual (theoretical *and* practical) aspect of Deleuze's work is what this book will seek to emphasise. Transcendental empiricism is the method that allows thought to access the real or immanent conditions of experience and to experience the conditions themselves.

At the heart of the Deleuzian method lies a reversibility, which this book seeks to draw out.
4. WP, 11/5.
5. The talk in question, delivered at the FEMIS in 1987, is transcribed in TRM, 291–302/312–24.
6. See WP, 137–9/144–6, where Deleuze provides an amusing critique of opinion and communication.
7. See Descartes' Meditation Two in Œuvres et lettres (Paris: Gallimard 'Bibliothèque de la Pléiade', 1953), p. 275; trans. D. Cress, *Meditations on First Philosophy* (Indianapolis & Cambridge: Hackett, 1993), p. 18.
8. This, as we have already suggested, is what Deleuze calls an image of thought. At one point, and in order to demarcate his thought from all such objective *and* subjective presuppositions, Deleuze went so far as to aim to produce a thought *without* image. See *Difference and Repetition*, Chapter Three ('The Image of Thought'). This is where we find Deleuze's most systematic exposition of the irreducible 'image' and 'postulates' of western thought, along with his effort, especially in Chapters 4 and 5, to produce a thought of an altogether different nature.
9. DR, 169–80/129–38.
10. It would seem that *What is Philosophy?* is actually returning to the conception of the image of thought Deleuze began by developing in *Nietzsche and Philosophy* (1962) and *Proust and Signs* (1964). The former book contains a section entitled 'New Image of Thought' (III, 15). In it, Deleuze reveals Nietzsche's 'new image of thought', which he opposes to the classical, 'dogmatic' image of thought (represented by the likes of Plato, Descartes and Kant): sense and value, as opposed to truth, are now the decisive elements of thought. Furthermore, thinking is not the natural practice of an innate faculty, but depends entirely on the nature of the forces that seize it, and which it expresses. So long as thought is in the hands of reactive forces, so long as it finds its meaning in them, we cannot say that we are genuinely thinking. It is only when different, active forces will have taken hold of thought, that we shall be in a position to say that we are really thinking. But such a turning, such an event in thought, can only be the result of a certain violence coming from without. We are not naturally inclined to think. We can only be forced to think. Thinking is a matter of forces. *Proust and Signs* repeats the same idea, albeit in a different context. In the conclusion of the book, entitled 'The Image of Thought', Deleuze extracts a general critique of classical rationalism, and of its insistence on the veracity and the good will of the thinker, from Proust's strong reservations regarding the value of friendship in the search for truth. Friends, rationalism believes, are like philosophers, in so far as they are individuals of

good will. All that is lacking, in order to think properly, and discover the truth, is the adequate method. But one's basic, natural disposition towards truth is itself never called into question. What *In Search of Lost Time* teaches us is that truth – at least the non-objective, metaphysical truth it is after – cannot be discovered methodically, but only accidentally, cannot be communicated, but only interpreted. Deleuze's Proust is, in that respect, very Nietzschean, and presents a very similar 'new' image of thought. That being said, I shall also want to show that what Deleuze calls the plane – as a plane of *immanence* – is not entirely reducible to the 'new' image of thought developed by Nietzsche and Proust. In other words, I shall have to show how something additional is at issue in the characterisation of the image in Deleuze's later thought.

11. WP, 39/37.
12. WP, 39–40/37.
13. DR, 173/132.
14. The project of the self-foundation of thought, and the foundation of the real in thought, characterises the most ambitious project of modern thought, from Descartes to Hegel. It is true that, in Descartes, the idea of the infinite, which the *cogito* discovers within itself, complicates the project. It is only with Hegel, really, that the reconciliation of the finite and the infinite, of ground and what is grounded, of the plane and the concept, is realised fully.
15. TRM, 360/385.
16. TRM, 360/385.
17. Giorgio Agamben, 'L'Immanence absolue', in Éric Alliez (ed.), *Gilles Deleuze. Une vie philosophique* (Le Plessis-Robinson: Institut Synthélabo, 1998), pp. 165–88. The text to which this title refers is: Gilles Deleuze, 'L'immanence: une vie . . .'. Originally published in *Philosophie* no. 47, 1995, it can now be found in *TRM*, 359–63/384–9.
18. 'Immanence is immanence only to itself and consequently captures everything, absorbs All-One, and leaves nothing remaining to which it could be immanent. In any case, whenever immanence is interpreted as immanent *to* Something, we can be sure that this Something reintroduces the transcendent' (WP, 47/45).
19. Jean-Paul Sartre, 'La Transcendance de l'Ego', in *Recherches philosophiques*, 1936–37; trans. F. Williams and R. Kirkpatrick, *The Transcendence of the Ego* (New York: Noonday Press, 1957).
20. LS, 120/98–9.
21. LS, 128/105.
22. LS, 30/18. I will return to this passage, and to its relevance for the question of sense, and logic, in Chapter 4.
23. LS, 149/123.

24. *DR*, 172/132.
25. *WP*, 7/1.
26. *WP*, 59/59–60.
27. Naturally, the definition of 'man' remained highly selective, as it excluded many types of males, and all women.
28. Jean-Pierre Vernant, *Les origines de la pensée grecque* (Paris: Quadrige/PUF, 1995), p. 101.
29. *WP*, 46/43.
30. Éric Alliez, *La signature du monde* (Paris: Les éditions du Cerf, 1993), p. 21.
31. *WP*, 97/101.

2
Ontology I: Genesis

1. Transcendence and Illusion

The time has come to address the question of how Deleuze himself adopts the standpoint of immanence. Whilst given from the start, as the very plane or horizon of philosophy, immanence always remains to be made, that is, conceptualised. This, however, does not amount to turning immanence into a concept. To produce a concept of immanence, as Hegel did, is not the same as to open concepts to the plane of immanence. Similarly, the plane of immanence is never given as such, or fully intuited; it needs to be drawn through the creation of concepts. In a sense, such a task is never-ending: it is the quest of a lifetime, a quest in which life itself is at issue, and in which life, in so far as it *mine*, dissolves and expands at the same time, in order to become *a* life, that is, the anonymous and impersonal life of immanence itself. As I'll try to show throughout this book, this is precisely the goal that Deleuze pursued in his own life and work. If the task of philosophy, understood as the creation of concepts for the sake of immanence, is infinite, it is not only because of the infinity of immanence itself. If, contrary to what Hegel believed, there is no end to, or of, that task, it is also because philosophy has an irreducible tendency, if not an urge, to turn its unthought, or its presupposition, into an instance of transcendence, created in its own image. Too often, and quite naturally, the space that separates philosophy from its own presupposition is turned into the space of transcendence. It's in this gap that the images of transcendence proliferate. Following Kant's vocabulary, Deleuze characterises the constant resurgence of transcendence as the transcendental or objective 'illusions' of thought itself, as mirages arising from the plane, 'like vapours from a pond'.[1] Thought constantly produces effects or traces of transcendence.

The illusions of transcendence come in various forms: God (at least a certain conception of God), the *cogito*, the transcendental consciousness – whether Kantian or phenomenological – the Other, the lived body and existence, all perpetuate the idea of a world

Ontology I: Genesis

essentially immanent, or given, to some ontologically distinct principle or origin. Concepts themselves, as the universals or categories *pros hen legomenon*, on the basis of which Being is said to be what it is, are instances of transcendence, in so far as they are thought in place of the plane of immanence itself. The greatest and possibly most dangerous illusion of all, however, is that of speculative dialectics, and of negativity, in so far as Hegel believes them to be the immanent source of movement and becoming. The illusion in question is one that, in his early work, Deleuze sought to criticise and avoid, precisely to the extent that it claimed to be the realisation of immanence as such, and so the completion of philosophy. Much, if not the whole of what Deleuze writes between 1954 and 1969 can be seen as a direct attack on Hegel, whom Deleuze 'detests'.[2] Up until *Logic of Sense*, Deleuze's philosophy is concerned with reconciling the genetic and structural standpoints by constructing a transcendental empiricism, or an ontological monism, which does not follow in the footsteps of Hegel, at least as presented by Hyppolite, most significantly in *Genèse et structure de la phénoménologie de l'esprit de Hegel* and *Logique et existence*.[3] Deleuze's 'detestation' of speculative dialectics stems from the fact that he sees Hegel's method as the figure of transcendence disguised as absolute immanence. On Hyppolite's reading, Hegel completes immanence by overcoming the distinction between the phenomenal and the intelligible world. What Hegel calls the Absolute is not a transcendent 'beyond', but the infinite movement of thought that is identical with the phenomenal world:

> Hegelian logic recognises neither the thing-in-itself nor the intelligible world. The Absolute is not thought anywhere else than in the phenomenal world. Absolute thought thinks itself in our thought. In our thought, being presents itself as thought and as sense. And Hegel's dialectical logic, like the logic of philosophy, is the expression of this doctrine of complete immanence.[4]

Deleuze's most sustained and systematic critique of Hegel is perhaps to be found in *Difference and Repetition*.[5] It is summarised in the following quotation: 'Hegel's audacity [*audace*] is the final and most powerful homage rendered to the old principle [of identity and transcendence].'[6] Hegel's dialectic is movement, and even infinite movement. As such, it gives the *impression* of being produced immanently. But it produces movement and immanence with words and representations only. The movement and immanence of speculative dialectics are not real, but abstract, and false. Despite Hegel's claim that the negative is the very engine of actuality, it is in fact nothing real. It is only an illusion. The real itself is not produced or moved as a result of some intrinsic negativity, some self-opposing or contradictory logic. There is, however, such a thing as non-being, Deleuze claims: it is the being of what he calls the problematical, the being of the problem, or of the question. He also calls it the virtual.[7] Non-being, in this instance, refers to what is not actual, yet entirely real: it is the differential element, the multiplicity of pre-individual and purely positive singularities. It is only when we mistake non-being for the negative that contradiction is introduced into the real. In reality, however, contradiction is only an appearance or an epiphenomenon, the illusion that is projected by the problem itself, or the 'shadow' of the question.[8] The negative is a false problem, because it is only the 'effect' of a difference, or a play of differences, which precede identity. Deleuze's objection to Hegel, then, is that he's trying to pull the wool over our eyes, to present to us as real (and as reality itself) that which, in fact, is only an illusion, or the surface effect of a deeper, virtual reality:

> Forms of the negative do indeed appear in actual terms and real relations, but only in so far as these are cut off from the virtuality which they actualise, and from the movement of their actualisation. Then, and only then, do the finite affirmations appear limited in themselves, opposed to one another, and suffering from lack or privation. In short, the negative is always derived and represented, never original or present: the process of difference and differenciation [which is the process of the real as involving processes of individuation from virtual differentiation] is primary in relation to that of the negative and opposition.[9]

It is only by restricting thought to the actual that it becomes possible to turn the negative into the source of movement and the principle of generation. But genuine genesis and true movement are always played out elsewhere. Dialectical immanence is a fake or simulated immanence, a simulacrum of truth. Rather than oppose Hegel (and we have learned from Derrida how ultimately self-defeating such an opposition must be), Deleuze chooses to carry out the genesis, or even the genealogy of the negative, to reveal its mechanism by returning to its unspoken origin: 'The critique of the negative is radical and well grounded only when it carries out a genesis of affirmation and, *simultaneously*, the genesis of the appearance [in the sense of semblance: *apparence*] of negation.'[10] Chapter 5 of *Difference and Repetition* claims that the illusion of the negative lies in the fact that dialectics is able to recognise only the actual, or extended differences,

Ontology I: Genesis

in the real. In extensity, Deleuze claims, differences can indeed *appear* to be oppositions. But differences in extended time-space always presuppose their intensive depth, that is, differences that are inequalities, pure differentials without negation. Consequently, the illusion of the negative is not just transcendental: it is also physical. It is nature itself that produces these illusions, these effects of positivity. It is, as Deleuze claims, a 'transcendental physical illusion'.[11] Negation, opposition, contradiction remain at the surface of the real, at the level of its effects, without ever being in a position to intimate its virtually and purely differentiated depth. In the end, we may have to go so far as to recognise transcendence not only as the danger and risk of philosophy, but also as the inevitable corollary of immanence, as the supplement of thought itself, or the residue of reality. Ultimately, it will be a question of asking whether one can ever be done with transcendence.

2. Spinoza: *Immanence and Univocity*

If, for the very reasons I have just outlined, there can be no end of philosophy, there is perhaps the possibility of something like its completion, in the guise of the appropriation of its own internal conditions, or of the difference that makes it possible, and to which its concepts would testify. This, at least, is what, according to Deleuze, Spinoza managed to achieve: 'He completed [*il a achevé*] philosophy, because he fulfilled its pre-philosophical presupposition.'[12] In saying this, Deleuze seems to agree with Hegel's own praise of Spinoza, and the privileged position which he occupies in the history of philosophy:

> It is therefore worthy of note that thought must begin by placing itself at the standpoint of Spinozism; to be a follower of Spinoza is the essential commencement of all Philosophy. For as we saw above when man begins to philosophise, the soul must commence by bathing itself in this ether of the One substance, in which all that man has held as true has disappeared.[13]

Yet Deleuze reads Spinoza *against* Hegel, and sees in a positive light what Hegel eventually criticises in Spinoza, that is, his non-dialectical, formal, deductive method, and his inability to trace the 'inner movement of its subject matter'.[14] In other words, Deleuze sees Spinoza precisely as a way out of Hegel and the false movement of dialectic. Against Hegel, and against Hegel's own nuanced, but ultimately critical, assessment of Spinoza, he understands Spinoza as having revealed the inner movement of his subject matter.[15] Before making immanence in his own way and with his own concepts, then, Deleuze discovers it in Spinoza, whom he calls the 'prince' and the 'Christ' of philosophers.[16] Of course, it is not as if it were already there, ready-made as it were. In fact, as we shall see, Spinoza doesn't even speak of immanence as such, but of immanent causality. With a degree of hermeneutic violence, Deleuze needs to extract immanence from Spinoza's thought. His approach is rather idiosyncratic: it is seemingly the work of an historian of philosophy, yet it is also, and above all, that of an original thinker responding to that which, in Spinoza, opens up a future for thought:

> It was on Spinoza that I worked most seriously according to the norms of the history of philosophy – but it was Spinoza more than any other that gave me the feeling of a gust of air that pushes you on the back each time you read him, a witch's broomstick that he mounts you atop.[17]

If, according to Deleuze, Spinoza is the philosopher *par excellence*, it is because he laid out the plane of immanence that was to become the reference for all future philosophy. In Spinoza, and for the first time in the history of philosophy, there is a concept of immanence that coincides completely (and not only partially) with that of God, or Being. With him, in a way, there is no longer a difference between the plane of immanence and the concepts of thought, between the horizon of thought and thought itself: thought has become truly infinite. Up until Spinoza, immanence was already at work in philosophy, but always as a goal that could never quite be fulfilled. Why? No doubt because it was the most dangerous theme: when God begins to be envisaged as an immanent cause, there is no longer any possibility of distinguishing clearly between it and its creatures, between the cause and the effect. In the whole history of heresies, the accusation of immanentism was the most damning, and the confusion of God and his creatures amounted to the most serious fault. In fact, it is such an accusation that caused Spinoza's excommunication from the Jewish community of Amsterdam in July of 1656.[18] Although given from the start, as the horizon and the demand of philosophy, immanence couldn't be realised, nor manage to find a place within the concepts of philosophy, so long as it remained subordinated to a version of transcendence. With Spinoza, and for the first time, reality (made up of modes and attributes) is no longer immanent *to* the substance (or God), and the substance is itself entirely immanent.

Ontology I: Genesis

The whole of the *Ethics* is constructed on one primordial proposition, which can be characterised as theoretical or speculative, and which stipulates the following: there is one absolutely infinite substance only, that is, one substance that possesses all attributes, and what we call the creatures are precisely not creatures, but the modes or the ways of being of that substance. And if they are the ways of being of the substance that possesses all attributes, then they must exist or be contained in the attributes of the substance. The immediate consequence, to which we shall return, is the levelling (or the ironing out) and the flattening – the *aplanissement* and *aplatissement* – of a vertical and hierarchical structure, of a sequence of concepts: there is no hierarchy, no sequence between the attributes, or between thought and extension, but a single fixed plane on which everything takes place. This is what Deleuze calls the plane of immanence. It is the plane that is at work, from the start and always, as the presupposition of philosophy, the plane that underpins the history of philosophy. At the same time, however, this plane always needs to be drawn, established and secured. It's always there, but never as something entirely given. Concepts are the tools with which the plane of immanence is assembled.

Deleuze's concern with immanence, then, is intimately bound up with his reading of Spinoza. It emerges explicitly within the context of his *thèse complémentaire* of 1968 which, as a thesis in the history of philosophy, is concerned to inscribe Spinoza within a historical perspective. The choice of Spinoza is highly significant, especially when considered alongside Deleuze's other, more systematic thesis (*Difference and Repetition*). In other words, there is a broader context, and a more systematic problematic, which frames the historical work in question. This is the problematic concerned with identifying the *real* and immanent conditions of experience, and this means, for Deleuze, the *genetic* conditions of reality itself – a goal that requires the invention of philosophy as transcendental empiricism, and the defence of ontology as univocal. In so far as philosophy is concerned with the conditions of experience, it is transcendental. In so far as it is concerned with the real – and not merely possible – conditions of experience, it is empirical. Against Kant's transcendental philosophy, Deleuze argues two things: first, there is a real difference, or a difference of kind, between the empirical and the transcendental (Kant could only model the transcendental field after the empirical, and thus introduce a relation of resemblance between the two); second, philosophy must be able to explore the transcendental field for itself, and thus experience it in a way that is quite specific (for Kant, and by definition, the transcendental could not be turned into an object of experience). The difficulty is then to know how this clear distinction between the transcendental and the empirical does not amount to a dualism, but is in fact the only way to establish philosophy as univocity. This is where Spinoza proves to be crucial: his thought is a decisive stage on the way to immanence. As such, Spinoza is more than just a figure in the history of philosophy.

In Chapter 11 of *Expressionism in Philosophy: Spinoza*, Deleuze comes very close to providing a synthetic account of immanence in the history of philosophy leading up to Spinoza. Let it be said from the start that, according to Deleuze, the concept of expression is precisely the one that enables Spinoza to achieve the standpoint of absolute immanence in philosophy. Expression is introduced as an alternative to the concepts of participation (to which it is also related), imitation, creation and emanation. Expression, therefore, is seen as a key moment in the realisation of philosophy as immanent ontology. The question that Deleuze raises at the outset of the chapter is the following: What are the logical links between immanence and expression? And what is the historical link between the two concepts? In order to answer these questions, we first need to establish the link between immanence and emanation.

A. EMANATION

In the *thèse complémentaire*, and following Spinoza's own thought, Deleuze introduces the theme of immanence through the classical problem of causality.[19] God, or Nature, Spinoza claims, is the cause of all things. However, he is quick to add that 'God is the immanent cause of things, and not the transitive cause.' A 'transitive' cause lies 'outside' its effect. A watchmaker, for example, is the transitive cause of his watch. An 'immanent' cause is in some sense 'inside' or 'together with' that which it causes. The nature of a circle, for example, is the immanent cause of its roundness. Spinoza's claim is that God does not stand outside the world and create it; rather, God exists *in* the world and subsists together with what it creates: 'All things, I say, are in God and move in God.' This is precisely the extent to which God is identical with Nature, or Being. In other words: God is an *immanent* cause. This is a type of causality that, ultimately, has the advantage of reconciling the Aristotelian and Scholastic efficient causality, still at work in Descartes, with the Neoplatonic 'emanative cause', which it extends and transforms. How?[20]

Ontology I: Genesis

In order to answer this question, we need to go back to the Platonic problem of participation,[21] understood in the following ways: to participate is to be a part of something; but it is also to imitate,[22] and also to receive something from a demon.[23] As a result, participation is interpreted at times materially, at times imitatively, and at other times still 'demonically'. But in each case, Plato seeks the principle of participation on the side of what participates. Participation is something like an accident that happens to what is participated, something of the order of a violence imposed on the participated. If participation is a matter of being a part and of taking part, literally as it were, it is difficult to see how the participated would not suffer from such an intrusion, division, or separation. If, on the other hand, to participate means to imitate, there is the need for an artist, who takes the Idea as his model. The role of the intermediary, whether artist or demon, is to force the sensible to *reproduce* the intelligible, while also forcing the Idea to allow itself to *be participated* by something alien to its own nature.

Faced with this problem, Neoplatonic thought decides to invert it: it seeks to identify a *principle* that would make participation possible, only, this time, from the point of view of the participated itself. This is how the One comes to be posited as the highest principle, over and beyond everything else, including Being. In the One, there is no division or distinction. It is absolutely simple, undifferentiated. As such, it isn't really anything, and can't be described. And yet, at the same time, it is everything, because it is the potentiality of all things. It is very much like the One of Plato's *Parmenides*,[24] of which everything can be affirmed and denied at the same time. In fact, Plotinus (205–70 CE) borrows his idea of the One as the highest principle from the Platonic dialogue. But Plato's *Republic*, Book 6, is also a source of inspiration: the One is equally the Good, in so far as it provides each thing with its being, or gives beingness to all beings. This, in turn, means that, like the Good, it is itself 'beyond being' (επέκεινα της ουσίας), since *to be* for Plato is necessarily to be *something*. So, whilst not an essence or a substance, the One is a *hypostasis*: it is a reality but one that, unlike the divine intellect, being, or life, is absolutely indeterminate. No positive attributes of any kind can be attached to it, not even those of 'one' and 'good', which are introduced only in relation to the following, subordinate hypostases. The question, then, is one of knowing why the One does not remain forever contracted within itself, why, unlike the Aristotelian unmoved mover, it feels compelled to cause or produce anything.²⁵ In fact, it does not feel compelled to do anything, and its production is entirely unconscious and involuntary. It is simply attributable to a kind of excess or abundance, which, like water flowing out of a fountain, produces effects of itself. Its production is purely a function of its perfection. This process is known as emanation, but is best described as a procession, that is, as the production of something that proceeds from the highest principle. Whilst flowing or proceeding from the One, the product seeks to remain as close to the source as possible, and to turn towards it so as to contemplate it. In this turning back, or this conversion, the second hypostasis – that of Intelligence, the intelligible world, and Being – is born.²⁶ As a consequence, the Neoplatonist universe is composed of hierarchically distinct things. At the same time, however, all things are part of a single continuous emanation of power from the One.

The Neoplatonists no longer start with the characteristics of what participates (as multiple, sensible, and so on), in order to ask about the type of violence by which participation becomes possible. Rather, they try to discover the internal principle and movement that grounds participation in the participated as such. The participated does not in fact enter into what participates in it. What is participated remains within itself. It is participated in so far as it *produces*, and produces in so far as it *gives*. But in order to produce or give, it need not leave or be separated from itself. This, according to Deleuze, is Plotinus' project: to start at the highest point, with the highest reality, to subordinate imitation to genesis or production, and substitute the idea of a *gift* for that of a violence. As a result, the participated is not divided, is not imitated from without, or constrained by intermediaries that would do violence to its nature. Participation is neither material, nor imitative, nor even demonic. Rather, it is *emanative*. Entities are said to 'emanate' from such a principle. Emanation is at once a principle of causation and an operation of donation: it causes by giving, or gives by producing. It's the participated that does the work now, and what participates is only an effect of that cause. Because everything emanates from it, because it *gives* everything, it is itself not something which entities take part in, or are a part of. This is also the basis of Proclus' theory of the Imparticipable: participation only occurs through a principle that is itself imparticipable, but that gives something in which to take part, or to be a part of.²⁷ In Plotinus' words: the One is necessarily above its gifts as it is above its products, participable only through what it gives. It is not what it gives, and does not have what it gives. In itself or as itself, it is imparticipable.²⁸

Ontology I: Genesis

On the one hand, then, this theory constitutes a progress with respect to the Platonic theory of participation, in so far as it shifts the emphasis from the participant to the participated, or from imitation to causality. On the other hand, it is able to do so only at the cost of reintroducing an order of transcendence between being and its cause. When Plotinus claims that the One has 'nothing in common' with the things that emanate from it,[29] it is with a view to emphasising the fact that the emanative cause is superior not only to its effect, but also to what it provides the effect with. And this is precisely the reason why the One, and not Being, is identified as the primary cause: since it gives being to all beings, it is necessarily *beyond* being or essence. So, emanation, in its pure state, is inseparable from a system of the One-above-being, inseparable, that is, from a hierarchy ultimately incompatible with the ontological (as well as ethical and political) univocity Deleuze seeks to establish. Needless to say, the first hypothesis of the *Parmenides* dominates Neoplatonism as a whole.[30]

B. EXPRESSION

What do the immanent and the emanative cause ultimately have in common? The fact that neither externalises itself: both produce something *while remaining in themselves*. Spinoza himself makes the connection between the two causes in the *Short Treatise*.[31] The two causes differ significantly, however, with respect to the way in which they produce. The emanative cause remains within itself, but the effect that it produces doesn't. The emanative cause produces through what it gives, but actually remains *beyond* what it gives. In the end, then, an effect emerges from its cause, exists only through that process, or is determined in its existence only through the cause from which it came. A cause is immanent, on the other hand, when the effect is itself 'immanate' ('*immané*') in the cause, and not when it simply 'emanates' from it. What defines the immanent cause, then, is the fact that the effect it produces remains within it, albeit as something else. As a result, the difference in essence between the cause and the effect can never be interpreted as a *degradation*. From the point of view of immanence, the distinction of essence does not exclude, but rather implies, an equality of being: it is *the same* being that remains in itself in the cause, and in which the effect remains as in something else. There is a further fundamental difference between the two causes. Whilst immanence implies a pure, positive ontology, or a theory of Being for which the One is not even an attribute or a universal of Being (or Substance), but only one of its many characters, emanation is a theology, or an onto-theology, for which the One is necessarily *beyond* Being. Its ontology is, as a result, negative and analogical: it respects the eminence of the principle or cause.³²

Analogy, it is well known, was introduced to avoid the risk of anthropocentrism in natural theology and, more importantly, of the confusion between the finite and the infinite. Aquinas (who, it is true, developed this argument not in relation to the Platonic tradition, but to Aristotelian metaphysics primarily) states that the qualities we attribute to God do not imply a community of form between the divine substance and its creatures, but only an analogy, that is, a relation of either proportion or proportionality. According to the former, God possesses *eminently* a perfection that exists only derivatively or formally in his creatures (Goodness, for example), whereas, according to the analogy of proportionality, God possesses *formally* a perfection that remains extrinsic in the creatures (the divine goodness is to God as human goodness is to man). The theory of analogy allows philosophy to maintain the transcendence of God, and not think his being under the same category as the being of his creatures. Univocity, on the other hand, by declaring being the one principle common to all beings (including God), or what can be predicated of everything that is, subsumes the difference between God and all other beings under a single essence. As such, it threatens to erase the singularity of God, and subsumes theology under metaphysics understood as the science concerned with what is primarily knowable, or the highest principle, namely, the being common to all beings (*ens commune*).³³ Spinoza reverses the problem by claiming that it is analogy, and equivocity, not univocity, which are guilty of anthropocentrism. Every time we proceed analogically, he claims, we borrow certain features from the creatures, and attribute them to God, either equivocally (formally) or eminently. In his view, attributes are forms that are common to God, whose essence they constitute, and to the modes or creatures, in which they are implicated. The same forms are affirmed of God and his creatures, despite the fact that God and his creatures differ both essentially and existentially. In other words, creatures differ from God in both essence and existence, and yet, at the same time, *formally*, God possesses something in common with the creatures, namely, the attributes. The modes *implicate* or *envelop* the attributes, whereas God is *explicated* in them. Attributes are univocal forms of being, forms that do not change in nature when changing 'subjects'. This means: their sense does not change, whether we predicate them of infinite being or finite beings, of the substance or the modes, of God or the creatures. To that extent, Spinoza is the inheritor and follower of Scotus. Yet univocity in Scotus was compromised by the desire to avoid pantheism. The theological, and this means, creationist perspective forced him to conceive of univocal Being as an indifferent, neutral concept, indifferent to the finite and the infinite, the singular and the universal, the perfect and the imperfect, the created and the uncreated. For Spinoza, on the other hand, the concept of univocal Being is perfectly determinate, as what is predicated in one and the same sense of substance in itself, and of modes that are in something else. With Spinoza univocity becomes the object of a pure affirmation. It is the same thing that, *formaliter*, constitutes the essence of substance and contains the essences of modes. What the idea of the immanent cause does, then, is to extend that of univocity, liberating it from the indifference and the neutrality in which it was held in the theory of divine creation. It is with the Spinozist conception of immanence that univocity finds its genuinely philosophical formulation: God is said to be the cause of all things *in the very sense* (*eo senso*) that he is said to be his own cause.[34] There lies the major difference with Descartes, for whom God is *causa sui*, but in a sense other than the sense in which it is the efficient cause of the things it creates.[35] As a result, being cannot be said in the same sense of everything that is, of divine substance and created substances, of substances and modes, etc. It is only by analogy with the efficient cause that God can be said to be *causa sui*. By contrast, Spinoza's *causa sui* cannot be said in a sense other than the efficient cause. On the contrary: it is the efficient cause that is said in the same sense as the *causa sui*. God produces or creates exactly as he is or exists. Spinoza's remarkable achievement is to have developed an ontology that is opposed to any eminence of the cause, any negative theology, any method of analogy, and any hierarchical conception of the world.

In the end, emanation is the principle of a universe in which the difference between beings in general is conceived as a hierarchical difference: each term, as it were, is the image of the superior term that precedes it, and is defined by the degree of distance that separates it from the first cause or first principle. Pure immanence, on the other hand, requires as a principle the equality of being, or the positing of equal Being: not only is Being equal in itself, but it is equally present in all beings; not only is it said of everything that is, but it is said in the same *sense* – as 'expression'. From the point of view of being, all beings – stones, animals, rational and irrational human beings – are equal, that is to say, worth the same. Similarly, the cause is equally close everywhere: there is no remote causation. Beings are not defined by their rank in a hierarchy, as in Neoplatonism; they are not more or less remote from the One. Rather, each depends directly on God, takes part in the equality of being, and receives all that it can receive within the limits of its essence. This means that, in its pure state, immanence requires a univocal Being, or a Nature that consists in positive forms (which Spinoza calls attributes) only, common to the producer and the produced, to the cause and the effect. In immanence, there is indeed a superiority of the cause over the effect (Spinoza retains the distinction between essences), but one that involves no eminence, that is to say, no positing of any principle beyond the forms that are themselves present in the effect. Participation must be understood entirely positively, and not on the basis of an eminent gift. Anarchy, and not hierarchy, is the defining feature of immanent causality.

For Spinoza, to be an entity at all is to exist 'in' or 'through' the one substance, to be a *modification* of that substance's essence. Nothing can be or be conceived outside of substance, which is infinite. All things are 'in' it. Univocal Being is immanent in its diverse manifestations. The essence of substance, Spinoza insists, is absolutely infinite power, and more specifically, the absolutely unlimited power to exist and generate effects. Spinoza equates essence and power at several points in the *Ethics*. But things are not the same with respect to the existence of substance, or to the manner in which it actually is. Substance actually exists as mode, as the 'things' that follow from its essence and express that essence determinately. Substance actually exists not as the power to generate effects, but as those effects. And each expresses, to the extent that it can, substance's essence. As essence, substance is *natura naturans*, that is, nature in its infinite power of expression. As existence, however, it is *natura naturata*, that is, nature realised or actualised – expressed – in this or that manner, as this or that mode. At the same time, 'the existence of God and his essence are one and the same'.[36] The possibility of viewing God, or Nature, from two different perspectives does not imply the existence of two distinct ontological realities. *Natura naturans* and *natura naturata* are not two different things. Rather, the former is expressed immanently in the latter.

But in truth, the Spinozist logic of expression involves two distinct levels of expression: 'expression, through its own movement, generates a second level of expression'.[37] Substance expresses itself first as essence, or attribute, and then as existence, or mode – or, if one prefers, first as power, and then as act. Each attribute 'expresses eternal and infinite essence',[38] but in one determinate way.[39] The first level of expression corresponds to a process of determination, which generates forms. Thus Thought and Extension both express the essence of substance, but determine that essence into different forms. Once this first expression has taken place – once substance is considered under one attribute rather than another – substance re-expresses itself at a second level. More specifically, 'the attributes are in their turn expressed: they express themselves in modes which designate them, the modes expressing a modification'.[40] Each mode expresses the power of substance, after its own fashion and to the extent that it can. So 'this second level defines production itself: God is said to produce things, as his attributes find expression'.[41] And since production is always of particular modes, Deleuze says that 'the production of modes [takes] place through differentiation'.[42] Thus expression comprises two movements: one from substance to attribute, the other from attribute to mode. The first is qualitative expression, through which substance renders itself determinate in certain (infinite) forms. The second is quantitative expression, through which these forms express themselves in turn through the production of particular modes. Expression comprises both determination and differentiation.

This, then, is how Deleuze is able to isolate expression as the category that establishes the principle of immanence for philosophy. In doing so, he follows Koyré's thesis, according to which the concept of expression constitutes an extension of, and an alternative to, not only that of emanation, but also those of 'complication' and 'explication', which already establish the priority of the immanent cause over the emanative cause.[43] The sixth century CE and 'last' Neoplatonist, Damascius (480–550), had already suggested that between the One and its many hypostases, or between the One and the Many, there is a double relation of comprehension and explication: whilst the Many is concentrated or *comprised* in the One, the One is *explicated* in the Many. At about the same time, Boethius applied the terms *comprehendere*, *complectiri* to eternal Being.[44] The nominal couple *complicatio-explicatio*, or the adjectival *complicative-explicative*, takes on great importance in Boethius' commentators, notably in the twelfth-century School of Chartres. But it is above all in Renaissance philosophy, in Nicholas of Cusa (1401–64) and Bruno (1548–1600), that these concepts acquire their rigorous philosophical character.[45] The central idea is that whilst all things are present in God, who *complicates* them, God is present in all things, which *explicate* and implicate him. The crucial evolution is that the successive and hierarchically ordered emanations of Neoplatonism now give way to the co-presence of two correlative movements. Things remain in God while also explicating and implicating him. Similarly, God remains in himself as he complicates them. The presence of things in God constitutes an 'inherence', just as the presence of God in things constitutes an 'implication'. God is this complicative principle that is explicated through things: 'God is the universal complication, in the sense that everything is in him; and the universal explication, in the sense that he is in everything'.[46] In place of a hierarchy of hypostases, we now have the equality of being; for things are present in the same Being, which is itself present in things. Immanence corresponds to the unity of complication and explication, of inherence and implication.

Deleuze himself draws the connection between expression and the dyad complication-explication in *Proust and Signs* (1964), in many ways a Neoplatonic book. In that book, Deleuze claims that the Proustian world is a world of signs – social, erotic, sensible (or material), and, above all, artistic – that *express* essences.[47] If those essences are eternal, it is precisely in the sense that they constitute the complicated state of time itself, and not the absence of change, or even the extension of a limitless existence: 'Certain Neoplatonists used a profound word to designate the original state that precedes any development, any deployment [*déploiement*], any "explication": *complication*, which envelops the many in the One and affirms the unity of the multiple.'[48] Thus, there is an essence of Combray, which Marcel's cup of tea explicates, or develops; similarly, that essence remains implicated, or enveloped, in the cup of tea. There is an essence of Swann and Odette's love, which the Vinteuil sonata, or a moment of it, explicates. In thus explicating itself, however, that essence doesn't exhaust itself. Rather, it reveals itself as the complication, or the mutual implication, of the sign and its meaning. First of all, meaning is implicated in the sign; it is like one thing wrapped or coiled (*enroulée*) in another. But implication does not go without explication: the sign develops, uncoils (*se déroule*) at the same time that it is interpreted. 'Implication and explication, envelopment and development: such are the categories of the *Recherche*.'[49] Thus, we see how, through his jealousy, the lover (Swann or Marcel) develops the possible worlds enclosed within the beloved. Similarly, the man

Ontology I: Genesis

guided by the signs of the sensible liberates the 'souls' implicated in the material world. Meaning itself coincides with this development of the sign as the sign coincided with the involution or the envelopment of meaning. As for Essence, it is the third term that dominates the two, their 'sufficient reason': essence complicates the sign and its meaning; it *complicates* them by putting one in the other. In that respect, Charlus is perhaps the most 'complicated', and the most fascinating, of all the Proustian characters. He seems to be concentrating an infinity of signs, and to be expressing an endless series of worlds and 'souls', which send the narrator on a deciphering frenzy.

That being said, immanence is constantly threatened by the demand to maintain and guarantee the transcendence of the divine being. Such is the reason why, in the Renaissance, as well as in modern times, philosophy is constantly accused of heresy (immanence and pantheism), and why philosophers themselves are so eager to avoid this accusation. For the most part, the way in which the transcendence of the Creator is saved is through an analogical conception of Being, or at least through an eminent conception of God that limits the consequences of Being as equality. In actual fact, the principle of equality of Being is itself interpreted analogically: it is the same God, the same infinite being, which is affirmed and explicated in the world as immanent cause, and which remains inexpressible and transcendent as the object of a negative theology that negates everything that was affirmed of its immanence. There, immanence appears as a limit-theory that is contained and attenuated through the perspective of emanation and creation. With Spinoza, on the other hand, participation finds its principle not in some emanation of which the One would be the source – with varying degrees of distance – but in the immediate and adequate *expression* of an absolute Being that comprises all beings and explicates itself through their individual essence: all beings manifest or express a ground with which they are in some sense identical. With the concept of expression, philosophy is once and for all free of emanation and resemblance: the things produced are modes of the divine, that is to say, they implicate the same attributes as those that constitute the nature of this divine being. Ultimately, the concept of expression is able to bring together the Neoplatonic and Renaissance notions of complication, explication, inherence and implication. In doing so, it is also able to realise immanence: immanence turns out to be expressive, and expression turns out to be immanent, in what has become a system of logical (and no longer simply historical) relations. With Spinoza, philosophy is finally at home, finally 'completed'.

3. Expression and Differentiation

In many ways, Deleuze's two doctoral theses, namely, *Difference and Repetition* and *Expressionism in Philosophy: Spinoza*, complement one another. The absence, or, better said perhaps, the discrete presence of Spinoza in *Difference and Repetition* cannot be taken as an indication of his limited role in the elaboration of the problematic of difference, and the thesis of univocity. Rather, we should understand the book on Spinoza as the necessary theoretical and historical supplement to *Difference and Repetition*, one that Deleuze will continue to develop and modify after 1968. In fact, what *Difference and Repetition* identifies as its own method of '*dramatisation*', and the twofold principle of '*différent/ciation*' it locates at the heart of being, is a direct equivalent of what the book on Spinoza refers to as 'expression'. The semantic similarities between the two terms are obvious. Yet they also function in a way that is equivalent: they are both concerned with the possibility of a presentation without representation, with the 'theatre' of the world and its conditions of existence: 'What we call drama resembles particularly the Kantian schema.'[50] It resembles the Kantian schema, but is not identical with it, precisely in so far as it designates not just the manner in which a concept or an idea can be presented in an intuition, but the manner in which phenomena themselves come to *be*, or are generated, in the first place. The category of expression, like that of dramatisation, reveals phenomena with respect to their conditions of existence, and not only with respect to their conditions of appearance. It is an ontological category. It is concerned with the being of phenomena themselves, but in the sense of their coming into existence, or their *genesis*. A such, it is an ontogenetic category. Unlike past theories of genesis and individuation, however, those of expression and dramatisation do not posit the principle or the condition of existence of phenomena outside of or above the phenomena themselves, in a cognitive faculty of the subject, for example. It is in that respect that they can be said to be immanent. This is the point at which the thesis of immanence coincides with that of univocity.

What *Difference and Repetition* recognises as a crucial move in the thesis regarding the univocity of being is a threefold possibility: the possibility, first of all, of a unified ontology through the recognition of an essential ontological sameness between not just God and the human, but all things. This sameness in no way signifies that God and the human being, or indeed all beings, are identical: ontological

Ontology I: Genesis

sameness does not imply ontical identity. Rather, it signifies that their very difference stems from a single being that is itself entirely indifferent to this difference as well as to its many differences. It means that if being can be said or predicated of this difference, as well as of all its other differences, it is always *in the same sense*. Being is equal (and equally indifferent) to all its individuating differences, yet these differences are precisely not equal amongst themselves. Being is said in one and the same sense of all its differences or intrinsic modalities, but these differences do not have the same sense. Univocal being essentially relates to individuating differences, but these differences do not have the same essence, and are precisely not 'variations' of the essence of being. In other words, it is not a question of annulling the difference between God and man, or between any two given phenomena, but of showing how, paradoxically perhaps, all modalities and differences are, to use Spinoza's own term, *expressions* of a single being or substance: 'One and the same voice [*voix*] for the thousand ways of the multiple [*le multiple aux mille voies*], one and the same Ocean for all the drops, one clamour of Being for all beings.'[51] Following Spinoza, Deleuze allows all differences to be expressions of a single being. Far from signifying the end of differences, therefore, the univocity of being constitutes their sole affirmation:

> There are not two 'paths', as Parmenides' poem suggests, but a single 'voice' of Being which includes all its modes, including the most diverse, the most varied, the most differentiated. Being is said in one and the same sense of everything of which it is said, but that of which it is said differs: it is said of difference itself.[52]

Paradoxically, then, univocity opens directly onto an ontology of difference. This is the second possibility, and one that is not explicitly developed in Spinoza: Being is said in one and the same sense of all its differences or intrinsic modalities, but these differences do not themselves have the same sense. They are all *expressions* of the same sense of being, which, in *Difference and Repetition*, is identified with difference itself. Specifically, and as I was suggesting a moment ago, Being, or Nature, is seen as involving a twofold movement of different/ciation equally real, yet not equally actual. Only the latter type of differen*c*iation coincides with a process of actualisation. The former, on the other hand, coincides with the distribution of *virtual* singularities across an intensive field, the differential potential of which forces a given system (*any* system) to resolve or actualise itself through the creation of divergent and bifurcating lines.

For Aristotle, and for an entire tradition after him, difference remained caught up within the identity of the concept (of the genus or of essence), its many forms as *specific* difference always presupposing the form of identity within generic concepts. As such, difference was never itself a concept. With Deleuze, on the other hand, being is said of difference alone, and this in such a way that the very form of the concept no longer presupposes that of identity. With univocity, ontology frees itself from the primacy of the identity of the concept, which is also always a primacy of the concept of identity. Finally, with univocity and expressionism, differences are no longer simply *in quid*, attributable to being as to the identity of a concept, but actually determining and, above all, individuating. As a result, and as I was alluding to a moment ago, ontology becomes a philosophy of individuation, or a philosophy concerned with the genesis of individuated entities; it becomes *ontogenesis*. This means that, in the wake of Nietzsche, Bergson and Heidegger, Deleuze is able to reconcile being with time, and the univocity of being with the ever-changing flow of becoming. When, Deleuze argues, we claim that univocal being relates immediately and essentially to 'individuating factors', we need to understand that they are precisely not individuals, or individuated entities. For univocity implies impersonality. Rather, what we have in mind is the transcendental principle (or, better said perhaps, the transcendental potential) coextensive with the process of individuation at the heart of these individuals. Such a principle (the 'virtual'), Deleuze claims, is just as capable of dissolving and destroying individuals as it is capable of constituting them temporarily. These 'individuating factors' are intrinsic to being, moving from one 'individual' to the next, circulating, and communicating beneath forms and matters. Individuation actually *precedes* all elements pertaining to the constituted individual: matter and form, species and parts, etc. The univocity of being demands that we show how individuating differences within being precede generic, specific and even individual differences. In other words, the movement and process of individuation, to which univocity alone leads, is altogether heterogeneous to the traditional operation of specification, as well as to the individuation through form and/or matter, both presupposing the analogy of being. In *Difference and Repetition*, being avoids analogy, and becomes univocal, by becoming genetic, and, more specifically, hetero-genetic. In that respect, it is an extension of Spinoza's expressionism: it is concerned with the manner in which Substance produces its own attributes, and then its own modes. This is what, in connection with Spinoza, Deleuze characterises as the two levels of expression. But the principle of production is now difference: in *Difference and Repetition*, expression becomes different/ciation.[53] Difference is now the transcendental horizon of all beings, or the condition of existence (and not possibility) of phenomena.

Notes

1. WP, 50/49.
2. See Deleuze's 'Lettre à Michel Cressole'. The letter was first published in *La Quinzaine littéraire*, no. 161, 1 April, pp. 17–19, and reprinted in *Pourparlers* (Paris: Éditions de Minuit, 1990) under the title 'Lettre à un critique sévère', pp. 11–23. The passage in question reads: 'What I detested the most was Hegelianism and dialectic' (p. 14).
3. Jean Hyppolite, *Genèse et structure de la phénoménologie de l'esprit de Hegel* (Paris: Aubier, 1947), trans. Samuel Cherniak and John Heckman, *Genesis and Structure in Hegel's 'Phenomenology of Spirit'* (Evanston: Northwestern University Press, 1974); *Logique et existence: Essai sur la logique de Hegel* (Paris: Aubier, 1952), trans. Leonard Lawlor and Amit Sen, *Logic and Existence* (Albany: SUNY Press, 1997). Those two books influenced an entire generation of French philosophers, from Deleuze to Foucault and Derrida, and it would not be an exaggeration to say that their thought started off as a response to Hyppolite's interpretation of Hegel. In 1954, Deleuze himself published a review of *Logic and Existence* for the *Revue philosophique de la France et l'étranger* (Vol. 144, pp. 457–60), a translation of which can be found as an Appendix to *Logic and Existence*. Whilst expressing his admiration for the manner in which Hyppolite rectifies the overly anthropological reading of Hegel inherited from Kojève, offering in its place a convincingly ontological interpretation of Hegel's thought as a whole, Deleuze wonders whether a different ontology, based on the concepts of difference and expression (concepts that organise Deleuze's *Difference and Repetition* and *Spinoza and the Problem of Expression*), should not take precedence over the Hegelian ontology of negation and contradiction.
4. Hyppolite, *Logic and Existence*, pp. 58–9.
5. DR, especially Chapters 1 (63–74/43–52), 4 (261–9/202–8), and 5 (303–4/235–6).
6. DR, 71/50.
7. See DR, Chapter 4. I deal with Deleuze's notion of the virtual and his own conception of movement and genesis in *Truth and Genesis: Philosophy as Differential Ontology*, Chapter 8 ('Virtual Multiplicities').
8. DR, 89/64.
9. DR, 267/207.

10. *DR*, 266/206.
11. *DR*, 294/228.
12. *WP*, 50/48.
13. *Hegel's Logic*, trans. W. Wallace (Oxford: Clarendon Press, 1975), p. 257.
14. For a precise account of the manner in which Deleuze uses Spinoza against Hegel, see Michael Hardt, *Gilles Deleuze: An Apprenticeship in Philosophy* (Minneapolis: University of Minnesota Press, 1993), pp. 65-71.
15. Regarding Hegel's interpretation of Spinoza, see his *Lectures on the History of Philosophy*, Volume III, in G. W. F. Hegel, *Werke*, Band 20 (Frankfurt am Main: Suhrkamp Verlag, 1986), pp. 157-96, and especially pp. 185 ff.
16. *WP*, 49/48 and 59/60, respectively.
17. *Dialogues*, 22/15.
18. The excommunication, or *cherem*, was read before the ark of the synagogue of Amsterdam on 27 July 1656. It speaks of the 'abominable heresies which he practiced and taught and about the monstrous deeds he did' and concludes that Spinoza 'should be excommunicated and expelled from the people of Israel', before formulating the following curse: 'Cursed be he by day and cursed be he by night; cursed be he when he lies down and cursed be he when he rises up. Cursed be he when he goes out and cursed be he when he comes in.' For an account of this episode and the events that led to it, see Matthew Stewart, *The Courtier and the Heretic: Leibniz, Spinoza and the Fate of God in the Modern World* (New Haven & London: Yale University Press, 2005), Chapter 2.
19. See Spinoza, *The Ethics* in *Complete Works* (Indianapolis & Cambridge: Hackett, 2002), edited, with introduction and notes, by Michael L. Morgan, trans. Samuel Shirley; Part I, Proposition 18.
20. See *Ethics*, I, Prop. 25.
21. Plato's most systematic, and aporetic, exposition of the problem of participation is perhaps to be found in *Parmenides*, 129a–134e.
22. With respect to the question of imitation we need only recall, for example, Socrates' description of the movement of the soul (*Phaedrus*, 246a–249d, *Republic*, Books V–VII), specifically in connection with the beautiful and the erotic (*Phaedrus*, 249d–257b; *Republic*, 473c–476d), his account of poetry, art and craftsmanship (*Republic* 393c–398b, 595a–607c), or his discussion of language, names and naming (*Cratylus*, 421c–427e).
23. According to Allan Bloom, demons are 'gods of lower rank, as it were, links between gods and men' and 'can become identified with personal geniuses' (Allan Bloom, *The Republic of Plato* [New York: Basic Books, 1968], p. 450). Such is the case of what, in the *Apology* (31d,

27d–e), Socrates calls his own 'voice', or *daimonion*. This is the divine, Apollonian voice that, speaking from beyond the city, has held Socrates back from entering public life, and set him on the path of truth and the good (of philosophy). It is also the cause of his trial before the Athenian court.
24. Plato, *Parmenides*, 137c ff.
25. See Plotinus, *Enneads*, trans. A. H. Armstrong (Cambridge, MA: Harvard University Press, Loeb Classical Library, 1984), especially III 8. 1; V 1. 7, 9; V 3. 15, 33; VI 9. 5, 36.
26. See Plotinus, *Enneads*, V 1. 6; V 2; V 3. 13 ff; V 4.
27. For Proclus (412–84 CE), a series is a collection of things that have something in common (for example, 'being good'). For every series, there is an imparticipated, or a transcendent term, which is neither in one of the terms, nor in all of them, but which exists prior to them (the Good, in the case of our example); and there is a participated, or a character that is common to all those things (goodness) and the participants (the things that we call good). See *The Elements of Theology: A Revised Text with Translation, Introduction, and Commentary*, by E. R. Dodds (Oxford: Clarendon Paperbacks, 1992), Propositions XXIII and XXIV.
28. Plotinus, *Enneads* VI. 7. xvii. 3–6. It is perhaps useful, here, to quote the following passage from E. Gilson's influential *L'Être et l'essence* (Paris: Vrin, 1948), which Deleuze himself cites: 'In a doctrine of Being, inferior things have being only by virtue of the being of superior things. In a doctrine of the One it is, on the contrary, a general principle that inferior things have being only by virtue of a higher thing not being; indeed the higher thing only ever gives what it does not have since, in order to give it, it must be above it' (p. 42).
29. Plotinus, *Enneads*, V, 5, §4.
30. The hypothesis in question is developed in *Parmenides*, 137b–160c.
31. Spinoza, *Short Treatise on God, Man, and his Well-Being*, in *Spinoza: Complete Works*, Part One, Chapter III, p. 50.
32. For Spinoza's critique of eminence, see *Ethics*, I, Prop. 15, Scholium, and Prop. 17, Corollary 2, Scholium.
33. Duns Scotus is the first and seminal thinker of the *ens commune*, and in that respect Spinoza's predecessor. For a concise formulation of the theory of univocity, see his *Ordinatio*, Prologue, §142.
34. EPS, 58/67. See also *Ethics*, I, Prop. XXXIII, Scholium II.
35. Descartes expresses this view most clearly, and at length, in his response to Antoine Arnauld's objections regarding his conception of God as formulated in his third and fifth *Meditations*. See Descartes, *Œuvres et lettres* (Paris: Gallimard 'Bibliothèque de la Pléiade', 1953), pp. 449–62. See also Descartes, *Principles of Philosophy*, §§ 20–2, 51, in *Œuvres et lettres*.

36. *Ethics*, I, Prop. 20.
37. *EPS*, 92/105.
38. *Ethics*, I, Prop. 11.
39. On the difficult and controversial question regarding the role of attributes in Spinoza's thought, especially in connection with Deleuze's own interpretation, see Michael Hardt, *Gilles Deleuze: An Apprenticeship in Philosophy*, pp. 79–87, and Antonio Negri, *The Savage Anomaly: The Power of Spinoza's Metaphysics and Politics* (Minneapolis: University of Minnesota Press, 1991), especially pp. 48–59.
40. *EPS*, 92/105.
41. *EPS*, 93/105.
42. *EPS*, 166/182–3.
43. See A. Koyré, *Mystiques, spirituels, alchimistes du XVIème siècle allemand* (Paris: Armand Colin, 1947).
44. Boethius, *The Consolation of Philosophy*, Book V, prose 6, trans., with an introduction, by Victor Watts (London: Penguin, 1999).
45. Deleuze's main source of inspiration on Cusa is M. de Gandillac, *La Philosophie de Nicolas de Cues* (Paris: Aubier, 1942).
46. Nicolas Cusanus, *Of Learned Ignorance*, trans. G. Heron (New Haven: Yale University Press, 1954), Book II, Chapter 3, p. 79 (translation modified).
47. We'll return to Deleuze's Neoplatonist interpretation of Proust in the last chapter of this book.
48. *PS*, 58/45.
49. *PS*, 109/89.
50. *DI*, 138/98.
51. *DR*, 389/304.
52. *DR*, 53/36.
53. In that respect, the importance of Bergson for Deleuze cannot be emphasised enough. The two decisive texts are 'La conception de la différence chez Bergson' (1956), now published in *L'île déserte*, and *Le bergsonisme* (1966). I have dealt with this connection, and with a sustained reading of *Difference and Repetition*, in *Truth and Genesis: Philosophy as Differential Ontology*, Part Three.

3

Ontology II: Cartography

I began by asking what thought means for Deleuze, the sort of activity it is, and the conditions under which it can be achieved. As the creation of concepts, which are thought's response to the singular events, or the impersonal and pre-individual differences, to which it is exposed, thought is essentially concerned with what, in *What is Philosophy?*, Deleuze calls the plane of immanence and what, in his earlier work, he calls the transcendental field of experience. The plane in question always runs the risk of being buried under the identities and the solutions it generates, and immobilised in instances of transcendence. So far, immanence has turned out to be a matter for ontology and, more specifically, for ontogenesis. We saw how, with Spinoza, philosophy reaches a point when, between the substance, the attributes, and the modes, there is no longer a vertical, transcendent, organisation of emanation, but a necesssary relation of *expression*. With Spinoza, and for the first time, philosophy is constructed on a single plane – the plane of immanence. We saw how Deleuze's interpretation of Spinoza is echoed in his own ontological treatise, and how the notion of 'dramatisation', central to *Difference and Repetition*, is perfectly consistent with Spinoza's concept of expression. That being said, I also emphasised that Deleuze reaches his own standpoint of immanence, and his own ontology, by becoming genetic, and, more specifically, heterogenetic. He extends Spinoza's expressionism by showing the way in which Substance *produces* its own attributes and modes through a double process of *different/ciation*. With Deleuze, difference becomes the transcendental horizon of all beings, or the condition of existence of attributes and modes. The question, from now on, will be one of knowing whether there is more to the plane of immanence than ontogenesis, or whether genesis exhausts the project of a purely immanent philosophy. Is ontology itself *only* ontogenesis, or is there a dimension of ontology that exceeds the limits of the ontogenetic problematic? And if, as I shall argue in this chapter, the latter turns out to be the case, can the Deleuzian project be seen to exceed the Spinozist framework in which I have so far inscribed it, or is it rather by deepening his understanding of Spinoza that Deleuze manages to extend his own conception of immanence? Finally, what are the consequences of such an extension of immanence for the classical domains of logic (Chapter 4), ethics (Chapter 5), and art (Chapter 6)?

Taking into account the trajectory of this book as a whole, and taking my lead from a few pages from *A Thousand Plateaus*, I would now like to distinguish between two different, equally legitimate and compatible projects, which Deleuze carried out in the course of his life, each involving immanence in its own way, or from a particular point of view. The first project, which Deleuze develops at length in *Difference and Repetition*, *Logic of Sense*, and in his readings of Spinoza, Kant and Bergson, can be described as ontogenetic. Yet ontogenesis doesn't exhaust ontology as such; the project that consists in extracting the (virtual) conditions of existence of (actual) phenomena doesn't exhaust the possibilities of thought itself. As I have already emphasised, the method of transcendental *empiricism* also involves the possibility of experiencing the virtual world of intensive singularities. To such a possibility corresponds the concept of *becoming*, which we will see at work in *Logic of Sense* and, more significantly, *Anti-Oedipus*.

Let me begin this new analysis by turning to *A Thousand Plateaus*, and to the tenth plateau in particular, entitled 'Memories of a Plan(e) Maker [*planificateur*]', where Deleuze introduces the distinction I shall be concerned with. Now in ordinary French, a *planificateur* is really a plan maker more than a plane maker, and we will see the extent to which Deleuze retains this idea of plan, as designating one possible, and even necessary sense of the French *plan*, and one that he himself adopts.[1] The 'memories' in question involve a retrospective look at Deleuze's own work, and his attempt to 'make' immanence philosophically by extracting the plane of immanence of thought and creating its concepts. We do not have, and never will have, a critical edition of the texts Deleuze wrote with Guattari. But it is clear that all the 'Memories' of the plateau entitled 'Becoming-Intense, Becoming-Animal, Becoming-Imperceptible', and especially the 'Memories of a Plan(e) Maker', refer back to some of Deleuze's most important texts and problems. In those few pages, Deleuze seems to take the full measure of the difficulty of drawing this plane of immanence, of returning thought to pure immanence, and goes as far as to develop an implicit yet, I would argue, crucial and illuminating evaluation

Ontology II: Cartography

(which, I will argue, is not be mistaken for a critique) of his own earlier attempt at constructing a univocal, immanent ontology.

He begins by formulating a hypothesis, or putting forward a thesis, the tentative nature of which is signalled from the start: 'Perhaps there are two planes, two different ways of conceiving the plane.'[2] This tentativeness is not rhetorical. Rather, I want to suggest, it points towards a fundamental complexity and ambiguity, which I shall eventually turn to. Deleuze's thesis states that there are two planes, or two ways of conceiving the plane. Now these are not the same thing: it is one thing to say that there are two planes, and another to say that there is only one plane, but two ways of conceiving it, two ways in which it can be seen. Ultimately, it's the latter that will turn out to be more adequate: in the same way that, in *Difference and Repetition*, Deleuze argued tirelessly that being knows of one sense only, he now claims that there is only one plane, the plane of immanence, from which another plane derives. Let me emphasise from the start what he is *not* claiming, and that is the co-originarity of two distinct planes, the connection of which would almost inevitably reintroduce the analogical ontology he had already overcome in his early work. Let me also emphasise from the start that those two planes, or those two ways of envisaging the plane of immanence, or nature, will turn out to be not just compatible, but complementary. They will designate two sides of the same coin (Nature), two ways or flows which, depending on the phenomenon in question, will be characterised as genesis and becoming, evolution and involution, stratification and destratification, etc. But once again, in order for those two 'ways' not to amount to a dualism, it is of the utmost importance to show that they are rooted (so to speak) in one and the same plane, in much the same way in which Swann's way and the Guermantes way turn out to merge in Proust's novel.

1. *Plane of Organisation and Development*

In the first instance, the plane can be understood as something like a principle, a *hidden* principle that allows us to see what we see (*donne à voir ce qu'on voit*), to hear what we hear, etc. It is a principle that accounts for the given as such, for the fact that it is given, in this or that state, at this or that moment. In this characterisation, we recognise the classical principle of sufficient reason, or ground. Now it is striking to see Deleuze characterise part of his own project, and especially his early work, in precisely those terms. This would be enough to suggest that there is no opposition, and no incompatibility, between the two ways of approaching the plane of Nature. This is what *Difference and Repetition* has to say about the way in which 'difference', as the central concept around which its ontology is articulated, needs to be understood:

> Difference is not diversity. Diversity is given, but *difference is that by which the given is given* as diverse . . . Every phenomenon *refers* to an inequality by which it is *conditioned*. Every diversity and every change refers to a difference which is its sufficient reason . . . Disparity – in other words, difference or intensity (difference of intensity) – is the sufficient reason of all phenomena, the condition of that which appears.[3]

A couple of pages later, Deleuze states again that 'difference is the sufficient reason of change'.[4]

What is most significant about this plane is that it is itself never given as such, but only in and through what it gives: it can only be inferred or induced from what it gives, whether simultaneously or successively, synchronically or diachronically. In so far as it is both at once, it can be characterised as a transcendental horizon *as well as* an empirical field, as a plane of organisation *as well as* of development. As such, it needs to be distinguished from the image of thought *Difference and Repetition* tried to overcome. But, as we shall see in some detail, it also needs to be distinguished from another plane, or another sense of plane, which it presupposes, and which *A Thousand Plateaus* is precisely attempting to draw, I would say once again, and more clearly. More specifically, it needs to be distinguished from another way of approaching the plane of Nature.

Difference and Repetition defines the transcendental field as the realm of Ideas.[5] Far from being essences or generalities, though, Ideas are *virtual multiplicities*. A multiplicity is a set of singularities engaged in relations of determination through differentiation. What characterises the elements of a multiplicity is the fact that they are a) inseparable from an ontological potential, in such a way that 'being' is understood as a horizon of virtual tendencies, and not as an actualised and locally individuated being; b) determined by reciprocal relations; and c) actualised or incarnated in a variety of *terms* and *forms*.[6] As such, the Idea (or the multiplicity) is both structure and genesis, both the principle of organisation of the real and its principle of development, or explication: 'Structure, the Idea, is the "complex theme", the internal multiplicity, in other words, the system of multiple, non-localisable connections between differential elements, which is incarnated in real relations and actual terms. In this sense, we see no difficulty in reconciling genesis and structure.'[7] Genesis (or development) is not incompatible with structure (or organisation) – far from it – *so long as* we understand genesis to take place not between one actual term and another actual term, but between the virtual and its actualisation. Then the general movement is from the structure to its incarnation, or from what Deleuze calls the conditions of a problem (which are not its conditions of possibility, but precisely of genesis) to the cases of its solution, from the differential elements and their ideal connections to actual terms and diverse relations that constitute at each moment the actuality of time.

The Idea, or the Problem, is not an essence, or a generality, of which the solutions would be simply particular instances, but an event. In other words, it isn't simply the case that problems, or Ideas, lead to solutions as to events. Rather, the differential elements constitutive of a pre-individual multiplicity themselves function as events. In this sense, Deleuze argues,

> it is correct to represent a double series of events which develop on two planes, echoing without resembling one other: real events on the level of engendered solutions, and ideal events embedded in the conditions of the problem . . . *The ideal series enjoys the double property of transcendence and immanence in relation to the real*.[8]

How should we understand this echo without resemblance? Every phenomenon echoes its noumenon, presupposes it, but the noumenon, itself entirely real, is nothing 'like' the phenomenon: born of it, the phenomenon repeats the noumenon, only always *differently*. At the same time, the noumenon, whilst entirely immanent to the phenomenon, remains in excess of it, its virtuality irreducible to its actualisation. There is a surplus of the ideal over the real, a transcendence of the problematic within the immanence of the solution. Between the problem and the solution, there is a relation of immanence: the solution presupposes the problem, but the problem exceeds the solution. The world of virtual tendencies is vaster than that of actualised differences. Between the two, there is a relation of heterogeneity, not homogeneity. Whilst the solution is entirely immanent to its own problematic horizon, this horizon transcends the solution that it produces. This is because the problem, the virtual, constitutes a world that is much larger and infinitely richer – rich with potentials, and not mere actualities disguised as possibilities – than that of the actual. If Deleuze's materialism is also an idealism, it is to the extent that every physical and material phenomenon presupposes its own horizon of constitution or problematic individuation. And the ideal, whilst entirely immanent to the real, also marks the inscription of transcendence within immanence. But we should avoid all confusion regarding the relation between immanence and transcendence being proposed here. Transcendence is not superimposed onto immanence; it does not govern it from above. As a result, immanence is not immanent *to* transcendence. Rather, it is transcendence itself that is transcendent to the immanence within which it unfolds: instead of transcendence, therefore, we should speak, as Deleuze suggests, of trans-descendence. In *What is Philosophy?* Deleuze admits that the virtual *seems* to operate like a transcendent instance, by virtue of the fact it surveys (*survole*) states of affairs. In actual fact, however, it is pure immanence that gives it 'the capacity to survey itself by itself'. And what is transcendent, or, more accurately perhaps, 'trans-descendent', is 'the state of affairs in which the event is actualised'.[9] But the event itself is immaterial and incorporeal; it is pure *reserve*. The virtual is not in a position of transcendence with respect to the actual. Rather, there is something like a surplus of immanence within actualised immanence.

Because the plane of organisation is hidden, or never given as such, 'it exists only in a dimension that is supplementary to that to which it gives rise $(n + 1)$'.[10] Deleuze suggests we take the example of the tree: 'The tree is given in the seed, but as a function of a plan(e) that is not given.' The plan that gives the tree in the seed is itself not given, but hidden. We can always describe the plan(e), but as something apart, as something ungiven in what it gives rise to. In other words, the plane in question, the Idea-genesis-and-structure, is something like a supplement, a surplus, that accounts for the given, without which the given would be unthinkable and unpresentable, but which is itself never given, never present. As such, it can remind us of the supplement in the Derridean sense of the term, of what Heidegger called concealment (*Verborgenheit*), or of what Deleuze himself, following Lacan, referred to as the symbolic object, or the signifying that is always lacking in its own place (*qui toujours manque à sa place*). In every instance, it is a matter of identifying the condition of appearance and phenomenality – of what Heidegger called *das Seiende* – in a process, or an event, that is itself never given qua phenomenon (*das Sein*). It is, in short, a matter of marking the difference between beings and being as a genetic difference, or as the difference by which beings come into being (or manifestation):

'Difference', Deleuze writes in *Difference and Repetition*, 'is not the phenomenon, but the noumenon closest to the phenomenon'.[11] To be sure, difference is not the difference between the phenomenon and the noumenon, but the difference that is internal to the phenomenon. Still, difference is the principle (the sufficient reason) that accounts for the phenomenon in its phenomenality, a principle (a structure-genesis) that is itself non-phenomenal.

This is precisely the point at which, as a supplementary, withdrawn, or symbolic *dimension*, the Idea runs the risk of being turned into a plane of transcendence. It is the point at which what Deleuze calls the transcendental field of pre-individual and impersonal singularities, or of being in contradistinction with beings, runs the risk of being interpreted as the *eminent* term of a *development*, or as the *proportional* relations of a structure, and thus as a plane of analogy. In that respect, one can understand Badiou's claim that, despite Deleuze's best efforts, his conception of the virtual doesn't quite manage to avoid transcendence and analogy.[12] One can understand the tendency and the temptation, which Deleuze not only resists, but also deconstructs, to interpret the relation between the virtual and the actual, between the Idea and the sensible, or between the problem and its solution, as analogical and metaphorical. Ultimately, though, it is a matter of understanding the nature of the relation between the plane of immanence, in which the conditions of a problem are generated, and the plane of actuality, in which the problem finds its solution, as a relation of expression and production, immanent to the real itself.

Whereas the model that enabled Deleuze to think the realm of the problematic, or of the virtual, was mathematical, and was captured under the notion of differen*t*iation, the model that serves to formalise the movement of actualisation from the virtual to the actual is biological, and very much thought through Bergson, although only up to a point. It is that of differen*c*iation, that of the manifestation of the new, of species and organisms, from a series of divergent moves or bifurcations. Yet it is not as if the movement from one level to the next were a passage from one field to another, from mathematics to biology. It is a single problematic that is being unfolded here, one that is philosophical, and more specifically ontological through and through: 'mathematics and biology appear here only in the guise of technical models which allow for the exposition of the virtual and the process of actualisation, along with the exploration of the two halves of difference, the dialectical half and the aesthetic half'.[13] In the same way that differential calculus serves to conceptualise or formalise a field that is not primarily mathematical but dialectical, so differentiation formalises the other side of the object, its phenomenal or aesthetic side. Differenciation is a universal concept that applies to all modes of actualisation, whether biological, physical, musical, social, artistic, etc. At the same time, however, biological systems constitute privileged examples of individuation, in so far as actualisation through differenciation is most evidently at work in such systems.[14] And it is because biological differenciation, and embryology in particular, functions as a model for the process of actualisation, that Deleuze likens the world to an 'egg', thus suggesting a system rife with virtual tendencies, tendencies which certain spatio-temporal processes alone can actualise. It is through a series of differenciations that the relatively undifferenciated (yet fully differen*t*iated, or determined) egg or the still developing embryo reaches its final stage, and this in such a way that the finished product does not resemble its virtual distribution. This is the sense in which the world, or being, can be said to be an egg.

What is most peculiar to the process of differenciation is that, whilst actualising virtual tendencies, it also tends to equalise, reduce or negate in actuality those very differences constitutive of the process itself. Such is the reason why, in experience, we know only forms of energy that are already localised and distributed in extension (*extensum, étendue*), differences that are reduced or identified, and so intensities (*intensio, intensité*) inseparable from their own extensity (*extensio, extensité*) and developed within extension:

> Intensity is difference, but this difference tends to negate or to cancel itself out in extensity and underneath quality. It is true that qualities are signs that flash across the interval of a difference. In so doing, however, they measure the time of an equalisation – in other words, the time taken by the difference to cancel itself out in the extensity in which it is distributed . . . [D]ifference is the sufficient reason of change only to the extent that the change tends to negate difference.[15]

The existential or, better said perhaps, *vital* problem that Deleuze faced from the very beginning and addressed through his readings of Spinoza, Nietzsche or Proust, was the following: how can we – as thinking, feeling and sensing beings – generate the conditions under which those very intensities, which tend to cancel themselves out in extensities, can be brought back to life, and *into* life? How can we affirm difference beyond its own tendency to negate itself in identity?

Ontology II: Cartography

How can our concepts, affects and percepts wrest themselves from fixed identities – essences, neuroses and clichés – and experience the world of intensities? This, as I will show in Chapter 5, is what's at stake in schizoanalysis. The problem of the schizophrenic is precisely one of disorganisation. It is a matter of knowing how to become a body without organs, cross the thresholds of organisation and become reunited with the field of virtual intensities. That problem is quite different from, albeit compatible with, the problem that consists in conceptualising the conditions of emergence of phenomena – different, that is, from the question regarding the development of forms and the constitution of subjects. As a matter of life, Deleuzianism is not reducible to ontogenesis. If, from that other perspective, Deleuzianism is still an empiricism, it is no longer as an epistemology, or a genetic ontology, but as an ethics: the question is no longer that of experience, and of its conditions, but that of the experience, and the experimentation, of the real, or the plane of immanence.

This plan(e), which constituted the focus of *Difference and Repetition*, is articulated in *A Thousand Plateaus* as essentially concerned with the development (or genesis) of forms and the formation (or organisation) of individuals (or substances), or, to use a more Spinozist vocabulary, with the *expression* of God (or nature) in attributes and modes. This point is made quite clearly in *A Thousand Plateaus*: 'expression' designates the manner in which matter gives birth to forms and substances, independently of any process of signification, independently, that is, of the 'idealist' conception of expression, which we saw Deleuze criticise and reject in the previous chapter. Deleuze's use of the concept of expression in *A Thousand Plateaus* is entirely consistent with that of *Expressionism*, and aims to define the same process: nature, or God, *expresses* its own essence in attributes and modes. In the vocabulary of *A Thousand Plateaus*: matter (which, as we shall see, consists of a multiplicity of pre-individual singularities, or 'haecceities') expresses itself in forms and individuals. Deleuze also refers to pure, pre-individual matter, as Nature, or the Earth. Such is the reason why he identifies every level of expression with a process of stratification, and every expression of the Earth with a stratum.[16] God, or nature, expresses itself by *stratifying* itself: 'To express is always to sing the glory of God. Since every stratum is a judgment of God, not only do plants and animals, orchids and wasps, sing or express themselves, but so do rocks and even rivers, every stratified thing on earth.'[17] As Montebello puts it, every strata expresses, without signifying anything. At the same time, every stratum is a 'judgment of God' because it relies on the power 'to organise infinitely'.[18]

In the plateau entitled 'Geology of Morals', Deleuze and Guattari introduce their thoughts on stratification via a conceptual character named 'Professor Challenger'. The pages devoted to the imagined Professor and his lecture are extremely funny. The Professor begins by explaining that the Earth, which is a body without organs, 'permeated by unformed, unstable matters, by flows in all directions, by free intensities or nomadic singularities, by mad or transitory particles', is actually and at the same time subjected to a very different phenomenon, 'beneficial in many respects and regrettable in many others: stratification'.[19] The process in question is also described as 'inevitable': one cannot escape it. It is 'beneficial' because it provides life and matter with a minimum of structure and stability. It is 'regrettable', though, in so far as something is always lost, or forgotten, in the process:

> [Strata] consisted of giving form to matters, of imprisoning intensities or locking singularities into systems of resonance and redundancy, of producing upon the body of the earth molecules large and small and organising them into molar aggregates. Strata were acts of capture, they were like 'black holes' or occlusions striving to seize whatever came within their reach. They operated by coding and territorialisation upon the earth; they proceeded simultaneously by code and by territoriality. Strata were judgments of God; stratification in general was the entire system of the judgment of God (but the earth, or the body without organs, constantly eluded that judgment, fled and became destratified, decoded, deterritorialised).[20]

Following Deleuze, let us take the example of geological stratification. Geological stratification consists of a process of organisation – of territorialisation, sedimentation and fixation of intensities and singularities – through which structures (or stable forms) emerge and molar assemblages (substances) take place. At the geological level, we could say that the initial process of sedimentation, in which units of cyclical sediments are piled up according to a statistical order, is followed by a process of folding, which establishes a stable, functional structure and facilitates the sediments' passage to the sedimentary rocks.[21] In the case of sedimentary rock, such as sandstone or limestone, every layer of rock contains additional layers, each of which is composed of small pebbles that are nearly *homogeneous* in size, shape and chemical composition. Now, given that pebbles in nature do not come in standard sizes and shapes, the question is one of knowing by what kind of 'sorting mechanism' this highly improbable distribution is achieved. In other words, a specific device is needed to deposit a multitude of heterogeneous pebbles in more or less uniform layers. Such would be the role of rivers, which transport rocky materials from their points of origin (such as mountains undergoing erosion) to the ocean, where they then accumulate. During this process, pebbles of variable size, weight and shape tend to be differently affected by the water transporting them, and it is these effects of moving water that sort them out, with smaller pebbles reaching the ocean sooner than larger ones. Once the raw materials have been sorted into more or less homogeneous deposits at the bottom of the sea (that is, once they have become *sedimented*), a second process occurs that transforms these loose collections of pebbles into units of a larger scale: sedimentary rock. This process – *cementing* – is carried out by soluble substances (such as silica, or hematite in the case of sandstone) that penetrate the sediment through the pores between pebbles. As this percolating solution crystallises, it *consolidates* these pebbles' temporary spatial relationship into a more or less permanent 'architectonic' structure. Thus a double operation – a 'double articulation' – transforms structures at one scale into structures at another scale. This, according to DeLanda, is precisely what Deleuze and Guattari designate as the twofold process of *content* and *expression*. Throughout 'The Geology of Morals' from *A Thousand Plateaus*, they warn us against confusing this process with the old distinction between 'substance' and 'form', since each of these two articulations involves both substances and forms. *Sedimentation* is not just a matter of accumulating pebbles (substance) but also entails sorting them out (form), while *consolidation* not only effects new architectonic couplings between pebbles (forms) but also yields a new entity, sedimentary rock (substance). Moreover, DeLanda goes on to say, these new entities may in turn accumulate and sort out (for example, the alternating layers of schist and sandstone that compose alpine mountains), then consolidate when tectonic forces cause the accumulated layers of rock to fold and become an entity of an even larger scale – a mountain.

Although stratification is a notion borrowed from geology, it applies to various natural phenomena, such as organisms. This is how DeLanda describes the parallel between genetic selection at the level of the species and sedimentation at the geological level:

> According to neo-Darwinists, for example, species are formed through the gradual accumulation and selection of genetic materials . . . Genes, of course, are not merely distributed or deposited at random, but are sorted out by a variety of selection pressures, including climate, the action of predators and parasites, and the effects of male and female mating choices. Thus, in a very real sense, genetic materials 'sediment' as pebbles do, even if their 'sorting device' is completely different.[22]

The parallel goes further still, as genetic accumulation also presupposes a process of consolidation, akin to that found in geological stratification:

> Furthermore, these loose collections of genes may, like sedimented pebbles, be lost under some drastic change of conditions (such as the onset of an ice age) unless they become consolidated. Genetic consolidation occurs as a result of *reproductive isolation*, that is, by the closure of the gene pool when a given subset of a population becomes incapable (for ecological, mechanical, behavioural, or genetic reasons) of mating and reproducing along with the rest. Reproductive isolation acts as a 'ratchet mechanism' which, by conserving the accumulated adaptive traits, makes it impossible for a given population to devolve into unicellular organisms.[23]

DeLanda is now in a position to conclude that 'through this dual process of selective accumulation and isolative consolidation, a population of individual organisms comes to form an entity of a larger scale: a new species'.[24]

We are now in a better position to understand why, according to Deleuze and Guattari, the organism is not at *all* the body, or the BwO, but only a *stratum* on the BwO: it consists of 'a phenomenon of accumulation, coagulation, and sedimentation that, in order to extract useful labor from the BwO, imposes upon it forms, functions, bonds, dominant and hierarchized organizations, organized *transcendences*'.[25] But the BwO itself is that 'glacial reality', that plane of immanence, 'where the alluvions, sedimentations, coagulations, foldings, and recoilings that compose an organism occur'.[26]

Let me turn to one final example of stratification, and emphasise the fact that Deleuze associates it with a process of transcendence. I only mention it here, as I will return to it in greater detail in Chapters 5 and 6. In art, and in music in particular, there is a transcendent principle of composition that is not of the order of sound, that is not 'audible' by itself or for itself, yet through which everything that is audible becomes audible, and that is the source not just of all possible interpretations, but also of the need for interpretation. We need to think only of Stockhausen, who feels the need to expose the structure of his sound forms as existing 'outside' them, since he is unable to make it audible. And in the realm of literature, we need to think only of Proust, who reveals the plan(e) of organisation and development of his work in something like a meta-language.[27] What generates thought, Deleuze insists in *Proust and Signs*, are the sensible signs. The sensible is what *provokes* thought, what sets it into motion. But the sensible provokes *thought*, and not just the senses, in so far as its elements are signs to be deciphered, interpreted. They refer to something outside them, or folded into them, something that is never given as such, but that can only be deduced: the essences. The world of essences is the meta-language of the language of signs: essences 'complicate' the sign and the sense, they put one into the other and so hold them together in this state of complication. The sense is implicated in the sign, and the sign is explicated in the sense.

2. *The Plane of Consistency, Immanence, or Nature*

In addition to the plane of organisation and development, and as the plane from which it grows, Deleuze is concerned to draw (or draw out) an altogether different plane, namely, the plane of consistency, or immanence. It is as if the ontological problematic of *Difference and Repetition*, and its emphasis on the virtual as designating the differential conditions of the real itself, had gone only so far in carrying out the project of immanence. In other words – such, at least, is the hypothesis I want to put forward – ontogenesis can take us only so far in the direction of immanence and can fulfil the task of philosophy – such as I have tried to define it in the opening chapter – only to an extent. Looking back at his first attempt to develop a univocal ontology and a logic centred around the ideas of genesis and structure – motivated in part by his anti-Hegelianism and Hyppolite's *Genesis and Structure of Hegel's Phenomenology's Spirit*,[28] in part by the structuralism of Lévi-Strauss, Althusser, Lacan and Foucault – Deleuze emphasises the one-sidedness of that attempt, and the need to distinguish it from a different project, and a different way of drawing out the plane of immanence: not qua organisation, development, and expression, but qua disorganisation, becoming and destratification: '[T]here is no reason to think that all matter is confined to the physico-chemical strata: there exists a submolecular, unformed Matter.'[29]

Structure and genesis – or, if you prefer, expression – define the Earth, or the plane of nature, from a certain point of view. It is an illusion, however, to believe that they would be 'the earth's last word'.[30] For the earth is also – above all, in fact, and primarily – a body without organs, that is, a surface 'permeated by unformed, unstable matters, by flows in all directions, by free intensities or nomadic singularities, by mad or transitory particles'.[31] We need to distinguish, then, between being as genesis, or as the development of forms and subjects, and being as pure becoming (or pure virtuality), in which forms and subjects dissolve, not into pure nothingness, but into a type of individuation that bypasses what *Difference and Repetition* called actualisation, or differenciation. The difference between the two is a matter of direction, or inclination: whereas the first traces actual phenomena back to the world of pre-individual and impersonal singularities, from which they originated, and so accounts for their genesis, the second points to the possibility of the reversed process, and the manner in which singularities themselves constantly come about, exceeding, traversing and opening forms and subjects onto their own becoming. In distinguishing between those two projects, we must avoid the pitfall of introducing other distinctions, such as that between theory and practice, to which they would correspond: it is not a matter of distinguishing between a purely theoretical (ontogenetic) and a purely practical (ethical) side of thought. Nor is it, for that matter, a question of understanding the distinction as strictly chronological, and identifying the project of ontogenesis with Deleuze's early work, and *Difference and Repetition* in particular, and the project of becoming-*x* with the later work. Whilst *Anti-Oedipus*, for example, would seem to confirm such a chronological division, *A Thousand Plateaus* is itself concerned with both projects. As such, it constitutes a gathering, and possibly the culmination, of Deleuze's thought as a whole – a gathering made possible by what Deleuze calls the 'plane of immanence', the 'plane of consistency', or the 'BwO'.

It is worth noting that, just as the first systematic interpretation of Spinoza accompanied the first systematic ontology of *Difference and Repetition*, the second series of lectures accompanies the second ontology of *A Thousand Plateaus*. To be sure, *Anti-Oedipus* is an essential stage along that path, as it achieves immanence in the field of desire, wresting it from its classical ontological straightjacket (in which it is envisaged as lack, and so as negativity) and its hermeneutical framework (which understands it as fantasy, as a sign in need of its own interpretation). In *A Thousand Plateaus*, Deleuze and Guattari draw a parallel between the biological egg, as the model of the body without organs, and the world as the totality of all bodies without organs, or as the cosmic egg, before raising the following question: 'After all, is not Spinoza's *Ethics* the great book of the BwO?'[32] And they go on to write: 'Drug users, masochists, schizophrenics, lovers – all BwO's pay homage to Spinoza.'[33] Why is that? Because, each in their own way, they all explore the question of what a body can do, how far it can go, what intensities it can produce. Each crosses thresholds of organisation and extensity, and lives according to a different regime, closer to the undifferenciated egg than the fully differenciated organism. *A Thousand Plateaus* constitutes Deleuze's most significant ontology after *Difference and Repetition*, and one which, I hope to show, he develops in parallel with a renewed interpretation of Spinoza, though an interpretation no longer rooted in the concept and problematic of expression.[34]

Let me now turn to the detail of that other plane, or that other conception of the plane. Here, it is no longer a matter of a plan, of a design, but of a plane only. We are no longer dealing with forms, or development of forms, with organs and functions; but neither are we dealing with subjects or substances and their formation. There is no structure, any more than there is genesis. This is the *other* plane that Spinoza also reveals, and which Deleuze wants to extend. It is perhaps most clearly and programmatically defined in the following passage:

> In short, if we are Spinozists, we will define something neither by its shape, nor by its organs or its functions, neither as a substance nor as a subject. To borrow medieval terms, or geographical ones, we will define it by *longitude* and *latitude*. A body can be anything; it can be an animal, an acoustic body, a soul, or an idea; it can be a linguistic corpus, a social body, a collectivity. We call longitude of any given body the ensemble of relations of speed and slowness, of rest and movement, between particles that constitute it from this point of view, that is, between *unformed elements*. We call latitude the ensemble of affects that occupy a body at each moment, that is, the intensive states of an *anonymous force* (force to exist, capacity to be affected). Thus we establish the cartography of a body. The ensemble of longitudes and latitudes constitutes Nature, the plane of immanence or of consistency, always variable and never ceasing to be altered, constituted, reconstituted, by individuals and collectivities.[35]

The emphasis is no longer on the logic of expression, or different/ ciation, as accounting for the nature of the relation between substance, attributes and modes, or, to use Deleuze's own vocabulary, between virtual singularities and actualised systems. The emphasis is now on those singularities themselves, and the way in which they interact on a horizontal plane.

On this other plane, then, there are only relations of movement and rest, of speed and slowness between elements that are not formed, between submolecular particles and molecules and particles of all kinds. There is Matter, but pure matter only, that is, relatively unformed and unstructured energy flows from which strata and aggregates emerge. It is the sea, perhaps, more than the Earth, which captures the pure, flowing surface, or the 'smooth' space of the plane of consistency, before it can be identified with a 'content' and its 'expression' in actual forms, or with a space that is itself 'striated' or 'metric'. This primordial level or plane is what Deleuze and Guattari call the 'body without organs'. It is without organs because it is not yet organised, not yet differentiated into structures and substances. But it is not dead, on the contrary: 'The body without organs is not a dead body but a living body all the more alive and teeming once it has blown apart the organism and its organisation.'[36] There is a life – Life itself – that is nonorganic, and that coincides with the BwO. Primary Matter is the universal body that is not yet formed, or stratified, and the set of submolecular and even subatomic particles, of pure intensities and free, prephysical and prevital singularities that flow on such a body. It is the primary level of 'instability', which is followed by a 'metastable' (or 'molecular') phase, and then by a final, 'stable' (or 'molar') phase. It is the originary chaos from which order emerges. At that level, on the plane of immanence or consistency, there are unformed elements that can be distinguished according to their speed and their capacity to be affected only, and which exceed the movement of an organic form and the determination of organs. Nothing *develops* on that plane, but things arrive late or early, and form this or that assemblage, depending on the composition of their speed. It is not a plane of organisation (a structure) and development (a genesis), therefore, but a plane of composition and consistency. If it is also, and primarily, referred to as a plane of immanence and univocity, it is because, unlike the plane of organisation, no matter how many dimensions it may have, it never has a dimension that is supplementary to that which takes place on it (*ce qui se passe sur lui*). It is simply not a supplement, a surplus, simply not of the order of something that remains withdrawn in what it gives rise to, simply not of the order of the ground, albeit redefined as abyss, unground or *effondement*. It is a geometrical plane, but of a very unusual, if not paradoxical, nature, since its number of dimensions increases with every event, whilst losing nothing of its 'planitude'. This, I believe, is what Deleuze already had in mind when he spoke of Ideas as 'multiplicities' in *Difference and Repetition*. The mathematical vocabulary to which he now has recourse is that of topology, rather than algebra: the plane of immanence is a formless 'object' made not of dimensions, but of directions. Neither a surface, nor a volume, it is best described as a fractal object, a kind of infinity in which thought delves, without losing anything of the infinite.[37] It is the plane on which events take place, and assemblages proliferate. But this proliferation of material has nothing to do with the development of a form or the filiations of forms, nothing to do, then, with an evolution (and this, again, is a striking difference with the Bergsonism of *Difference and Repetition*, in which Deleuze was concerned to include evolution in the concept of different/ciation). Nor does it have anything to do with a regression leading back to a principle, in short, with a retrovolution or a revolution as grounding. Rather, it is an *involution*, in which form is constantly being dissolved, and in so doing frees speeds and affects, longitudes and latitudes. This is the plane I must now turn to, the impetus of which Deleuze finds, once again, in Spinoza.[38]

Since I have already introduced the example of the organism in connection with the problematic of genesis and structure, let me turn to it once again, this time from the point of view of the plane of immanence, or consistency. Unlike Cuvier, Geoffroy Saint-Hilaire manages to move beyond the standpoint of organs and functions, and reaches abstract elements, which he characterises as 'anatomical'.[39] By that, and in contemporary terms, we need to understand biochemical materials and genetic information, which, combined in various ways, constitute specific organs, and take on specific functions. At that level, it is speeds and slowness, or relations of movement and rest, which assume priority over structures and other types of development. Deleuze and Guattari note that it is less a question of form and function, and more of speed. In line with new research developments in fertility, they ask: 'do the paternal chromosomes arrive early enough to be incorporated into the nuclei?'[40] What we have here is the fixed plane of life, where everything moves, slows down, or accelerates. There is a single Abstract limb as it were, or, more generally, a single abstract Animal for all the assemblages that effectuate and actualise it. There is a single plane of consistency, or composition, for the cephalopod and the vertebrate. This is precisely what, according to Deleuze, Geoffroy Saint-Hilaire was able to intimate: 'For the vertebrate to become an octopus, all it would have to do is fold itself in two fast enough to fuse the elements of the halves of its back together, then bring its pelvis up to the nape of its neck and gather its limbs together into one of its extremities.'[41] This is what Deleuze and Guattari refer to, when, following Spinoza, they say that we do not know what a body is capable of, what a body can *do*. As an individuated, organised body, we know exactly what it can do. But as a plane of consistency, as a virtual, anorganic body, the possibilities are infinite:

> We must try to conceive of this world in which a single fixed plane – which we shall call a plane of absolute immobility *or* absolute movement – is traversed by nonformal elements of relative speed that enter this or that individuated assemblage depending on their degrees of speed and slowness. A plane of consistency peopled by anonymous matter, by infinite bits of impalpable matter entering into varying connections.[42]

It is only at the cost of positing such a plane, of understanding the real as a space in which connections between nonformal elements of matter are established, in which assemblages occur as a result of varying degrees of speed and slowness, that the standpoint of analogy can be overcome, and univocity established once and for all. Immanence, in other words, can be realised only as materialism.

Besides speeds and slowness, movement and rest (longitude), bodies are also characterised by their ability to affect and be affected (*affectio*, latitude). Biologists and naturalists, such as J. von Uexküll, are really Spinozists, when, turning to the tic, they identify it with three affects: the tic is affected by light when it climbs on top of a branch; it is affected by smell when it drops on the mammal that happens to pass under the branch; and it is affected by heat when it seeks the warmest part of the mammal's body. Of a thing, or a body, Aristotle used to ask: 'What is it?' Of an animal, he would ask: 'Of what kind?' or 'what species?' The question was one of essence, of definition, and the *logos* coincided with the *horismos*. Essence was the sense in which everything could be said to be. With Spinoza, as I have tried to show in Chapter 2, the body is no longer an essence, but an event, that is, something that *does* something, and so cannot be contained within a definition. Unlike the Aristotelian, the Spinozist (or the ethologist) asks: what can this animal *do*, what is it capable of? Every single being is defined by what it can do, by its own degree of power, which is itself determined by the type of relations that

Ontology II: Cartography

characterise it as an individual. At stake is something like a register of the powers of the animal in question. This one can fly, that one eats grass, and that third one eats meat. Diet, for example, is a question that concerns *modes* of existence, as opposed to substances, or quiddities. All bodies are modes of a single substance, of a single plane of Nature. They all express a longitude and a latitude, that is, a composition of extensive parts that come together to produce a distinct degree of power. The plane of immanence is not a plan, a design, or a programme, but a diagram, a problematical field, that is, a field where distinct problems find local and concrete solutions, whether biological, social, artistic, libidinal, etc. In itself, however, the plane of immanence is neither biological nor social, neither physical nor libidinal.

In a way that echoes Proust's famous characterisation of those states induced by involuntary memory, and which *Difference and Repetition* appropriated when describing the field of virtual singularities, the plane of consistency of Nature is compared with 'an immense abstract, yet real and individual Machine'.[43] If this machine (and no longer, as was still the case in the earlier work, this stage or this theatre) is made of parts, its parts must be understood, once again, precisely not as organs or functions, but as assemblages, that is, as the various individuals that 'group together an infinity of particles entering into an infinity of more or less interconnected relations'.[44] Deleuze's materialism – his 'machinism' – is therefore not a straightforward mechanism. The immediate consequence of this is the unity of the plane in question: there is one plane, and one plane only, which applies equally to the animate and the inanimate, the artificial and the natural. The greatest mistake, then, would be to understand the plane of Nature as distinct from that of Culture, or to establish a difference in kind between the animate and the inanimate, between animal life and vegetal life, or between human life and animal life. There are differences, naturally, but those are of degree, not kind. Another mistake would be to equate this plane with a plan, or a design, in other words, with something like a hidden project or end, whether hidden in the mind of God or in Nature itself. Finally, this plane must be firmly distinguished from anything like a ground, or a structure, which would remain buried deep within things. At this point – and this, perhaps, is a difference with the earlier work, and *Difference and Repetition* in particular, where the vocabulary of depth and surface, ground and effect was still in place – there is only a surface, a flat plane, on which 'everything is laid out'. It is itself nothing other than the intersection of all forms, nothing more than the machine of all functions. Desire is a machine (the unconscious machine), the novel is a machine (the literary machine), and the embryo is a machine (the organic machine): they all 'function' or operate by cutting into the hyletic continuum of a single plane of immanence. Of those, we do not ask: 'What are they?' or 'What do they mean?' but 'How do they work?'

3. *The Connection between Planes*

I introduced the two planes by saying that the distinction between them was rather tenuous and delicate to pin down. Yet Deleuze insists on the difference, on the need to distinguish between a plane of organisation and development on the one hand, and a plane of consistency and immanence on the other. The question, now, is one of knowing how they relate to one another. In 'Memories of a Plan(e) Maker', Deleuze seems to suggest that, although we always begin from the plane of immanence, there seems to be – generated from within as it were – something like a drive or an inclination towards transcendence:

> Why does the opposition between the two kinds of plane lead to a still abstract hypothesis? Because one continually passes from one to the other, by unnoticeable degrees and without being aware of it, or one becomes aware of it only afterward. Because one continually reconstitutes one plane atop another, or extricates one from the other. For example, all we need to do is to sink the floating plane of immanence, bury it in the depths of Nature, instead of allowing it to play freely on the surface, for it to pass to the other side and assume the role of a ground that can no longer be anything more than a principle of analogy from the standpoint of organisation, and a law of continuity from the standpoint of development.[45]

This possibility can, once again, be seen as a reference to Deleuze's own attempt, in *Difference and Repetition*, to 'ground' univocity, and therefore return it to transcendence. But it can and also must be seen as intrinsic to the philosophical gesture itself which, taking its impetus or clue *from* immanence, grants it a certain depth, and so begins to understand Being in terms of depth and surface, cause and effect, in what amounts to a series of hierarchised oppositions, in which one term is said to precede and ground the other, and in which the second is seen as deriving from the first. The plane of

Ontology II: Cartography

organisation is always introducing depth, hierarchies, strata and roots. The plane of consistency, on the other hand, implies a generalised destratification of all of Nature. It does away with depth, roots and strata by introducing lines (lines of flight), diagonals, rhizomes. The fact is that pure relations of speed and slowness between particles imply movements of deterritorialisation. They are not arborescent, but rhizomatic, not vertical, but horizontal. But one plane does not replace the other, whichever way we look at it. There never is just one plane. The two planes co-exist, and are always engaged in undoing one another. The first has always and already begun to give way to the second. 'The plane of organisation is constantly working away at the plane of consistency, always trying to plug the lines of flight, stop or interrupt the movements of deterritorialisation, weigh them down, restratify them, reconstitute forms and subjects in a dimension of depth.'[46] At the same time, however, the plane of consistency is constantly extricating itself from the plane of organisation, causing particles to spin off the strata, scrambling forms by dint of speed or slowness, breaking down functions by means of assemblages.

Let me return to the example of the sea, which I introduced very briefly. On one level, Deleuze and Guattari tell us, the sea is the archetype of smooth space. Yet 'it was the first to encounter the demands of increasingly strict striation'.[47] Maritime space was striated as a function of two astronomical and geographical gains: *bearings*, obtained by a set of calculations based on exact observation of the stars and the sun; and *the map*, which intertwines meridians and parallels, longitudes and latitudes, plotting regions known and unknown onto a grid. Slowly, and beginning in the fifteenth century, the striated progressively took hold, turning an intensive, directional, non-metric multiplicity into an extensive, dimensional, metric multiplicity. More recently, however, it is as if the sea had regained some of its smoothness, but only through the perpetual motion of the strategic submarine, which outflanks all gridding and invents a neonomadism in the service of a war machine still more disturbing than the States, which reconstitute it at the limit of their striation. All of this shows that, whilst absolutely distinguishable in principle (*de jure*), smooth space and striated space are in fact always intertwined: 'smooth space is constantly being translated, transversed into a striated space; striated space is constantly being reversed, returned to a smooth space'.[48] Smooth space is filled by events or haecceities, whereas striated space is filled with formed and perceived things.

Smooth space is a space of affects, whereas striated space is a space of measures and properties. Smooth space is intensive (*Spatium*) rather than extensive (*Extensio*): a body without organs as opposed to an organism and a plane of organisation. What one perceives (or feels) in a smooth space are intensities: wind and noise, sonorous and tactile qualities, the creaking of ice and the song of the sand, as in the desert, steppe or ice. In the absence of fixed points, characteristic of the striated space, 'the navigator of the desert relies on the "song of the sands" and other shifting sets of relationships (haecceities) – as the mariner relies on the differential tastes of the sea'.[49] It is through affect, not representation, that one navigates such spaces. Striated space, on the contrary, is overdetermined ('canopied') by the sky as measure and by the measurable visual qualities deriving from it, whether at sea or in the desert.

Another example – which Deleuze and Guattari could not have possibly written about in the early 1980s – is the internet. Born within the state apparatus, it was initially designed for the US military with a view to enhancing communication and intelligence in the chain of command, allowing the latter to operate in a less vertical manner. But the phenomenon took an unexpected turn when passed on to civilian use, cutting across nation-states and government control, allowing for the free circulation of material deemed threatening for one reason or another (from Islamic terrorism to child and animal pornography, music and cinema pirating, or simply undesirable information). In the light of this phenomenon, we see considerable efforts on the part of states, the police, the judiciary and big business, to control, appropriate or reterritorialise it. This essentially fluid and smooth space is being subjected to an increasingly aggressive striation by the forces of Capital as well as by individual states (and for different reasons, whether we take the example of the United States or that of China and the restrictions it imposes on information services and internet service providers).

What we are slowly realising, then, having distinguished between the two planes, is the extent to which they call for one another, presuppose one another, so that, in the end, we can wonder with Deleuze whether it is not necessary 'to retain a minimum of strata, a minimum of forms and functions, a minimal subject from which to extract materials, affects, and assemblages'.[50] These 'Memories of a Plan(e) Maker' began with a hypothesis, a tentative 'perhaps'. They end with an interrogation. This interrogation is taken up again and reinforced in the conclusion of the book:

Ontology II: Cartography

What movement, what impulse, sweeps us outside the strata (*metastrata*)? Of course, there is no reason to think that all matter is confined to the physicochemical strata: there exists a submolecular, unformed Matter. Similarly, not all Life is confined to the organic strata: rather, *the organism is that which life sets against itself in order to limit itself*, and there is a life all the more intense, all the more powerful for being anorganic. There are also nonhuman Becomings of human beings that overspill the anthropomorphic strata in all directions. But how can we reach this 'plane', or rather how can we construct it, and how can we draw the 'line' leading us there? For outside the strata or in the absence of strata we no longer have forms or substances, organisation or development, content or expression. We are disarticulated; we no longer even seem to be sustained by rhythms. How could unformed matter, anorganic life, nonhuman becoming be anything but chaos pure and simple? Every undertaking of destratification (for example, going beyond the organism, plunging into a becoming) must therefore observe concrete rules of extreme caution: a too-sudden destratification may be suicidal, or turn cancerous. In other words, it will sometimes end in chaos, the void and destruction, and sometimes locks us back into the strata, which become more rigid still, losing their degrees of diversity, differentiation, and mobility.[51]

We always run the risk of being torn apart by anorganic life, which attempts to limit its own power by organising itself. This, we recall, is what the schizophrenic endures. Thought itself, when it opens itself to the body without organs, runs the risk of being engulfed in pure chaos, and is always on the verge of collapsing into nothingness. Yet it is precisely there, on the verge, on the edge of the abyss, that thought comes into its own. Pure immanence is a reality, yet one that thought can experience only to an extent, only mixed, and never in its absolute purity. There is something monstrous, literally inhuman about pure immanence, and so it is only by exercising the greatest caution that thought can hope to approach it. The question, in other words, is one of knowing how a breakthrough can avoid turning into a breakdown, how the body without organs can avoid total closure, and catatonia. When exposed to the brute and intensive forces of anorganic Life, the activity of thought becomes dangerous. If madness and destruction threaten thought in its effort to wrest itself from the stratified, so does a greater attachment to the very strata it seeks to escape. An all too-sudden and ill-prepared journey will result in a more stratified and cancerous return:

> The BwO howls: 'They've made me an organism! They've wrongfully folded me! They've stolen my body!' The judgment of God uproots it

from its immanence and makes it an organism, a signification, a subject. It is the BwO that is stratified. It swings between two poles, the surfaces of stratification into which it is recoiled, on which it submits to the judgment, and the plane of consistency in which it unfurls and opens to experimentation . . . What does it mean to disarticulate, to cease to be an organism? How can we convey how easy it is, and the extent to which we do it every day? And how necessary caution is, the art of dosages, since overdose is a danger. You don't do it with a sledgehammer, you use a very fine file. You invent self-destructions that have nothing to do with the death drive. Dismantling the organism has never meant killing yourself, but rather opening the body to connections that presuppose an entire assemblage, circuits, conjunctions, levels and thresholds, passages and distributions of intensity . . .[52]

To avoid death, a minimum level of organisation needs to be retained: 'You don't reach the BwO, and its plane of consistency, by wildly destratifying.'[53] This is because the BwO

is always swinging between the surfaces that stratify it and the plane that sets it free. If you free it with too violent an action, if you blow apart the strata without taking precautions, then instead of drawing the plane you will be killed, plunged into a black hole, or even dragged toward catastrophe. Staying stratified . . . is not the worst that can happen; the worst that can happen is if you throw the strata into demented or suicidal collapse, which brings them back down on us heavier than ever.[54]

There are (at least) two extreme ways in which thought (as well as other modes of experimentation) can fail, then: it can dissolve into pure chaos, and become a flux without form, or it can solidify into ever more rigid strata. Thought must not choose between those two extremes, though, and privilege chaos over order, absolute fluidity over total reification, or pure becoming over brute being. Instead, it needs to create the concepts that map the manner in which, at any given point, chaos is being ordered and order is being carried away into chaos. Its concepts are not fixed, rigid forms; but they are not purely fluid entities either. They need to avoid the process of reification and solidification that characterises representational thought, whether metaphysical or scientific (both are metaphysical in the sense of being representational); but they can hope to map the becoming of immanence only asymptotically, by multiplying images and concepts that will approach and intimate their object, much in the way that Bergson evokes the possibility of conceptualising duration. Thought, Deleuze and Guattari argue in the Conclusion to *What is Philosophy?*, does not protect us from chaos in the way that opinion does. This is because its victory over chaos results from its immersion in it, and not from its mere opposition to it. Yes, thought extracts planes of different kinds from pure immanence. But those planes and the concepts that delimit them are akin to the very chaos it masters.[55] Concepts must have the fluidity of Chaos, while avoiding dissolution into nothingness the moment they are born. They must retain a minimum of consistency if they are to be concepts in the first place. If, in a way, concepts can only begin with forms and substances, and, above all, with this form we call the Self, it must be with a view to accessing the formless and the substance-less in them, including in the Self. Thought must learn to move freely and effortlessly between the sphere of pure Chaos, in which all things originate, but which also harbours the danger of madness, and the sphere of fully individuated substances, facts and states of affairs, which harbours the danger of ossification and lifelessness. The problem of philosophy, Deleuze and Guattari claim in *What is Philosophy?*, is 'to acquire a consistency without losing the infinite into which thought plunges'.[56] Thought plunges into chaos, and extracts a consistency from it. It draws its own plane by carving out a section of chaos.[57] 'To carve out', as one commentator puts it, 'can only mean to grasp (define, retain) a "slice", as it were, of a chaos that remains free (and infinitely free) in all other directions and dimensions'.[58] As for chaos itself, it isn't an 'inert or stationary state'. It 'makes chaotic [*chaotise*] and undoes every consistency in the infinite'.[59] To carve out a section of chaos, then, doesn't only mean to extract, select and fixate. For thought, to carve out means first and foremost to 'dive' into the infinity of chaos. And this 'dive' into chaos is precisely what distinguishes philosophy from science, which 'seeks to provide chaos with reference points [*references*], on condition of renouncing infinite movements and speeds, and of carrying out a limitation of speed first of all'.[60] The plane of science is not that of consistency, or immanence, but that of reference. Where philosophy provides chaos with consistency, without losing anything of the infinite, or of Becoming, science sacrifices Becoming and relates space to 'reference points', that is, to fixed states of affairs. Science and philosophy differ only in relation to the nature of their relation to chaos. It is that difference alone, however, which allows Deleuze to claim that philosophy is the science of the pure event.

In that respect, philosophy is more akin to artistic creation. By situating themselves in relation to a Chaos, which they do not tame, but from which they extract concepts, affects and percepts (which

Deleuze is very careful to distinguish from metaphysical categories, as well as lived experiences and perceptions), philosophy and art live on the edge of chaos, and constantly run the risk of being engulfed by it. Before turning to art, however, I would like to show how Deleuze takes up the challenge of thinking at the edge of chaos in relation to the question of *sense* (Chapter 4) and *desire* (Chapter 5).

Notes

1. In the next and final chapter, I will show how Proust's work illustrates the two types of *plan* Deleuze mentions.
2. ATP, 325/265.
3. DR, 286/222. My emphasis.
4. DR, 288/223.
5. For a more detailed and exhaustive exposition of the role and function of the Idea in *Difference and Repetition*, and its connection with the actual, phenomenal world, see P. Montebello, *Deleuze*, pp. 146–55; J. Williams, *Gilles Deleuze's* Difference and Repetition: *A Critical Introduction* (Edinburgh: Edinburgh University Press, 2003), Section 5; M. DeLanda, *Intensive Science and Virtual Philosophy* (London: Continuum, 2002), Chapter 1; M. de Beistegui, *Truth and Genesis*, Chapter 8.
6. DR, 237/183.
7. DR, 237/183.
8. DR, 244/188–9. My emphasis.
9. WP, 148/156.
10. ATP, 325/265.
11. DR, 286/222.
12. I should qualify this claim straight away by saying that a *certain* interpretation of the virtual, and of Bergson's use of it, can lend itself to the charge Badiou formulates in *Deleuze*. *'La clameur de l'être'* (Paris: Hachette, 1997), pp. 65–81. In that respect, I would point to Deleuze's later use of that concept, especially in *Cinema 2*, and to his renewed interpretation of Bergson's *Matter and Memory*, as indicative of a slight yet decisive shift with respect to the manner in which he understood the virtual in his structural and genetic work. This revaluation of the virtual makes it entirely compatible with what *A Thousand Plateaus* calls the plane of immanence, or the body without organs. The key passage is in *Cinema 2* (C-2, 106–7/79–80), where Deleuze distinguishes very clearly between the virtual image as it is being actualised in states of consciousness and what he calls the virtual image in its *pure* state. The latter is not *another* image, different from the one being actualised, but the side or the aspect of the virtual image that will never be actualised,

that need not ever be actualised – the *purely* virtual. It is the virtual side of the actual image, its originary, non-actual doubling: 'It is the virtual image that corresponds to a particular actual image, instead of being actualised, of having to be actualised in a *different* actual image. It is an actual-virtual circuit on the spot, and not an actualisation of the virtual in accordance with a shifting actual. It is a crystal-image and not an organic image' (C-2, 107/80). It is a crystal-image precisely in so far as it crystallises with the actual image, doubles it as it were, instead of organising it. It is not a principle or a plane of organisation (of structure and genesis), but of disorganisation. It is the an- or pre-organic plane that is coextensive with the development of organs and organisms. As such, however, it is not the lifelessness that precedes the emergence of all living forms, but 'the mighty, non-organic Life that grips [*enserre*] the world' (C-2, 109/81). This is the Life to which thought must return, the plane on which philosophy must create its own concepts, and on which, as we shall see in connection with Proust and Francis Bacon, art thrives.

13. DR, 285/220–1.
14. We need to recall, however, that if Simondon does eventually turn to biological individuation (and even, later on, to psychic and collective individuation), he begins by analysing processes of individuation in physical systems.
15. DR, 288/223.
16. 'Forms and subjects, organs and functions, are "strata" or relations between strata' ATP, 330/269.
17. ATP, 58/43–4. Translation modified.
18. P. Montebello, *Deleuze*, p. 173.
19. ATP, 53–4/40.
20. ATP, 54/40. Translation modified.
21. See the opening pages of 'The Geology of Morals' in *ATP*. For more on this topic, and a finely nuanced appraisal of Deleuze and Guattari's 'geophilosophy', see Mark Bonta and John Protevi, *Deleuze and Geophilosophy* (Edinburgh: Edinburgh University Press, 2004), especially pp. 150–3 (on strata and stratification). In a highly illuminating article entitled 'Immanence and Transcendence in the Genesis of Form' (in Ian Buchanan, ed., *A Deleuzian Century* [Durham & London: Duke University Press, 1999], pp. 119–34), which I am here summarising, Manuel DeLanda shows how Deleuze and Guattari's argument can be extended and applied to a number of areas within science, and eventually leads to a 'philosophical physics' and a 'reinvigorated materialism' (p. 132). In other words, DeLanda is keen to show how a *systematic* philosophy of the genesis of form and structure (in areas as diverse as geology, biology and economics) can be derived from Deleuze's thought as a whole, from *Difference and Repetition* to *A*

Thousand Plateaus. *Difference and Repetition* already raised the question of morphogenesis, the question, that is, of knowing how specific forms of molecular or biological systems, from a soap bubble to a living organism or a limb, emerge and come to be what they are. By drawing on the work of Albert Lautman in topology and that of Simondon on individuation, Deleuze was able to claim that morphogenesis was a purely immanent, or material, process, and so overcome what Simondon had characterised as the hylemorphic model of classical philosophy. The spherical shape of the bubble, or the star-like shape of the crystal is a result of the interaction of constituent molecules 'as these are constrained energetically to "seek" the point at which surface tension is minimized' (DeLanda, 'Immanence and Transcendence', p. 120). An endogenous topological form, also known as a singularity, which designates a point in the space of energetic possibilities – otherwise known as a *phase space* – for a given molecular assemblage, governs the collective behaviour of the individual molecules and results in the emergence of a specific shape. *A Thousand Plateaus* expands those resources to analyse structures of different types – geologic, biologic, and even socio-economic. No one, I believe, has gone further in testing and extending the validity of Deleuze's ontogenesis than DeLanda.

22. DeLanda, 'Immanence and Transcendence', p. 123.
23. DeLanda, 'Immanence and Transcendence', p. 123.
24. DeLanda, 'Immanence and Transcendence', p. 123.
25. *ATP*, 197/159. My emphasis.
26. *ATP*, 197/159.
27. I return to Proust and to this question of the two planes in the final chapter.
28. J. Hyppolite, *Genèse et structure de la Phénoménologie de l'esprit de Hegel* (Paris: Aubier, 1947).
29. *ATP*, 628/503.
30. *ATP*, 55/41.
31. *ATP*, 54/40.
32. *ATP*, 190/153.
33. *ATP*, 191/154.
34. Deleuze's Vincennes lectures from 1978–81 are available on http://www.webdeleuze.com
35. *SPP*, 171/127–8. Translation modified.
36. *ATP*, 43/30.
37. On the question of fractal objects, see Benoît Mandelbrot, *Les objects fractals* (Paris: Flammarion, 1975). At times, Deleuze and Guattari talk of the plane of immanence as a special kind of space, which they call smooth, and which they contrast with striated space. The latter is a metric space, or a multiplicity, whereas the former isn't. Mandelbrot's fractals can be seen to provide a very general definition of smooth

spaces. Fractals are aggregates whose number of dimensions is fractional rather than whole, or else whole but with continuous variation in direction. A cube into which holes are drilled according to what's known as the principle of similarity becomes less than a volume and more than a surface. Similarly, a cloud is more than a surface, and less than a volume. So, we can call striated or metric any aggregate with a whole number of dimensions, and for which it is possible to assign constant directions. A smooth space, on the other hand, does not have a dimension higher than that which moves through it or is inscribed in it; in this sense it is a flat multiplicity, for example, a line that fills a plane without ceasing to be a line (*ATP*, 607–8/487–8).

38. See Spinoza, *Ethics*, II, Prop. 13.
39. The evolution of Deleuze's analysis on this point is worth noting. In *Difference and Repetition*, Geoffroy Saint-Hilaire was precisely praised as having extracted something like a structure of the organism which, because it designated a potential, or a set of virtualities, was entirely compatible with a more genetic approach. In *A Thousand Plateaus*, it is the very standpoint of structure and genesis that is criticised as reinscribing the plane of analogy, or transcendence. Deleuze's implicit suggestion, therefore, is that Geoffroy's work is on both sides of the plane, on both planes at the same time, that he extracted the plan(e) of organisation, or development, of the organism as well as its plane of immanence.
40. *ATP*, 312/255.
41. *ATP*, 312/255.
42. *ATP*, 312/255.
43. *ATP*, 311/254. Proust's characterisation reads as follows: 'real without being actual, ideal without being abstract' (*À la recherche du temps perdu* [Paris: Gallimard, 'Bibliothèque de la Pléiade', 1954], III, p. 873). Here, like in *A Thousand Plateaus*, 'abstract' is opposed to 'real': the 'abstract' machine is not an abstraction, or something unreal, but the plane that can be abstracted or extracted from the various events that populate it. Here, 'abstraction' must be understood in the artistic, pictorial sense, and coincides with what Deleuze also calls the virtual. The plane of immanence is an 'abstract' or 'virtual' machine, much like the egg which, wholly (but virtually) differentiated, under certain conditions, differentiates itself in organs and functions.
44. *ATP*, 311/254.
45. *ATP*, 330/269.
46. *ATP*, 330/270.
47. *ATP*, 598/478.
48. *ATP*, 593/474.
49. Bonta and Protevi, *Deleuze and Geophilosophy*, p. 76.
50. *ATP*, 331/270.

51. *ATP*, 628/503. My emphasis.
52. *ATP*, 197–8/159–60.
53. *ATP*, 198/160.
54. *ATP*, 199/161.
55. *WP*, 190–1/202–3.
56. *WP*, 45/42.
57. *WP*, 44/42.
58. Bento Prado Jr, 'Sur le "plan d'immanence"', in Éric Alliez (ed.), *Gilles Deleuze. Une vie philosophique* (Le Plessis-Robinson, Institut Synthélabo, 1998), p. 313.
59. *WP*, 45/42.
60. *WP*, 45/42.

4

Logic

Initially (and systematically) broached in *Spinoza and the Problem of Expression*, where it characterises the nature of the relation between substance, attributes and modes, the problem of expression reappears in *Logic of Sense*. Now the focus is on expression as what designates the operation of sense. In both instances, expression enables an immanent conception of its subject matter. Sense is no exception to what we could characterise as the metaphysical, or onto-theological, drive to transcendence. Indeed, too often, Deleuze argues, sense is represented as a Principle, Reservoir, Reserve or Origin. As a 'celestial' or 'divine principle', it is understood to be fundamentally forgotten and veiled; as a 'subterranean' (or human) principle, it is understood to be erased, hijacked or alienated. It becomes a question, therefore, of re-establishing or recovering sense beneath the erasure and under the veil, either in a God that one would have never sufficiently understood, or in a humanity that one would have never adequately explored. It is in vain that we replace Man with God, however, if we remain ultimately trapped in anthropomorphism. Equally, it is in vain that we replace the true and the false with sense and value, as Nietzsche suggests, if we persist in thinking the latter by means of the former, as if it were a question of discovering or uncovering something essentially hidden. Such is the reason why, for Nietzsche, the problem is primarily that of the overhuman, and not that of humanity. To think sense without transcendence presupposes that we cease to think of it as buried or veiled, and think it instead as the object of an encounter, that is, as something essentially *produced*. But who or what produces sense? How does it occur? We will see that the force by which sense is produced is always anonymous and impersonal, and that it is not legitimate or possible to infer sense from any transcendent entity without installing oneself in paradox. In this chapter, I show the extent to which Deleuze's account of sense relates to, and differs from, that of logical empiricism and Husserl's transcendental logic – in other words, I show how his ambition to construct a transcendental empiricism unfolds with respect to the question of sense and logic.

1. The Logical Positivism of the Vienna Circle

The impact and significance of the so-called linguistic turn which logical empiricism carried out at the beginning of the last century is well known: it consists in the systematic analysis of the propositions of knowledge as defined by the sciences of empirical reality, and in the dissolution of the false or pseudo-problems of metaphysics. In addition, logical empiricism is characterised by its method, the new logic, inherited from Frege and Russell. The task of philosophy is no longer to create theories, but only to clarify the sense and validity of propositions by logical means.[1] In other words, once we've purged what is traditionally called 'philosophy' of both pure nonsense and the questions that now belong exclusively to the empirical sciences, we are left with a unique activity (and not a theory) that bears on the *language* of science, and concerns logic. In Russell's own words: 'the study of logic becomes the central study of philosophy'.[2] In the same text, Russell recommends that the new method of logic be applied to questions that lie outside the mathematical domain and, through the use of specific examples, demonstrates how logical analysis can call into question the meaning and significance of a number of philosophical propositions and problems. For Russell, as for the members of the Vienna Circle inspired by his work, logical analysis was to become the exclusive method of philosophy and, at last, clear the way for a truly scientific philosophy. Yet in so far as it was never meant to be a system of propositions, it could not claim to be a science, strictly speaking. Still, given its extraordinary importance, it was destined to be worshipped as 'the queen of all sciences'[3] and thus carry out the original dream of philosophy.

A particular feature of modern logic is that it is entirely independent of experience: it is not concerned with the facts or states of affairs designated in the propositions it analyses, but only with the formal character of those propositions. The critical analysis of language, therefore, aims to distinguish between the propositions of science, endowed with sense, and the propositions of metaphysics, devoid of sense, yet without any reference to empirical reality. Such a distinction can be established only on the basis of a criterion of sense, which the neo-positivists of the Vienna Circle believed to have found in Wittgenstein. In their view, it is possible to interpret the *Tractatus Logico-Philosophicus* in the following terms: all metaphysical propositions are non- or pseudo-propositions, that is, propositions devoid of sense. 'Genuine' or 'meaningful' propositions, on the other hand, are derived from the truth of elementary or atomic propositions ('protocolary propositions'), which describe 'atomic facts', or facts that can be verified by observation. Hence the close, but not exclusive, relationship between sense, truth and verification.[4] Carnap, for instance, sees the verification principle as an essential criterion of demarcation between scientific propositions and nonsensical propositions. This is a view that virtually all members of the Vienna Circle shared, and one that is most clearly formulated in a famous article by Blumberg and Feigl from 1931, which introduced logical positivism to the English speaking world.[5] In the article, the authors claim that there is a unique and privileged way to arrive at a general axiomatisation of knowledge indicated by the verification procedure. In order to arrive at the atomic propositions, which constitute the core of the complex propositions of science, the most fertile approach is not to ask, as Descartes did, about what cannot be doubted, but to seek the conditions under which a proposition can be said to be 'true'. If the conditions cannot be given, then the proposition is meaningless. Now according to Wittgenstein's own definition in paragraph 4.024 of the *Tractatus*, the sense or meaning (*Sinn*) of a proposition is the 'what is the case' or the 'what is not the case' of the fact it expresses. Thus, to know the meaning of a proposition or statement is to know 'what must be the case' in order for the proposition to be true. A proposition is 'true' when the fact it affirms 'is the case'; a proposition is false when this fact 'is not the case'. The truth and falsity of a proposition can be established by comparing it with reality. Paragraph 4.06 of the *Tractatus* affirms that 'propositions can be true or false only by being a picture of reality'.[6] By returning from the complex to the simple, one ultimately reaches those immediate facts, of which the 'being the case' constitutes the meaning of the proposition. Given a complex proposition, logical empiricism will always ask how it can be verified.

Hitherto, and with a few notable exceptions which, following Deleuze, I will emphasise, the question of sense (*Sinn*) emerged in the context of a logic that envisaged it as the condition of what is usually called 'denotation' or 'reference' (*Bedeutung*), and which designates the relation between a proposition and a state of affairs. Thus, according to Frege, the *Sinn* of a sentence or a word is a distinct and public entity, which belongs to, or is associated with, the proposition, whereas the *Bedeutung* is the reality denoted by the sentence or the word.[7] By distinguishing so clearly between *Sinn* and *Bedeutung*, Frege breaks with the philosophical tradition that determined sense on the basis of certain mental terms, or at least on the basis of pre-linguistic elements. In the process, he recognises *Sinn* as independent from the thinking or speaking subject. He frees sense from denotation as well as from what Deleuze calls 'manifestation'.[8] In that respect, Deleuze remains indebted to Frege. Wittgenstein, whose *Tractatus* extends and modifies the distinction between *Sinn* and *Bedeutung*, goes further still: the proposition alone has sense, whereas a name or a primitive sign has a *Bedeutung* and represents an object.[9] Denotation associates words with specific pictures, to which correspond specific states of affairs. From the logical point of view, the criterion and element of denotation is that of the true and the false. A proposition or statement is true when its denotation is actually fulfilled by a state of affairs, or when it is the picture of reality, as Wittgenstein, followed by the Vienna Circle, argued. 'False', on the other hand, means that the denotation is not fulfilled, either because the pictures selected are inadequate, or because it is impossible to produce a picture that can be associated with the words in question. By *conditions* of truth, one needs to understand the totality of conditions under which a proposition 'would be' true. The conditioned proposition might well be 'false', in that it refers to a non-existent or non-verifiable state of affairs. Thus, by grounding truth, sense also makes error possible. Such is the reason why the condition of truth is not opposed to the false, but to that which is deprived of sense, and which can be neither true nor false. This is the very condition that Deleuze calls 'signification', and which he equates with the third dimension of the proposition (after 'denotation' and 'manifestation'). It is now a matter of the relation between words and universal or general concepts, and between syntactical connections and conceptual implications. This, modern logic claims, is the level of sense strictly speaking – the very level at which, as *formal* logic, it is to operate. The elements of a proposition 'signify' conceptual implications that can refer to other propositions and serve as premises for the original proposition. Signification is defined according to this order of conceptual implication in which 'the proposition under consideration intervenes only as the element of a "demonstration", in the most general sense of the word, either as premise or as conclusion'.[10] The linguistic signifiers are thus of the type 'implies' and 'therefore'. Whereas signification is always to be found in its corresponding indirect process, that is to say, in its relation to other propositions, from which it is inferred, or whose conclusion it renders possible, denotation, on the contrary, refers to a direct process. The logical value of

Logic

signification thus understood is no longer truth, but the *condition* of truth, that is, the set of conditions under which a proposition *would be* true.

By thinking sense in such a way, however, logic does not manage to reach the genuine condition of denotation or expression. By speaking of a condition of truth, classical logic does indeed move beyond the true and the false, since a false proposition too has a sense or a signification. The problem, however, is that this superior condition defines only the possibility for a proposition to be true. As Russell himself, whom Deleuze quotes, puts it: 'We may say that whatever is asserted by a significant sentence has a certain kind of possibility'.[11] Thus the possibility for a proposition to be true – its sense – is nothing else than the form of possibility of the proposition itself. Deleuze expresses his dismay before this 'odd procedure', which 'involves rising from the conditioned to the condition, in order to think of the condition as the simple possibility of the conditioned'.[12] Why, Deleuze wonders, move from the conditioned to the condition, if, ultimately, we can think of the condition only as the image of the conditioned, that is, as its mere *form* or its condition of *possibility*? Why model the condition after the conditioned? If the move to the condition, or to what some, notably Husserl, would call the foundation of truth statements, is to take place, should we not seek their real, rather than merely possible, condition? Formal logic does indeed reach the level of foundation, but what is founded remains what it was, unaffected by the very operation that grounds it. This is how 'denotation remains external to the order that conditions it, and the true and the false remain indifferent to the principle which determines the possibility of the one, by allowing it only to subsist in its former relation to the other'.[13] One is therefore perpetually referred from the conditioned to the condition, and also from the condition to the conditioned, in what amounts to a purely formal back and forth. For the condition of truth to avoid this defect, Deleuze goes on to say, 'it ought to have an element of its own, distinct from the form of the conditioned'.[14] In other words, it ought to be something *unconditioned* capable of assuring a real genesis (and not a merely possible conditioning) of the other dimensions of the proposition, namely, denotation, manifestation and signification. The condition of truth would then be defined as genuine sense, and no longer as mere conceptual form of possibility. In that, the 'logic of sense' would quite explicitly contravene the imperatives of logical positivism, which saw fit to remain at the level of the form of the proposition, or risk

81

falling back into psychologism. In addition, the logic of sense would no longer aim to be a meta-language, a mathematics, or a *mathesis universalis* of natural and scientific language. Finally, and as Deleuze himself emphasises, it would renew Husserl's ambition to develop a transcendental logic, that is to say, a logic that would aim at extricating the real conditions of experience underlying all meaningful operations, and all statements of truth. Whilst himself raising the question regarding the truth conditions of a proposition, Deleuze rejects the formalist approach. On the one hand, the latter claims to solve the question of sense independently of experience. On the other hand, it is the empirical reality itself, or 'what is the case', which in the end guarantees the validity of the atomic proposition. The way logical positivism conceives sense is too formal and its conception of reality is too empirical (in so far as it is determined by the empirical sciences). It is only by developing a logic not of form, but of content, and a conception of the real that is not positivist, but transcendental, that one can overcome the limits – and the limitations – of logical empiricism.

2. *Husserl's Transcendental Logic*

Husserl's great achievement with respect to the question of sense is to have facilitated the passage from formal to transcendental logic by redirecting the sense of the proposition to the horizon of immanence, or to the pre-predicative ground, from which it stems.[15] This transition does not amount to a mere dismissal of the linguistic procedures of formal logic. Rather, it consists in the demonstration of a layer of sense and experience that precedes such procedures. In short, it is a shift in the order of grounding. For Husserl, it was a matter of extracting the very condition of formal logic and, through such an extraction and its ambition to found the empirical sciences as such, to develop a theory or a pure idea of science. Such a theory, by means of which one would be able to distinguish the *a priori* possibilities to which science itself must conform if it is to be genuinely scientific, must indeed exist, if the ultimate justification for science does not reside solely in its successful organisation or its mere factual existence. Yet the entire question is whether *formal* logic can claim to be this science of science. Husserl's answer is clearly negative, and stems from the observation that traditional logic cannot cope with the increasingly complex and differentiated organisation of the sciences, and that modern logic borrows its methods and its style of demonstration from mathematical science itself, which remains a particular science. The science of sciences, or the truly scientific logic, on the other hand, can only be a *universal* science.

Husserl's *Formal and Transcendental Logic* is divided into two parts, which clearly indicate the aim and movement of Husserl's thought with respect to the question of logic. In the first part, he is concerned to analyse the structures and the sphere of objective formal logic, within which he identifies two distinct trends: 'apophantic analytics' and 'formal ontology'. Formal ontology is 'an eidetic science of any object whatever'.[16] It is a mathematical, *a priori* theory of objects, though a *formal* one, relating to the pure modes of anything whatever, conceived with the emptiest universality. As such, it is an all-embracing science, the forms of which can be conceived without reference to concretely designated objects.[17] Formal ontology is distinguished by its theme from formal apophantics, which itself is the *a priori* formal science of the judgement, more precisely of the predicative judgement, or of what Aristotle called *apophansis* (assertion). Apophantics is concerned with the categories of signification, such as subject, predicate, concept and proposition, while formal ontology is concerned with categories of the object, such as thing, set, number, property, quality, relation, identity, unity, equality and totality. If Husserl qualifies this logic as a whole as *objective* formal logic, it is to draw our attention to the fact that traditional logic (and that includes mathematised, symbolic logic) remains unilaterally focused on the object, that is, oriented towards thought-formations (*Denkgebilde*). Up until the end of the first part of the book, Husserl is concerned to distinguish between formal ontology and formal apophantics, and analyse the close ties between them. By gradually distinguishing the sense belonging to traditional logic, however, Husserl's investigation uncovers the presuppositions of logic, which reveal it to be a 'naïve' logic, one that never dreamt of questioning what it declares to be a matter of course, namely, its orientation towards objects or something in general. The specific plan of *Formal and Transcendental Logic* is that of reaching a logic that transcends objective logic by integrating it into a logic able to attain a full understanding of itself: 'our chief purpose is to show that a logic directed straightforwardly to its proper thematic sphere, and active exclusively in cognising that, remains stuck fast in a naïveté that shuts itself off from the philosophic merit of radical self-understanding and fundamental self-justification'.[18] Thus, in the second part of the book, the investigation into sense is led to criticise the evidences of logic, and hence to return to the constituting subjective activity and to the clarification of this activity. Logic, in other words, becomes reflective, that is, directed towards the specific mode of intending of formal logic. Only with the phenomenon of intentionality, and with the investigation into the manner in which judgements are produced, or 'constituted', do we arrive at the condition of meaningful or scientific propositions, and thus at a genuine foundation of science itself. The subjective orientation of this criticism eventually turns out to support the exclusively objective orientation of the theme of traditional logic.

Husserl's stroke of genius is not simply to have introduced the pole of subjectivity in matters of sense and logic, that is, to have shifted the terrain of logic from object to subject, but also, and above all, to have avoided the trap of psychologism in the process. It is by wanting to avoid this very trap that logical empiricism had thought it necessary to become a purely formal science. In so doing, however, it had cut off the operation of sense from that of consciousness, and separated philosophy and psychology absolutely. With the discovery of intentionality, however, it is no longer the empirical consciousness that is sought as the foundation of sense in general, but the transcendental consciousness. In other words, there is no longer any reason to interpret problems referring to subjectivity as problems of *natural* human subjectivity, hence as psychological problems in the empirical sense. The problems that the phenomenological criticism of logic deals with are the problems of *transcendental* subjectivity, that is, of a constitutive or sense-bestowing subjectivity.[19] Thus one comes to a logic that 'descends into the depths of transcendental interiority'. Only then can the sense of science in its true objectivity be fully understood:

> Only a science clarified and justified transcendentally (in the phenomenological sense) can be an ultimate science; only a transcendentally-phenomenologically clarified world can be an ultimately understood world; only a transcendental logic can be an ultimate theory of science, an ultimate, deepest, and most universal, theory of the principles and norms of all the sciences.[20]

Formal logic, even expanded into *mathesis universalis*, can only be an analytic criticism of cognition, a criticism of theories and of ideal processes that result in these theories. Only a transcendental criticism can truly set up a *universal* theory of science, for it is the criticism of the intentional, or subjective, life that itself 'constitutes' regions and theories.

Logic

Let us look briefly, then, at the task that falls to a transcendental theory of judgement.[21] Its ultimate aim is to rediscover the hidden essential grounds from which traditional logic springs. As such, it is a genetic analysis. Now Husserl's thesis is that all syntactical operations point back to *experience* as to their irreducible origin: his method of successive reductions leads us from true judgements of the higher level down to true judgements relating *directly* to the individual objects, which are given through experience. The primordial judgements, then, are judgements of experience: they are the most immediate judgements of the categorial form, where one has the 'evidence' that procures the presence of the things 'themselves'. The basic level of the categorial, the judgement of experience, contains in itself 'immediately' the source of experience. Hence we should place ourselves there in order to know what experience is. And by placing ourselves on the lowest level of the judgement, which is the judgement of experience, we come to discover that what one would believe to be pertinent to the predicative sphere, that is, certainty and its modalities, intention and fulfilment, etc., is already pertinent to the intentionality of experience. There is, then, a type of categorial activity, albeit of low level, which takes place in experience. This is what *Experience and Judgement*, devoted to a genetic theory of judgement, reveals most clearly.[22] Even something like perception, when accompanied with a minimum level of attention (*die betrachende Wahrnehmung*), Husserl claims, is an activity that must be distinguished from a mere passivity. No doubt, at the bottom of it all there is a believing in the existence (*Seinsglauben*) of the *pregiven* that is entirely passive. This is what Merleau-Ponty called perceptual faith (*foi perceptive*). There is, for instance, the barking of a dog that comes from the surrounding world, and which we hear 'without our paying the least attention to it'.[23] But from the moment we pay attention to it, from the moment we take it as an object of interest, there is an activity – an *antepredicative* activity, but an activity all the same. It is essential, therefore, that we distinguish the antepredicative and the pregiven, the passive synthesis of mere perception (which Hume qualified as *belief*) and the active synthesis of attentive perception. This is how Husserl is able to extend the concept of judging to include this antepredicative activity and not reserve it exclusively for the predicative judging, as traditional logic always does.

In a sense Deleuze is indebted to Husserl for having extracted a layer of sense beneath predicative sense, for having broadened the sphere of sense and judgement and included in it the antepredicative activity, that is, the life-world that is the horizon of any relation whatever. The problem, however, from Deleuze's own perspective, is that the life in question is *my* life: Husserl discovers the transcendental field, yet immediately proceeds to tie it to the form of the Ego, or to a synthetic consciousness. In doing so, he perpetuates one of the fundamental postulates of the western image of thought, which seeks to give sense a unique source (the Ego) and a unique destination or direction, namely the form of the object that corresponds to it. That is what *Difference and Repetition* calls *good* sense.[24] In addition, the postulate requires that, *qua* origin, sense be essentially shared, and thus able to constitute the ground of science itself and guarantee its objectivity. That is what Deleuze calls *common* sense. Between them, good sense and common sense constitute the two halves of *doxa*, or the unthought of western thought. Ultimately, the genesis of sense in Husserl's logic is nothing more than the genesis of good sense and common sense, that is, of sense as it is from the start subordinated to the imperatives of a synthetic consciousness. Such is the reason why this logic remains a logic of substance, or of the *substratum*: it seeks to delimit judgement in its identity. Sense remains bound to consciousness as the correlate of its intention in experience. In that respect, it cannot be distinguished from the *form* of predicative judgement. It is still modelled after that which it is supposed to ground (the predicative judgement): the structure of transcendental experience reproduces the form of the propositional structure.

Such is the reason why, ultimately, Deleuze seeks to solve the problem of sense by placing it on a different terrain altogether, that is, one that would be neither pure grammar, understood as a certain method, which Carnap would have described as 'syntactic',[25] nor intentionality, understood as a sense-bestowing activity. Sense, Deleuze believes, needs to be wrested from logical positivism *as well as* transcendental psychology. It must bind its fate neither to the world understood as the set of objects or facts as a whole, nor to the formal conditions under which expressions can denote such facts, nor, finally, to consciousness as the site of their original constitution. But if sense is produced neither in the proposition as such, nor in the subject from which the proposition emanates, nor, finally, in the objects that it intends, from what horizon does it unfold? The answer can be formulated in a few words, even though such words refer to a complex reality: in order to liberate sense from any intentionality, or horizon of fulfilment, it is necessary to envisage it as a pre-conscious or unconscious surface, a horizon, that is, not

Logic

of convergence, where each thing would find its place and its focus from a unique luminescent source, but of divergence, populated by differences as yet untamed and unresolved, and thus pregnant with an infinity of virtual worlds. No longer *my* life, but *a* life.[26] The transcendental field to which logic refers, and the genesis of which phenomenology aims to produce, is neither, contrary to what Husserl thought, an individuated consciousness, nor even, as Sartre believed, a pre-individual consciousness, to which sense would be immanent, but an impersonal and pre-individual unconscious, at once structural and genetic.[27]

3. Sense and Expression

This is the point at which structuralism takes over the project of phenomenology, and of a transcendental logic: in order to understand the operation of sense, one needs to envisage it as structure. In the sixth series of *Logic of Sense*, Deleuze argues that a structure must conform to the following minimal conditions. First of all, one needs at least two heterogeneous series, one determined as 'signifying' and the other as 'signified'. A unique series is therefore never sufficient in itself to form a structure. In addition, each series has to be constituted by terms that exist only through their reciprocal relations. To these relations, or rather, to the values of these relations, correspond specific 'events', that is, 'singularities' that can be assigned in the structure. We need to understand 'event' in the sense of a mathematical singularity. Structure is indeed quite similar to differential calculus, wherein the distribution of singular points corresponds to the value of differential relations. Thus, as structural linguistics reveals, the differential relationships between phonemes assign singularities to a particular language, and it's in the 'vicinity' of those singularities that the characteristic sonorities and significations of the language in question are constituted. As for sense, even though it is embodied in 'real' words (or in the real part of the word known as its 'sonority') and in 'images' or concepts associated with the words, according to determinable series, it is not reducible to them. In fact, it is 'older' than them, and more profound than the series it determines.[28] As structuring power, sense is this 'symbolic' element that accounts for the genesis of signification, manifestation and denotation, of the subject as well as the object. It is the genuine transcendental subject, but a subject that cannot be thought so long as it is envisaged in its actuality. Structure is a system of differences that always has a certain reality, an actuality, but one in which what actualises or embodies itself, here and now, are this or that relation, this or that differential, and not the structure or the system as a whole, which can be defined as the totality of its *ideal* differences. It is a kind of ideal reservoir or repertory, where everything coexists in its *virtual* state. This, then, is how the question of sense oscillates between 'structure' and 'genesis'.

We are left with the delicate question of knowing how to recognise the symbolic element, or the structure. Deleuze's answer is: by its 'position'. The position in question, however, is rather unique. Naturally, sense cannot occupy a *real* place, or a position in extension. It cannot even occupy an imaginary place, or the place of a substitute. Such is the reason why it is a space outside space, an empty square, or a 'transcendental' space. The new transcendental philosophy, which Deleuze extracts from structuralism, and with which he wants to link the question of sense, always privileges places over what fills them. This is how we need to understand the work of Foucault, for example: Foucault does not consider death, work, desire, or play as dimensions of empirical human existence, but as places or positions that allow those who occupy them to become mortal, working, desiring, or playing subjects. One finds, therefore, a new distribution of the empirical and the transcendental, the latter being defined as an order of places independent of those who occupy them empirically.[29] This is how empirical psychology, the social sciences as a whole, and empirical logic itself find themselves grounded in, and determined by, a transcendental topology.

A number of consequences derive from this local or positional definition of sense: if symbolic elements are characterised by neither an extrinsic denotation nor an intrinsic signification, but only by a sense of position, we must conclude that *sense or meaning always results from the combination of elements that are themselves not meaningful*. In other words, sense is produced as a result or an effect – akin to an optical, linguistic or surface effect – of non-signifying elements. This is precisely what Deleuze means when he claims that, in order to be a genuine condition, sense cannot be conceived in the *image* of signification, or as its mere condition of *possibility*. There is, therefore, something like a meaninglessness or significationlessness of sense, a nonsense of sense, which we must be careful to distinguish from what is normally referred to as the absurd. From the point of view of the philosophy of the absurd, it is sense that is lacking, essentially. From a structuralist point of view, however, there is always an excess of sense in relation to signification, and any process of signification amounts to a reduction of sense, or to its 'resolution' (in the algebraic sense of the term). Thus nonsense is not mere absurdity, that is, the opposite or negation of sense (as signification), but what gives it a value and what generates it by circulating in the structure.[30] Such is the reason why, throughout *Logic of Sense*, Deleuze draws on various examples of nonsense, especially from Lewis Carroll. Nonsense, in this instance, does not stem from a personal fondness for the absurd, which is only a lack of sense, and desperation in the face of it, but from a surplus of sense that is prior to the signifying procedures, and from which they themselves derive. If, in the end, Lewis Carroll's work is so jolly and humorous, it is because it invites the reader to pass to the other side of the mirror of sense (which is not its negation, its contrary or its contradiction), where the virtual conditions (distinct from its real and imaginary incarnations) of sense await us. Let us take the example of his 'portmanteau words'. Their role is exactly equivalent to that of Levi-Strauss's 'floating signifier' or that of an 'object = x': a symbolic or 'zero' value that circulates within the structure and enables it to function as such, and which, in a way, is also produced by it, but only as an optical or positional effect. Always displaced or at a distance from itself, this object, like Poe's purloined letter or Carroll's Snark, has the odd characteristic of never actually being where we expect to be, and of being found where it is not. With Lacan, we could say that 'it is lacking in its own place' or that 'it fails to observe its place'.[31] Should we attempt to treat the Snark as sign, we would be met with the following, bewildering explanation: 'because the Snark is a Boojum, you see'. In other words, our attempt to differentiate it from another signifier and connect it with a signified, or a signified chain, will always cause it to slide, slip, or float further. The same goes for the Knight who announces the title of the song that he is about to sing in *Through the Looking-Glass*:

> 'The name of the song is called *"Haddock's Eyes"'* – 'Oh, that's the name of the song, is it?' Alice said, trying to feel interested. – 'No, you don't understand', the Knight said, looking a little vexed. 'That's what the name of the song is *called*. The name really is *"The Aged Man"*.' – 'Then I ought to have said "That's what the *song* is called"?' Alice corrected herself. – 'No, you oughtn't: that's quite another thing! The song is called *"Ways and Means"*: but that's only what it's *called*, you know!' – 'Well, what *is* the song then?' said Alice, who was by this time completely bewildered. – 'I was coming to that', the Knight said. 'The song really *is* "A-sitting on a Gate"! . . .'[32]

On the other hand, as soon as we envisage it as a different kind of signifier, a *floating* signifier, we generate both the signifier and the signified, in one go as it were. The mistake, concerning the Snark, would consist in believing that it consists of two (or more) significations mixed together. In fact, it does not signify *stricto sensu*; it is otherwise than signifying, or beyond meaning, precisely to the extent that it signifies the operation of sense itself, the way, that is, in which sense is produced: 'sense is the Snark'.[33] Its nonsense is precisely a function of its sense, or of the fact that it *is* sense (but the sense of being of sense is precisely what is at issue here, and one that we will need to clarify).

According to Deleuze, the Snark, like Lewis Carroll's work as a whole, is traversed by the fundamental alternative, and duality, between eating and speaking, which it reveals and expresses in its constitutive tension. In *Sylvie and Bruno*, for example, 'the alternative is between "bits of things" and "bits of Shakespeare"'.[34] Similarly, at Alice's coronation dinner, 'you either eat what is presented to you, *or* you are introduced to what you eat'.[35] More importantly still, the alternative is often between speaking of food or eating words (Alice, for example, is 'overwhelmed by nightmares of absorbing and being absorbed' and 'she finds that the poems she hears recited are about edible fish'[36]). Ultimately, this duality synthesises that between things and propositions, or between bodies and language, in which the question of sense is played out: is sense produced in the depths of bodies or things, in 'their action and passion', and in 'the way in which they coexist with one another?'[37] Or is it a movement of the surface, produced in language alone? In fact, it is neither – neither the result of a given proposition nor the effect of a given state of affairs. Yet it is the condition for both, and for their irreducible relation. It is the joint, hinge, or articulation between the two series, which it allows to communicate with one other, without ever reducing the gap that separates them. It is always on the move, always circulating through the series, and thus defining the unity of the structure. The entire structure is propelled and made to function through this originary third term, this intruder that lacks an origin. It distributes differences within the structure, and causes the differential relations to vary through its displacements. In short, it is the differentiator of difference itself, or its 'paradoxical instance': sense manages to bring together the two series it runs through by constantly keeping them apart. As a word = x, it runs through a determinate series, that of the signifier. But as an object = x, it designates another series, that of the signified. Neither signifier nor signified strictly speaking, it is simultaneously more and less than both. As a word, it is most peculiar, in so far as it designates exactly what it expresses, and expresses what it designates. It expresses what it designates as much as its own sense. In a single operation, it manages to say something and the meaning of what it says: it says its own sense. In that respect, it is utterly unusual. For the law that governs all meaningful words is precisely such that their sense can only be designated by another name. The name that expresses its own sense can only be nonsense.

The logic of Stoicism can be shown to operate in the same way, and to underlie virtually the whole of Lewis Carroll's universe. In fact, the way it introduces and uses the pair *semainon/semainomenon*, or signifier/ signified, prefigures Saussure's own structural linguistics. The pair in question essentially presents two characteristics, which distinguish it from Aristotle's theory of language. Firstly, it doesn't work without the participation of a third term, the *tughkanon*, which functions like a reference point, and which is often compared with Frege's *Bedeutung*, inasmuch as it designates the corresponding external object. Literally, it means 'what's there' or 'lies out there'. Foucault translates it as *'conjoncture'* or 'state of affairs'.[38] It designates the external, corporeal, or physical substrate (the *hupokeimenon*, or what stands beneath), which corresponds to the vocal utterance (the *phone*). This *phone*, which one utters and hears, in its bodily materiality, is the signifier itself. It shows or manifests the signified. In Sextus Empiricus' own words, the latter is *'auto to pragma*, the matter itself as it manifests itself in the vocal utterance, and which we, in turn, understand when it presents itself to our thought, whereas the people who do not understand our language do not understand it, even though they hear the vocal utterance'.[39] The second characteristic of this invention is that the signified is not called only *semainomenon*, but also *lekton*, as if the Stoics wanted to mark their invention by creating a neologism. The term in question is a nominalisation of the verbal adjective of the verb *lego*, to say. Diogenes Laertius defines *lekton* as 'that which subsists according to', or 'in conformity with a logical representation'.[40] Sextus Empiricus takes up this definition, and refines it: according to the Stoics 'what can be expressed or spoken [*lekton*] is what belongs to a discursive representation [*logiken*]; a discursive representation is that in which what is represented can be made manifest in speech [*logos*]'.[41] Now what distinguishes the *logos* from the mere *lexis*, essentially defined as 'the voice articulated in letters', is that it is necessarily meaningful, precisely as a result of the presence of the *lekton*.

But what sort of presence is at issue here? What kind of thing is the *lekton*? This is the point at which the originality of Stoicism becomes apparent, and its opposition to the Aristotelian theory of language manifest: unlike the *logos*, understood as a collection of signifiers, and the denotation, associated with the state of affairs, the *lekton* is an 'incorporeal' (*asomaton*). Without a given *logos*, of which it is the effect, the *lekton* does not exist. It exists (*huparkhein*) only in the actual uttering of the speech. And yet, it does not simply cease to be outside its utterance; it remains something. It 'subsists' (*huphistanai*). The being of sense, therefore, is not existence. Besides existence, which designates the empirical reality, there is at least another sense of being, which belongs to the incorporeal. This amounts to another opposition to Frege and his disciples, for whom the various classical meanings of being can be reduced to that of existence (whether possible or actual).[42] The being of sense is even less equivalent to that of essence, which assumes the reality of an intelligible world, accessible by means other than the propositional. Rather, according to Diogenes Laertius, incorporeality is said of 'that which can be occupied by bodies, without actually being so occupied'.[43] Besides the *lekton*, the Stoics recognise three incorporeals: time, space and the void. This distinction between the corporeal and the incorporeal draws on the Stoic theory of causality. Following the Platonic definition of being as power (*dunamis*),[44] the Stoics understand the body as what can act or be acted upon. By contrast, they define the incorporeal as essentially inactive and impassive: 'According to them, the incorporeal neither acts on anything, nor is acted upon by anything.'[45] This view implies that whilst incorporeals do not interact with bodies, nor bodies with incorporeals, bodies do interact with one another. Yet a body can cause an incorporeal effect in another body, such as 'being burnt' or 'being cut'. This is how Émile Bréhier, from whom Deleuze draws his inspiration, puts it:

> when the scalpel cuts through the flesh, the first body produces upon the second *not a new property* but a *new attribute*, that of being cut. The *attribute* does not designate any real quality . . ., it is, to the contrary, always expressed by the verb, which means that it is not a being, but a way of being. . . . This way of being finds itself somehow at the limit, at the surface of being, the nature of which it is not able to change: it is, in fact, neither active nor passive, for passivity would presuppose a corporeal nature which undergoes an action. It is purely and simply a result, or an effect which is not to be classified among beings.[46]

Logic

It is clear, therefore, that the Stoics draw a radical distinction between two planes of being: on the one hand, real or profound being, force (*dunamis*); on the other, the plane of effects, which take place on the surface of being, and constitute an endless multiplicity of incorporeal beings (attributes).

Following Deleuze, we need to emphasise that the *lekton* is an attribute of the object, and not of the proposition: it is the predicate, for example 'green', which is the attribute of the subject of the proposition. It is precisely because of this attribute, which is affirmed of the object, without changing the nature of the object, that the signified object (*to semainomenon*) differs from the object as a corporeal, physical entity corresponding to the vocal utterance (*to tugkhanon*). In the proposition, the attributes of beings are expressed not by its epithets, which indicate properties, but by its verbs, which indicate acts. But it is the very meaning of the proposition, and of logic itself, which changes, when the emphasis shifts from predicates to attributes. 'Green' (*vert*) is certainly the predicate of 'tree'. But 'to green' (*verdoyer*) is its attribute. When I say: 'the tree greens', I do two things: on the one hand, I erase the reference to the copula, and with it the delicate question of knowing how subject and predicate relate to one another, or how to connect different classes of objects; in a sense, I place myself before the subject–predicate divide, in order to reach the subject in its being, or rather its becoming. On the other hand, I then erase the predicate itself, and replace it with an attribute, which designates the manner of being of the subject. As a result, this attribute is not that of the proposition itself, but the attribute of the state of things it designates. Thus, the action of a scalpel on the flesh does not produce a new property or quality, but an attribute of the type 'being cut'. Now an attribute is neither a being, nor a quality (green, or cut), but a way of being, what the Stoics, in their table of categories, called a *pos ekhon*. It is a manner of being that does not affect essences, and is not even an accident in the Aristotelian sense. In a sense, it is a manner of being that leaves the state of things always intact. In short, it is an event which occurs at the surface, an effect which slides alongside substantial beings, affecting neither existences nor essences, neither substances nor accidents, and which, as a result, is a matter for a 'logic' other than that of the subject and its predicates. Events are not like deep-sea creatures, but like crystals, which form or grow only around the edges. The event is a manner or a mode of being which escapes corporeal reality and its causal connections, its actuality and its chronology: the time of attributes is not that of being, but a parallel time, a pure becoming. From the point of view of this time, or this becoming, it is not impossible to grow and shrink at the same time, as Alice does. We need to distinguish clearly between what chrono-logy excludes, or what, from its own point of view, cannot take place at the same time, and this other time, which always doubles and redoubles the first, at *the same time*. In what amounts to a reversal of the Platonic order, sense no longer designates what is deep, but the surface; it no longer designates the origin, but the effect, no longer what is given from the start, but what is generated.[47] In every aspect, sense is opposed to the metaphysical essence, which it replaces. This is how sense escapes transcendence.

The attribute absorbs both the copula and the predicate. In other words, a proposition of essence disappears in favour of a proposition of modality, and a logic of substance is replaced with a logic of events. It is no longer the colour 'green' that is predicated of the substance 'tree', but the tree itself that appears from a primordial 'greening'. The attribute – the verb – is no longer the expression of a concept (an object or a class of objects), but of an event or a singularity in the vicinity of which both subject and predicate organise their relationship. In their classification of attributes, the Stoics do not distinguish them, as Aristotle did, according to the (more or less accidental) nature of their connection with the subject. On the contrary, in such attributes they see only the many ways in which an event can be expressed. It is by becoming a logic of the event that the logic also becomes a logic of immanence. The logic of predication was a logic of substance and essence, and essence – the transcendent reality – was opposed to becoming. The concept was modelled after such essence. It must now model itself after the event, or after what Deleuze calls pre-individual and impersonal singularities (it is because of this that the operation of sense is no longer indicative of an intuitive and sense-bestowing consciousness). At this level, all events are compatible: they express one another, or are 'inter-expressive' (*s'entr'expriment*).[48] Ultimately, the aim is 'to attain to the universal communication of events'.[49] Incompatibility only emerges with the individuals and the bodies in which events are effectuated. By allowing oneself to penetrate the plane of events, where actualisations through differentiation have not yet taken place, one reaches the point of view of God, for whom everything is, to use Leibniz's expression, 'compossible'. But this God is not that of onto-theology. It is the God of univocal being, the unique substance, which is said in one and the same sense of everything of which it is said. Thus, we see how the Deleuzian theory, inspired by Stoicism, extends his ontology of univocity and immanence, inspired by Spinoza: beings are not the properties of substance, but its manners of being, or its modes; they themselves are not individuals, but becomings.

From the start, and throughout, Deleuze's concern was to allow singularities to pierce through the crust of individuated realities, and extract sense from the surface of reality itself. In the end, this conception of philosophy could not be further from that of logical positivism, which envisages philosophy as that which can establish the sense or the nonsense of a proposition, but on no account *produce* it: the aim of philosophy, Wittgenstein affirms, is the logical clarification of propositions, and not the production of philosophical propositions.[50] For Deleuze, on the other hand, 'today's task is to allow the empty square to circulate and to allow pre-individual and impersonal singularities to speak – in short, to produce sense'.[51] Elsewhere, he describes the structure as 'a machine for the production of incorporeal sense'.[52] This, however, doesn't signal the reign of arbitrary, random sense. On the contrary, the mistake would be to think that, because it is produced, sense is necessarily produced by an 'I' or a 'self'. Inasmuch as it is pre-individual, 'I' cannot produce it. It is precisely by no longer being myself, that is, by rejoining the world of pre-individual and impersonal singularities, that I gain access to the world in the making, as opposed to the world as the totality of ready-made things. It is signification, not sense, that deals with such things, or, to use the terminology of logical empiricism, with the 'being-the-case' or the 'not-being-the-case' of the fact expressed in a proposition.[53] As soon as they are meaningful, predicative propositions designate states of affairs, or facts. At that level, however, everything has already been decided. One speaks, but not to say anything new. As logical empiricism argues, one speaks only to repeat, albeit in different, logical, terms what has already been said.[54] Yet what really matters is ignored. For what matters lies elsewhere, on the other side of the looking-glass, and not in the sky (whether open or closed) of a Sense given in advance, to which it would be a matter of returning, or which it would be a matter of discovering. But sense is the attribute of a state of affairs, and not the predicate of a substance: it expresses a singularity, or an event, and not a fact, or a quality. The event is not the accident of a substance that would preexist it. Rather, it is the substance itself – or the phenomenon – that is the effect, or the crystallisation, of such a system. To reduce the event to an accident is to fall back into vulgar empiricism. To reduce the event to an essence is to fall back into idealism and dogmaticism. Both vulgar empiricism and idealism fail to understand that true events are transcendental, and that they are singularities. As transcendental, singularities are precisely *not* actual. They are real, yet their reality differs from that of the *things* in which they actualise themselves. As events, they need to be distinguished from the states of affairs in which they both incarnate and resolve themselves. All states of affairs, or individuals, presuppose singularities as their origin. States of affairs are themselves the product of the resolution or the integration of singular points in ordinary facts and stable situations. This is how the real unfolds: from the transcendental events to the empirical subjects, from the singular to the ordinary, and from difference to identity. All too often philosophy seeks to impose another direction onto the real – the very direction or sense which it refers to as 'good sense'. By doing so, it takes the world back to front: it posits states of affairs as primary, stability as the norm, and subjects the world to the form of identity. Identity, however, whether of the world or of consciousness, is the effect of a sense that is first and foremost differentiated and multidirectional. Inasmuch as they connect singular points and differences of potential with one another, events are not stable. But neither are they simply unstable. Rather, they are 'metastable'. It is this world of singularities beneath states of affairs, these virtual events folded in individuals, that sense expresses; sense is their voice, or their trace inscribed at the surface of propositions. It is this entire horizon, this infra-individual and impersonal life that *Logic of Sense* seeks to grasp in this or that statement where it has surfaced. It is this, the bottomless, the Dionysian world of singularities (in opposition to the divine individuation of Apollo, and, naturally, to the human individuation of Socrates), which is the true subject of philosophy:

> What is neither individual nor personal are . . . emissions of singularities in so far as they occur on an unconscious surface and possess a mobile, immanent principle of auto-unification through a *nomadic distribution*, radically distinct from fixed and sedentary distributions as conditions of the syntheses of consciousness. Singularities are the true transcendental events . . . Only when the world, teaming with anonymous and nomadic, impersonal and pre-individual singularities, opens up, do we tread at last on the field of the transcendental.[55]

As we can see, logic cannot be separated from ontology. The sense that is at stake always exceeds the place that it is assigned in the

Logic

proposition. Yet that is where it surfaces. Whilst never where we expect it to be, whilst always missing in its own place, sense alone can bring us to the things themselves, to those things that are precisely not 'things', but their virtual conditions of existence – their singularities – which exist (or rather insist) independently of their *actual* existence. In the end, Deleuze's effort consists in displacing the very locus of the question of sense from the proposition, and its criteria of signification (of truth or truthfulness) to the truly *eventful* horizon that surfaces in, and precedes, the proposition.

By way of illustrating further the possibility of an actual experience of the field of the transcendental, and providing a transition to the following chapter, I wish to turn to the thirteenth series of *Logic of Sense*, entitled 'Of the schizophrenic and the little girl'. By introducing the problem of schizophrenia, and the figure of Artaud, Deleuze produces a tension within his book, one that will find its solution in *Anti-Oedipus*. To a large extent, it is the problem of schizophrenia that propels Deleuze beyond his own structuralism, and Artaud's own work that allows him eventually to reject Lewis Carroll's work as the paradigm of transcendental sense.

There is, Deleuze begins by claiming in that series, no such thing as nonsense. Rather, there is no *one* such thing as nonsense. The logician alone would have us believe that. But between the nonsense of *Alice in Wonderland* and that of some of Artaud's texts from his time in Rodez, including his own 'translation' of 'Jabberwocky', there is actually a world of difference. Between the portmanteau word of the little girl and that of the schizophrenic, there is ultimately no comparison. One could not seriously confuse Babar's song ('Patali dirapata cromda cromda ripalo pata pata ko ko ko), which resembles Carroll's, with Artaud's howls-breaths ('Ratara ratara ratara Atara tatara rana Otara otara katara . . .'). Why does Deleuze feel the need to distinguish between the two? What's at stake in that difference? Why, in other words, and despite his initial attraction for Lewis Carroll, does Artaud himself claim that his writing has nothing in common with that of Carroll? With this question, a new and decisive avenue is opened up, one that propels Deleuze's own thought into uncharted territory (in fact, into the deterritorialised domain of the body without organs). With this question, a new aspect or new configuration (for essential reasons, we cannot say a new *sense*) of immanence emerges. Now to answer this question, we need only emphasise the fact that Carroll's language is organised according to heterogeneous series (say, to eat/to speak, consumable things/expressible senses, in relation to orality), which are emitted at the surface of bodies. On this surface, a line is akin to the frontier between two series, propositions and things, or between dimensions of the same proposition. Along this line, sense is elaborated, both as what is expressed in the proposition and as the attribute of things – the 'expressible' of expressions and the 'attributable' of denotations. The two series are therefore articulated by their difference, and sense traverses the entire surface, even though it remains on its own line. Undoubtedly, this immaterial sense is the result of corporeal things, of their mixtures, and of their actions and passions. But the result has a very different nature than the corporeal cause. It is for this reason that sense, as an effect of being always at the surface, refers to a quasi-cause which is incorporeal. This is the always mobile nonsense, which is expressed in esoteric and in portmanteau words, and which distributes sense on both sides simultaneously. All of this forms the surface organisation upon which Lewis Carroll's work plays a mirror-like effect.

It is this structuralist approach that breaks down in the face of the language of schizophrenia. For the schizophrenic, there is no longer a surface. The surface has split open. Things and propositions no longer have a fixed frontier between them, precisely because bodies have no surface. The primary aspect of the schizophrenic body is that it is a sort of body-sieve. Freud emphasised this aptitude of the schizophrenic to grasp the surface and the skin as if they were punctured by an infinite number of little holes. The consequence of this is that the entire body is no longer anything but depth – it carries along and snaps up everything into this gaping depth which represents a fundamental *involution*. As there is no surface, the inside and the outside, the container and the contained, no longer have a precise limit; they plunge into a universal depth or turn in the circle of a present which is increasingly contracted as it is filled up. Hence the schizophrenic manner of living the contradiction: either in the deep fissure which traverses the body, or in the fragmented parts which encase one another and spin about. Body-sieve, fragmented body, and dissociated body – these are the three primary dimensions of the schizophrenic body.

In this collapse of the surface, the entire world loses its meaning. It maintains perhaps a certain power of denotation, but one that is experienced as empty. It maintains a certain power of manifestation, but one that is experienced as indifferent. And it maintains a certain signification, but one that is experienced as 'false'. Nevertheless, the world loses its sense, that is, its power to draw together or to express

Logic

an incorporeal effect distinct from the actions and passions of the body, and an ideational event distinct from its present realisation. Every event is realised, be it in an hallucinatory form. Every word is physical, and immediately affects the body. The moment that the world loses its sense, it bursts into pieces; it is decomposed into syllables, letters, and above all into consonants which act directly on the body, penetrating and wounding it. The word no longer expresses an attribute of the state of affairs; its fragments merge with unbearable sonorous qualities, invade the body where they form a mixture and a new state of affairs, as if they themselves were a noisy, poisonous food. The parts of the body, its organs, are determined in virtue of decomposed elements which affect and assail them. In this passion, a language-affect is substituted for the effect of language.

For the schizophrenic, then, it is less a question of recovering sense than of destroying the word, of conjuring up the affect, and of transforming the painful passion of the body into a triumphant action. Triumph may now be reached only through the creation of breath-words (*mots-souffles*), howl-words (*mots-cris*), in which all literal, syllabic and phonetic values have been replaced by *values which are exclusively tonic* and not written. To these values corresponds an organism without parts, a body that operates entirely by insufflation, respiration, evaporation and transmission. What defines this second language and this method, practically, is its consonantal, guttural and aspirated overloads, its apostrophes and internal accents, its breaths and its scansions, and its modulation which replaces all syllabic and or even literal values. It is a question of transforming the word into an action by rendering it incapable of being decomposed and incapable of disintegrating: *language without articulation*. It is a question of activating, insufflating, palatalising and setting the word aflame so that the word becomes the action of a body without parts, instead of being the passion of a fragmented organism. This is Antonin Artaud's 'body without organs'.

It seems entirely insufficient, consequently, to say – as Lacan does – that the language of the schizophrenic is defined by an endless and panic-stricken sliding of the signifying series (or the symbolic) towards the signified series (or the real). In fact, there are no longer any series at all; the two series have disappeared. Nonsense has ceased to give sense to the surface; it absorbs and engulfs all sense, both on the side of the signifier and on the side of the signified. In this primary order of schizophrenia, the only duality left is that between the actions and the passions of the body. Language is both at once. There is no longer anything to prevent the propositions from falling back onto bodies and from mingling their sonorous elements with the body's olfactory, gustatory, or digestive affects. Not only is there no longer any sense, but there is no longer any grammar or syntax either. Carroll needs a very strict grammar, required to conserve the inflection and articulation of bodies, if only through the mirror which reflects them. It is for this reason that we can oppose Artaud and Carroll point for point. The *surface series* of the 'to eat/ to speak' type have really nothing in common with the poles of depth of schizophrenia. The two *figures of nonsense* at the surface, which distribute sense between the series, have nothing to do with the two *dives into nonsense* which drag along, engulf and reabsorb sense (*Untersinn*). We must avoid confusing the nonsense of *Unsinn* and the non-sense of *Untersinn*, nonsense and infra-sense. Ultimately, the distance between Carroll and Artaud is the distance separating a language emitted at the surface and a language carved into the depth of bodies. It is the distance – in fact, the abyss – that separates the logic of sense (and nonsense) from what is otherwise than sense, the abyss that separates nonsense from madness (or what, in the second edition of *Proust and Signs*, Deleuze calls 'Anti-logos'). It is to 'madness' that we now need to turn.

Notes

1. This is more or less Schlick's position, directly inspired by Wittgenstein's *Tractatus*. See Ludwig Wittgenstein, 'Logisch-philosophische Abhandlung', in *Annalen der Naturphilosophie*, 1922, no. 14, pp. 185–262; trans. C. K. Ogden, *Tractatus Logico-Philosophicus* (London: Kegan Paul, 1922). Neurath goes further still by refusing to grant philosophy any constructive role, not even that of clarifying the concepts and propositions of science. Such a task, according to him, befalls a science that is entirely devoid of worldviews.
2. Russell, *Our Knowledge of the External World as a Field for Scientific Method in Philosophy* (London: George Allen & Unwin, 1914), p. 243. Quoted in Carnap, 'Intellectual Autobiography' (1963), in Paul Arthur Schilpp, ed., *The Philosophy of Rudolf Carnap* (La Salle, IL: Open Court, 1963), p. 13.
3. M. Schlick, 'Die Wende der Philosophie' (1930), *Erkenntnis*, 1, p. 8.
4. This is a feature that Frege rejected. First, according to him, the notion of truth precedes that of the correspondence between propositions and facts. Second, it is impossible to measure propositions against facts, since facts are only ever presented in propositions. See G. Frege, 'Logik

[1897]', in *Nachgelassene Schriften*, edited by H. Hermes, F. Kambartel and F. Kaulbach (Hamburg: Felix Meiner, 1970); trans. P. Lang and R. White, 'Logic', in *Posthumous Writings* (Chicago: Chicago University Press, 1979).
5. Albert E. Blumberg and Herbert Feigl, 'Logical Positivism. A New Movement in European Philosophy', *The Journal of Philosophy*, vol. XXVIII, no. 11, 21 May 1931, pp. 281–96. Karl Popper's 'critical rationalism', it should be said, constitutes a significant exception to this consensus. Whilst sharing some of the goals and assumptions of logical positivism, Popper refuses to see sense as the criterion of scientificity. Instead, he opts for 'falsifiability' (or 'refutability'), which is not a criterion of signification separating meaningful (or scientific) from meaningless (or metaphysical) propositions, but a criterion of 'demarcation' between scientific and metaphysical propositions thought to be *equally meaningful*.
6. 6 Wittgenstein, *Tractatus Logico-Philosophicus*, §4.06.
7. G. Frege, '*Über Sinn und Bedeutung*', in *Kleine Schriften*, edited by Ignacio Angelelli (Hildesheim: G. Olms, 1967); trans. Max Black et al., 'On Sense and Meaning', in *Collected Papers on Mathematics, Logic, and Philosophy*, edited by Brian McGuinness (Oxford: Blackwell, 1984).
8. LS, 23/13.
9. Wittgenstein, *Tractatus Logico-Philosophicus*, §3.3.
10. LS, 24/14.
11. Bertrand Russell, *An Inquiry into Meaning and Truth* (London: George Allen & Unwin, 1940), p. 179. Cited by Deleuze, LS, 29/18, note 7.
12. LS, 30/18.
13. LS, 30/19.
14. LS, 30/19.
15. See E. Husserl, *Formale und transzendentale Logik* (1929), edited by Paul Janssen (Husserliana XVII), (The Hague: Martinus Nijhoff, 1974); trans. D. Cairns, *Formal and Transcendental Logic* (The Hague: Martinus Nijhoff, 1974). In what follows, I have found inspiration in Suzanne Bachelard's *A Study of Husserl's* Formal and Transcendental Logic, trans. Lester E. Embree (Evanston: Northwestern University Press, 1968).
16. E. Husserl, *Ideen zu einer reinen Phänomenologie und phänomenologischen Philosophie, I. Buch: Allgemeine Einführung in die reine Phänomenologie*, edited by Karl Schuhmann (Husserliana III), (The Hague: Martnus Nijhoff, 1976), p. 22; trans. F. Kersten, *Ideas Pertaining to a Pure Phenomenology and to a Phenomenological Philosophy, First Book, General Introduction to a Pure Phenomenology* (Dordrecht/Boston/London: Kluwer Academic Publishers, 1983), p. 21.

17. Husserl, *Formal and Transcendental Logic*, pp. 77–8.
18. Husserl, *Formal and Transcendental Logic*, p. 153.
19. This feature is what distinguishes it from the Kantian transcendental subjectivity: aside from the mere form of intentionality, there is nothing that is simply given in the transcendental field: all meaningful acts are constituted, or *generated*. This genetic dimension of the transcendental is also crucial for Deleuze.
20. Husserl, *Formal and Transcendental Logic*, p. 16.
21. Here, I am following Suzanne Bachelard's *A Study of Husserl's* Formal and Transcendental Logic, pp. 136 ff.
22. E. Husserl, *Erfahrung und Urteil*, edited by Ludwig Landgrebe (Hamburg: Claassen, 1954); trans. James S. Churchill and Karl Americks, *Experience and Judgement* (Evanston: Northwestern University Press, 1973).
23. Husserl, *Erfahrung und Urteil*, p. 61.
24. DR, 133–4/175.
25. Carnap's thesis is most clearly and completely expressed in *The Logical Syntax of Language* (Vienna: Julius Springer, 1934). The language in question is that of science. It is necessary to distinguish, therefore, between the language on which the philosophical analysis bears and the meta-language in which this analysis takes place. According to Carnap, philosophical analysis must henceforth bear on the syntax of scientific language, which alone is meaningful. Specifically, it must bear on the set of rules that determine such a language, and which include, on the one hand, the rules of formation, which determine the expressions of a language that are correctly formed, and, on the other hand, the rules of transformation, which determine the deductive relation between different propositions. 'Syntactic' means that the definition of such languages and the characterisation of their properties refer only to the *form* and the *order* of the signs that constitute the expressions of the language in question, and not the *signification* of such signs.
26. 'Immanence: a Life' is the title of the last text that Deleuze published in his life-time. See *TRM*, 359–63/384–9.
27. In the remainder of this chapter, I look at sense as involving an operation of structure and genesis, which also governs the ontology of *Difference and Repetition*, as I have tried to show in detail in *Truth and Genesis: Philosophy as Differential Ontology* (Bloomington: Indiana University Press, 2004). In subsequent chapters, and in Chapter 5 in particular, I try to show the limits of such an approach, and the way in which Deleuze's later thought projects him beyond ontogenesis.
28. See Deleuze, 'How Do We Recognize Structuralism?', in *DI*, 238–69/170–92.
29. M. Foucault, *Les mots et les choses* (Paris: Gallimard, 1966), p. 329 sq.

Logic

30. In that respect, non-sense is the exact equivalent of the non-being of *Difference and Repetition* (see *DR*, 88–91/63–6), which Deleuze distinguishes from the negative in the Hegelian sense.
31. Lacan, *Écrits*, p. 25. Quoted by Deleuze, *LS*, 55/41.
32. *LS*, 42/29.
33. *LS*, 31/20.
34. *LS*, 36/23.
35. *LS*, 36/23.
36. *LS*, 36/23.
37. *LS*, 36/23.
38. Foucault, *Les mots et les choses*, p. 57.
39. See Sextus Empiricus, *Adversus mathematicos*, VIII, 11–12; trans. R. G. Bury, *Against the Logicians* (Cambridge, MA: Harvard University Press, 1997).
40. Diogenes Laertius, *Lives of Eminent Philosophers*, VII, 63 (Cambridge, MA: Harvard University Press, 1925); Greek text facing an English translation by Robert Drew Hicks; reprint with an introduction by Herbert Strainge Long, 1972.
41. Sextus Empiricus, *Adversus mathematicos*, VIII, 70.
42. When Quine, for example, asserts that 'to be is purely and simply to be the value of a variable', he is actually saying that *to be* is equivalent to being the *possible* instance of a concept. See 'On What There Is', in *The Review of Metaphysics*, II (1948), p. 32. Quine modified the wording of his article in *From a Logical Point of View* (Cambridge, MA: Harvard University Press, 1953), p. 13: 'To be assumed as an entity is, purely and simply, to be reckoned as the value of a variable.' The latter formulation better captures his conviction that semantics can only reveal the ontological commitments of language, but cannot establish definitively what there is (pp. 15–16).
43. Diogenes Laertius, *Lives of Eminent Philosophers*, VII, 140.
44. Plato, *Sophist*, 247e.
45. Sextus Empiricus, *Adversus mathematicos*, VIII, 263.
46. Émile Bréhier, *La Théorie des incorporels dans l'ancien stoïcisme* (Paris: Vrin, 1997), p. 12. Cited by Deleuze, *LS*, 14/5.
47. The play of depth and surface in *Alice in Wonderland* is fundamentally Stoic. In the second part of the story, we see surfaces prevail over depths: the animals from the depths give way to playing cards, to figures without depth, and Alice herself returns to the surface and disavows the abyss.
48. *LS*, 208/177.
49. *LS*, 208/178.
50. Wittgenstein, *Tractatus Logico-Philosophicus*, §4.112.
51. *LS*, 91/73.
52. *LS*, 88/71.

53. According to Albert Blumberg and Herbert Feigl, to know the meaning of a proposition is 'to know what must be the case if the proposition is true' ('Logical Positivism. A New Movement in European Philosophy', p. 287). This idea is one that Wittgenstein had already formulated in proposition 4.024 of the *Tractatus Logico-Philosophicus*: 'To understand a proposition is to know what is the case, if it is true.'
54. Blumberg and Feigl stipulate very clearly that, being concerned only with the internal structure of language, and therefore without relation to experience, logic defines the rules that allow one to repeat entirely or in part what has been said in a different form ('Logical Positivism. A New Movement in European Philosophy', p. 283). The propositions of logic are tautological, or analytic. They are not statements, that is, they say nothing regarding the existence or non-existence of a given state of affairs. It is precisely this tautological dimension, or the dimension which, in the eyes of logical positivism, defines philosophy as a whole and as a legitimate enterprise, which Deleuze rejects entirely: it is the sign of a miserable and sad conception of philosophy that is not worthy of philosophy. Not that philosophy ought to concern itself with states of affairs after all: its sole concern, rather, should be for events.
55. LS, 124–5/102–3.

5

Ethics

1. Ontology and Ethics

Between ontology and ethics, there is no difference in kind, no gap, and no complex mediation, but a continuity: the being of man is entirely co-extensive with that of nature. If Spinoza is the highest expression of philosophy, or the 'prince of philosophers', it is because he realised that the greatness of thought, and the human conatus, consisted not in its ability to distinguish and abstract itself from the plane of nature, and posit its own being on the basis of a being (whether itself, or God) in excess of nature, but to express nature in its infinity. His greatness, in other words, consisted in his ability to associate the power of the human with the infinite power of nature, and to distinguish the power in question from an expression of transcendence. I would like to begin this chapter by considering some of the practical consequences of Spinoza's ontology for the existence of modes, and especially for the human being as one such mode, or one such expression, of Substance. The rest of the chapter will show the extent to which Deleuze's thought after *Expressionism in Philosophy* remains indebted to Spinoza.

The discourse concerned with modes, and their various and peculiar ways of being (and modes are nothing but ways in which the substance *is*, or comports itself) is what Spinoza calls ethics. Ethics is entirely different from morality. Ethics is not concerned with values, judgement, or duty, but with ontological potentials, powers and bodily or physical states. It is closer to ethology and natural law than the moral law. At the same time, however, it is concerned with the highest good for man (beatitude), and with the way of attaining it. In a lecture at Vincennes from February 1980, Deleuze claims that morality can never be derived or extracted from ontology.[1] Similarly, if we begin with ontology, and especially with an ontology of immanence, we will never arrive at morality. Why? For the simple reason that morality always implies something higher than, or beyond, being, a One or a Good on the basis of which everything, including being itself, can be judged. Morality is 'the system of judgement' that posits a principle beyond being, a transcendent value, according to which the comportment of human beings is judged, and in which the essence of man is supposed to be realised.[2] Contrary to what Levinas claimed, much of the history of ontology is actually a systematic subordination of ontology to morality, a transcendent ontology, or an onto-theology. In other words, and as I have tried to show by following Deleuze's own interpretation of the historical unfolding of the problematic of imitation and emanation, much of the history of ontology and metaphysics is in fact moved and motivated by moral values. Such a diagnosis is of course deeply Nietzschean, and it is with the eyes of a genealogist that Deleuze reads and understands the history of philosophy. By freeing ontology from morality and transcendence, and by following Spinoza and Nietzsche in the process, Deleuze also and *de facto* frees up the possibility of ethics.

Now modes, according to Spinoza, comprise three main features.[3] First, modes are characterised by their *essence*. But essence, far from designating an idea, or a general concept – far, that is, from dividing itself into genus and species – designates a degree of *power*, or potency (*potentia*). Yet this essence always expresses itself in a distinct *relation*, or a certain capacity to be affected (*affectio*):[4] a thing is designated not (only) by what it is, but by what it can (do); its being is its power. To define something not according to its essence (for example, man as the rational animal), its genus, or species, but according to its power, and so to align essence with power, is to follow in the footsteps of Nicholas of Cusa, who had coined the term *possest* precisely to designate the identity of possibility (qua power, or capability [*posse*]) and being (*esse*) in God and the beings that explicate it.[5] Finally, modes can be seen from the point of view of their *existence*, or from the point of view of the extensive parts subsumed in this relation – from the point of view, that is, of their affects (*affectus*), or emotions.[6] By mode, then, we need to understand a certain essence (understood as a degree of power and a singular expression of substance), which has the capacity of being affected by other modes, and is thus characterised by specific affects, which define its existence.

All modes, including the human mode, are defined according to this triad. It is the nature of all modes to exercise their power, or attempt to realise their essence. All modes, therefore, can be designated according to their specific tendency to persist in their own being, or their *conatus*. It is a matter of recording the different powers of the modes, of registering their capacities and their affections. For any given mode, then, the question is one of knowing what its powers are, *what it can do*, or of what it is capable.[7] This statement should be qualified by saying that it is not *in principle* or *structurally* that we do not know what a given body can do. It is only that we do not know *a priori* what it can do. In other words, we cannot define the power, affections and affects of a body according to a metaphysical essence defined in advance, but only according to its nature, and the effects it produces. Modes are characterised by their ability to be affected and affect, or suffer and act, in a certain way. And this is something that we can know only through experience, and *as* a body. Hence Deleuze's insistence that onto-ethology, and not metaphysics or onto-theology, is the discourse that is adequate to characterise living things in general, and human beings in particular. Thus, we will distinguish between a frog and a horse, or even a racehorse and a plough horse, not according to traditional lines (genus, species, family, etc.), but according to their respective powers and capacities.

For Deleuze, and following Spinoza's philosophy of immanence, it is a matter of dissociating the ethical, or onto-ethological, question, from the moral question, and of thinking ethically where we have grown accustomed to thinking morally. Instead of asking what we *ought* to do, subordinating our action and our natural inclination to our moral duty, Spinoza asks what we *can* do. Ethics is a matter of power, not duty. It is only once we know what we can do, the sort of affections we are capable of *as bodies*, that we know what we should, or want to, do: for what we seek to actualise, like all other modes, is precisely our ontological potential, and what we seek to feel is the joy and general fulfilment that accompanies this actualisation. On this particular point, Spinoza is anti-Cartesian. Descartes assumed that the body was passive, and the mind active, or that when the body was active, the mind was only passive.[8] On the basis of such an assumption, and up until Kant, morality came to be viewed as the attempt on the part of the mind to dominate the body and its passions. According to the *Ethics*, on the other hand, what is action in the mind is *also* and *necessarily* action in the body, and what is passion in the body is also and necessarily passion in the mind.[9] Such is the substance of Spinoza's doctrine of 'parallelism', which not only denies all relation of real causality between mind and body, but also rejects any form of eminence of the former over the latter. Consequently, by *truly* knowing the powers of the body, or by knowing what bodies are capable of, beyond the mere effects that they produce on consciousness, we will be able to discover the powers of the mind.

Bodies or modes are not the only ones that can be affected: ethics, or ethology, extends to Nature as a whole. As a specific type of power (*potentia*), the essence of God also possesses this power to be affected. This is what Spinoza calls his *potestas*. The difference between God and the existing world is the following: in the case of substance, the power of affection is necessarily active; it consists in purely active affections. God is necessarily cause of all his affections, which can all be explained by his nature. God's affections, then, are all actions: they are the modes themselves, whether as essence or existence. In the case of existing modes, their ability to be affected is always and in each case exercised, albeit first and foremost by affections and affects of which the mode itself is not the adequate cause. Their affections are produced by other, external existing modes; the modes' affections are like second-degree affections, or affections of affections. It's understandable, then, that existing modes be subjected to changes that their nature alone cannot explain. Their affections and affects are first and foremost the result of imaginations and passions, of inadequate ideas, or ideas of which they are not the cause. That situation is the one in which human beings are themselves thrown from the start: 'All men are born ignorant of the causes of things.'[10]

The crucial question, then, is that of knowing whether, and how, existing modes can produce active affections and adequate ideas. That is the genuinely ethical question. Supposing, however, that modes actually manage to produce such affections, and free themselves from the infantile state in which they are 'most dependent on external causes',[11] the state in question will never disappear altogether, and the modes will never destroy entirely their passive emotions; rather they will reach a stage in which that state constitutes the least part of themselves.[12] This, in turn, means that the ethical question is already played out at the level of passive affections. As long as the capacity to be affected is filled by passive affections, it is reduced to its minimum. For Spinoza, the power to suffer, or be passive, doesn't express anything positive. In every passive affection, there is something imaginary, which stops it from become real. Our passivity and our passions are the result and the expression of our imperfection: 'For it is certain that what is active acts through what it has and that the thing which is passive is affected through what it has not.'[13] We suffer as a result of an encounter with something else, distinct from us; we have a force of suffering, therefore, which is distinct from our force of action. But our force of suffering is only the imperfection, the finitude, or the limitation of our force of action.

Ethics

Our force of suffering does not affirm anything, because it does not express anything: it only 'envelops' our powerlessness. In reality, our power to suffer is our powerlessness, our own form of bondage, and the limitation of our power to act.[14] In passive affections, we remain imperfect and powerless; we are separated or disconnected from our essence, our degree of power – separated, that is, from what we are capable of, what we can do. To be sure, the passive affections that we feel fill our power of affection; but they do so only to the extent that they have reduced that power to its bare minimum, and separated us from what we are capable of (our power to act), ever since we were children. Such is the reason why, following Spinoza, Deleuze constantly returns to the following question, as to the question with which ethics needs to begin: we don't even know what we are capable of, the sort of affections we can produce, nor how far our power reaches.[15] We don't know what that active power consists of, or how to acquire or regain it. The goal of the *Ethics* is precisely to find out, and make us active (again).

Regarding affects, or emotions, Deleuze emphasises the following. Emotions are exactly the form that the *conatus* takes when it is determined to do something, as a result of being affected in a certain way. In so far as an existing mode possesses a very great number of extensive parts, it can be affected in a very great number of ways, and its parts can always be forced to enter into a new relation, yet one that always corresponds to its essence, or its degree of power. This is how the relation between parts that characterises an existing mode (a horse, a fish, a man) can increase or weaken, and even die.[16] In that respect, we need to distinguish between two different types of relation, or encounter, between existing modes – two ways, that is, in which relations between parts can be composed, decomposed and recomposed. On the one hand, using myself as an example, I can meet a body whose relation combines with my own. This will produce a joyful emotion, which increases my power of action:

> (This itself may happen in various ways: sometimes the body encountered has a relation that naturally combines with one of my component relations, and may thus contribute to the maintenance of my overall relation; sometimes the relations of two bodies may agree so well that they form a third relation within which the two bodies are preserved and prosper.) Whatever the case, a body whose relation is preserved along with my own is said to 'agree with my nature', to be 'good', that is, 'useful', to me. It produces in me an affection [in fact, what Deleuze has in mind here is actually an affect, rather than an affection] that is itself good, which itself

agrees with my nature. The affection is passive because it is explained by the external body, and the idea of the affection is a passion, a passive feeling. But it is a feeling of joy, since it is produced by the idea of an object that is good for me, or agrees with my nature.[17]

Whilst being a passion, and thus an expression of my powerlessness, the affection thus produced 'envelops' a degree, however small, of our power of action. In other words, when 'the feeling affecting us itself agrees with our nature, our power of action is then necessarily increased or aided'.[18] Our own power has been facilitated by that of another body, and the joy that it generated is added to the desire that follows from such an affection. Whenever our nature or *conatus*, which Spinoza defines as our effort, or desire, to persevere in existence, is determined by an affection that is good or useful to us, our power of action increases.[19] To the extent that our feeling of joy increases our power of action, it determines us to desire, imagine, do, everything in our power to preserve this joy and the object that generated it. In short, we don't altogether cease to be passive, or separated from our power of action, but we tend to be less separated from it, and get closer to it.

My encounter with other bodies can also lead to the opposite situation, and produce a feeling of sadness. I meet a body (another person, a climate, food) whose relation cannot be combined with my own:

> The body does not agree with my nature, is contrary to it, bad or harmful. It produces in me a passive affection which is itself bad or contrary to my nature. The idea of such an affection is a feeling of sadness, a sadness corresponding to a reduction of my power of action.[20]

What ethical consequences should we draw from this? Firstly, the fact that 'good' and 'bad' only apply to what agrees or disagrees with my own nature. And in so far as God and Nature are one and the same, 'good' and 'bad' cannot be mistaken for, or indeed subsumed under, another, moral order, defined in terms of 'good' and 'evil'. For a philosophy of immanence such as Spinoza's, there is simply no room for morality: 'The evil suffered by a man is always, according to Spinoza, *of the same kind as indigestion, intoxication or poisoning.*'[21] In that respect, his interpretation of Adam's misfortune is exemplary. The divine prohibition to eat from the fruit should be understood as a purely natural recommendation, and not as the expression of divine, transcendent law. Rather, there is no difference between divine and natural law. Everything unfolds on the plane of nature, that is, on the plane of the connection between causes, and

Ethics

their effect on bodies. All the law stipulates is that eating from the fruit will result in the decomposition of the relation between parts that constitute Adam. It's a fruit that doesn't agree with his nature, and so one that he should avoid. To Adam, the fruit is poison. To another mode, it could be something else. Because the prohibition is not a matter of morality, Adam is not guilty of anything. His only 'sin' amounts to an error of judgement, a lack of reasoning. Because Adam knows things only through the effects that they produce (including on him), because he is ignorant of their causes, he *believes* that God's prohibition is an arbitrary, moral one. But God, who knows things through their causes, and knows himself as his own cause and as cause of the world as a whole, only reveals to Adam the natural consequences of his action. We should, Deleuze tells us, 'imagine Adam as a child: sad, weak, enslaved, ignorant, left to chance encounters'.[22] Spinoza rejects entirely the theological idea of the perfection of the original man, and he does so on *natural* grounds. It is not Adam's sin that explains his weakness, but his weakness, and the weakness of the original stage of humanity, which explains the myth of original sin. The moral standpoint, and the belief in transcendence, is only the expression of a theoretical confusion that fails to understand the natural order.

Secondly, whereas joy generates love, benevolence and other such positive desires, until they fill our entire power of affection, 'out of sadness is born a desire, which is hate'. Negative emotions only generate negative emotions, and destructive desires: antipathy, derision, contempt, envy, anger, etc. Even in sadness, our power of action is not entirely inhibited. For sadness, no less than joy, defines our *conatus* or essence. Even in sadness, we endeavour to triumph over, or destroy, its cause. If, when confronted with sadness, our power of action diminishes, it is because 'the feeling of sadness is not added to the desire that follows from it'.[23] On the contrary, the feeling inhibits the desire, and the power of the external body escapes our own.[24] Our power of action is progressively diminished; it tends towards its lowest degree, and reaches the point at which it can only *react*.

If, on Deleuze's interpretation of Spinoza, the ultimate goal of ethics is to know how to produce active affections (an operation that presupposes the production of common notions and adequate ideas, and so a transition from the life of imagination to that of reason), a preliminary step consists in knowing how to experience a maximum of joyful passions.[25] In a modal and subjective sense, *good* or *virtuous* (or free, strong and reasonable) can be said of a subject who strives to organise his encounters according to his own nature, to compose his relation with relations that agree with his nature, and thus to increase his power of action. *Bad* – or enslaved, weak and unreasonable – on the other hand, can be said of the existing mode who lives according to random encounters, and merely suffers their effects, moaning all the while, and even accusing something or someone every time the effects in question don't agree with him and expose him to his own powerlessness. This, according to Deleuze, accounts for the birth of resentment, with which we poison others, and guilt, with which we poison ourselves. Such is the reason why Spinoza denounces all passions rooted in sadness, which separates us from life and our power of action. There is no doubt that Deleuze sees Spinoza as a proto-Nietzschean, and his ethics as a way of thinking and living beyond good and evil.[26] Like in Nietzsche, there is a philosophy of life in Spinoza, one that denounces all transcendent values, which turn against life itself: good and evil, right and wrong, praise and blame, sin and redemption.[27] The moral, transcendent standpoint judges the world, and sees it from the point of view of an *ought*. The ethical, immanent standpoint, on the other hand, seeks to understand the world and the degrees of power that each mode expresses. It is rooted in a theory of power, not duty. Joyful affections require that we shift our standpoint, from the moral to the ethical, and from the imaginary to the real (or the rational). This, then, is how ethics, understood as the typology of the immanent modes of existence, replaces morality, which always relates existence to transcendent values. The moral standpoint is a function of man's tendency, and the illusion that follows, to attribute a transcendent value to those things that are useful to him, and to consider the world itself as if it had been created for him.[28] To adopt the moral standpoint, we need only not understand, or grasp the laws of nature as if they were divine commandments, adopt the standpoint of judgement rather than that of reason, and suffer rather than act. When we don't understand a law of nature, we tend to inject it with a moral value, and see it as an *ought*. The Law is always the instance of transcendence that determines the opposition between good and evil. Knowledge, however, is always the immanent power that determines the qualitative difference between good and bad as modes of existence.

Ultimately, though, it is not enough to avoid sad passions, seek joyful affections, and augment our power of action. For none of that is sufficient to render us active. It is a first, crucial effort of reason, but one that is not sufficient. Eventually, we need to free ourselves

Ethics

entirely from passions, however joyful. For passions will never give us the power of action we seek. To the extent that joyful passions themselves are born of inadequate ideas, they can only indicate the *effect* that another body has on us. Ultimately, we need to know bodies, including our own, not through the effects that they suffer, but through their causes. What's required is that, using joyful passions as our guide, we form the idea of what's common to the external body and our own. Only that idea, or 'common notion', is adequate. It's only in the transition to this second stage that the ethical standpoint is actually reached. Only then do we begin to understand and act, rather than suffer and judge. Only then do we become reasonable. This is also the point at which an active joy is added to our passive joy; and from that active joy reasonable desires, which follow from an adequate idea, are born.

Chapter 2 began by showing how, for Deleuze, Spinoza was the first philosopher of immanence, the first, that is, who was able to align philosophy with the plane of immanence. The plane in question first appeared as an ontological one. Progressively, though, it appeared that it was also, and from the start, practical, and thus signalled a decisive shift from the transcendence of morality and the 'ought' to the immanence of ethics and the 'is'. According to Deleuze, Spinoza substitutes the opposition between values (good–evil) with the difference between modes of existence (goodness–badness), and morality as a theory of duty with ethics as a theory of power and desire. It should come as no surprise, then, that Deleuze's own ethics, developed in collaboration with Guattari in the 1970s and 1980s, focuses on desire, and repeatedly appeals to Spinoza as a precursor. In that respect, his collaboration with Guattari can be seen as a way of extending and realising the onto-ethical programme set out in his early work, and especially in connection with Spinoza. In other words, having delineated his plane of immanence, or what he also calls the transcendental field, as an ontogenetic plane, in which two basic tendencies, the virtual and the actual, find themselves enmeshed, Deleuze seeks ways of experiencing the transcendental field itself. Increasingly, therefore, it becomes a question of knowing how, if at all, the human mind and body can counter-actualise the movement of organisation and individuation, or loop back into a state of thought, feeling and perception that is not yet codified, fixated or bound. This, we recall, is a dimension of Deleuze's thought (and of life itself) that was there from the start: what he calls transcendental empiricism is not just a theoretical or ontogenetic enterprise, but one that is also immediately practical or experimental. Whilst the ultimate aim of ethics is to know how to produce active affections, its temporary goal is to know how to experience a maximum of joyful passions, and rid ourselves of the transcendent apparatus that generates the negative passions of hatred, *ressentiment* and guilt. Thought is itself practical, or experimental, in that sense. But thought is not just philosophical thought. As will become apparent in the final chapter, literature, painting, music and film, also 'think', although not with concepts. They too are engaged in processes that seek to extract the realm of intensities from that of extensities, and the energy that moves there freely from its bound and limited state. Non-philosophy (and literature especially) is most relevant to philosophy, and can allow it to see and experience beyond its own boundaries.

Crucially – such, at least, is the hypothesis I wish to formulate in this chapter – the problem of ethics, and of life, especially in the 1970s, focuses on desire as the distinctly human (and over-human) *conatus*, as the concept that designates the question of what we are capable of, how far we can go, and how we can overcome the human, all too human condition. Desire, we recall, 'is the very essence of man, that is, the conatus whereby man endeavours to persist in his own being'.[29] This suggests that desire does not add anything or any content to the *conatus*: it is not a desire for an object (or a desire) that would be external or transcendent to it. Since the *conatus* is the tendency to persevere in one's essence, that is, the tendency to be what one *can* be, desire is a power of expression (of the substance, or nature), and not, as classically conceived, the sign of a human deficiency oriented towards the possession of an object that is lacking, or, worse still, of a transcendent Law. Desire, in short, is not the expression of an originary, structural lack, but of plenitude, and an ontological potential (*puissance*) that seeks its own expression. Like consciousness itself, desire is not intentionally structured: it is not '*désir de* . . .' (desire *for*, or *of* something). Rather, it *is* something (which Deleuze, especially in his collaborative work with Guattari, identifies with the unconscious), and something that is immediately real, immediately productive.[30] As such, the products of desire aren't images, fantasies, or symbolic objects, but real objects, or bits of reality: desire struggles with the real itself, and with the real in its entirety. Such is the reason why, in *Anti-Oedipus* and beyond, the question of desire comes to occupy such a central ground: it is the practical or ethical testing ground of the ontology of immanence,

Ethics

expression and production, developed in the 1960s. The problem of desire designates the cornerstone of the transcendental in its experimental or practical dimension. Deleuze's critique of psychoanalysis, his readings of Kafka, Sacher-Masoch, Proust and Artaud, his books on Bacon and cinema, can all be attributed to this insistent questioning regarding what *our* body can do, the processes of creation (of affects, percepts and values) it reveals, and the power of life and action it generates.

In order to be fulfilled, the programme that consists in thinking and living desire immanently requires a critical engagement with psychoanalysis, and especially with its idealist, transcendent interpretations, which converge in the centrality of castration and Oedipus. It requires that we understand how Oedipus came to play such a role for psychoanalysis, and why, according to Deleuze and Guattari, it is the main problem, or obstacle, to overcome, in order to arrive at an immanent understanding of the mechanisms of desire, and a liberation of its potential. Only then will we be able to turn to Deleuze and Guattari's alternative solution to the transcendent turning of psychoanalysis, which they characterise as schizoanalysis. The solution in question consists in a 'disoedipalising' or 'schizoising' of the unconscious. This operation consists in wresting desire from the symbolic, the Law, or the plane of transcendence, to which it was artificially attached, and bringing it back on the plane of reality, Nature, production, or indeed expression in the technical, Spinozist sense previously identified. Ultimately, we need to distinguish between expression in a Spinozist, materialist sense and expression in the representational, idealist sense.[31]

Needless to say, Deleuze's encounter with Guattari in the summer of 1968, followed by their immediate collaboration, played a crucial part in that evolution. As a psychiatrist and analyst mostly concerned with the problem of schizophrenia, Guattari had a practical and professional, as well as theoretical, relation to psychoanalysis. At the clinic of La Borde, he experienced first-hand the theoretical and practical limitations of psychoanalysis, especially in relation to schizophrenia. His basic idea was that psychoanalysis tries to think schizophrenia on the basis of a theoretical framework – the Freudian theory of neurosis, and the Lacanian theory of paranoia – which can't account for its singularity. At the same time, as a political activist and revolutionary concerned with the institutional aspects of psychiatry, and the need for a new social order, Guattari saw psychoanalysis' insistence on the family nucleus, understood as the primal scene of all conflicts and trauma, as a reductive and essentially bourgeois practice, which marginalised the social as the real and only realm in which the unconscious operates, and as reinforcing the bourgeois-capitalist order. It's that framework which, according to him, the schizophrenic shatters, his delirium being directly and immediately social, historical, or political. That being said, and as I have tried to show, Deleuze himself, especially through his reading of Artaud in *Logic of Sense*, had begun to reflect upon the singular status of schizophrenia, and the manner in which it poses a problem for, if not a radical challenge to, psychoanalysis. In a way, and despite its continued allegiance to Lacan's structuralism, *Logic of Sense* had already planted the seeds of this break with the concepts and presuppositions of psychoanalysis. A remarkable tension runs through that book, pulling it in two different, ultimately incompatible directions, one represented by Lewis Carroll, and the other by Artaud. Ultimately, it is the latter that prevailed, and allowed Deleuze to carry the question of sense and expression beyond the boundaries in which he had tried to confine it in *Logic of Sense*.

However, there is no doubt that, as a result of his encounter with Guattari, and of the social and political background against which it took place (May '68), Deleuze began to philosophise differently. This is what Deleuze had to say regarding the 'revolution' of May '68, which he saw as an irruption of the real (and of desire as reality), incompatible with its symbolic, or imaginary, interpretation:

> *Anti-Oedipus* was about the univocity of the real, a sort of Spinozism of the unconscious. And I think '68 was this discovery itself. The people who hate '68, or say it was a mistake, see it as something symbolic or imaginary. But that's precisely what it wasn't; it was reality breaking through [*c'était une intrusion du réel pur*].[32]

On a purely formal level, which contrasts with the academic, scholarly, and at times heavy style of Deleuze's early work, we need to stress the extent to which the two volumes of *Capitalism and Schizophrenia*, and *Anti-Oedipus* especially, appear carefree, and often lacking in rigour. They include many repetitions, unnecessarily long developments, and significant fluctuations in conceptuality. But those characteristics are themselves the result of a deliberate strategy, and a singular encounter between two modes of thought and different writing styles. This is how Deleuze recounts the initial stages of his collaboration with Guattari in an interview from 1972, the year of the publication of *Anti-Oedipus*:

Ethics

So Félix and I decided to work together. It started off with letters. And then we began to meet from time to time to listen to what the other had to say. It was great fun. But it could be really tedious too. One of us always talked too much. Often one of us would put forward some notion, and the other just didn't see it, wouldn't be able to make anything of it until months later, in a different context. And then we read a lot, not whole books, but bits and pieces. Sometimes we found quite ridiculous things that confirmed for us the damage wrought by Oedipus and the awful misery of psychoanalysis. Sometimes we found things we thought were wonderful, that we wanted to use. And then we wrote a lot. Félix sees writing as a schizoid flow drawing in all sorts of things. I'm interested in the way a page of writing flies off in all directions and at the same time closes right up on itself like an egg. And in the reticences, the resonances, the lurches, and all the larvae you can find in a book. Then we really started writing together, it wasn't a problem. We took turns at rewriting things.[33]

The two volumes of *Capitalism and Schizophrenia*, and the first one in particular, are filled with pages that seem to run in all sorts of directions, in an uncontrolled, almost erratic way. They indeed carry all sorts of things, precious stones as well as the mud from which they were extracted. They are singularly aneconomical. It should come as no surprise, then, that Deleuze and Guattari were, and still are, criticised not only as sloppy, careless 'philosophers', but also as irresponsible apologists of schizophrenia and free, anarchic desire.[34] As we shall see, such charges apply only to a superficial understanding of what Deleuze and Guattari were trying to achieve, and especially of what, according to them, was fundamentally at stake in schizophrenia, namely, desire. According to them, both schizophrenia and May '68 revealed something about the profound nature of desire. It's precisely in so far as Deleuze and Guattari were seeking to develop a positive and immanent conception of desire, the blueprint of which Deleuze found in Spinoza, that they needed to engage with the then dominant discourse on desire, namely, psychoanalysis. Given the singularity of Deleuze and Guattari's collaboration, and their methodological and stylistic decision, it cannot be a question of providing a rigorous and close commentary, nor even a summary of *Anti-Oedipus* and the texts surrounding it. Rather, it can only be a question of extracting key problems and notions, in order to show how desire, or the unconscious, can be rendered immanent, or revealed according to its immanent criteria.

2. The Three Syntheses of the Unconscious

Drawing inspiration from Kant's critical enterprise, Deleuze and Guattari summarise their programme for an immanent conception of desire in the following terms:

> In what he termed the critical revolution, Kant intended to discover criteria immanent to understanding so as to distinguish the legitimate and illegitimate uses of the syntheses of consciousness. In the name of *transcendental* philosophy (immanence of criteria), he therefore denounced the transcendent use of syntheses such as appeared in metaphysics. In like fashion we are compelled to say that psychoanalysis has its metaphysics – its name is Oedipus. And that a revolution – this time materialist – can proceed only by way of a critique of Oedipus, by denouncing the illegitimate use of the syntheses of the unconscious as found in Oedipal psychoanalysis, so as to rediscover a transcendental unconscious defined by the immanence of its criteria, and a corresponding practice that we shall call schizoanalysis.[35]

Leaving aside, for the moment, the question of the syntheses of the unconscious, to which I shall return, let me say a few things about Deleuze's crucial reference to Kant, which requires some explanation. Deleuze and Guattari suggest that we follow in the footsteps of Kant's Copernican revolution, and subject the unconscious, as the faculty of desire, to an immanent critique of its powers and uses, and thus establish philosophy as schizoanalysis. Naturally, we shall have to ask why Deleuze and Guattari felt it was necessary to replace psychoanalysis with schizoanalysis, and why they single out schizophrenia as the type that designates the legitimate or immanent use of the syntheses of the unconscious. Before turning to their discussion of schizophrenia, though, and by way of clarifying Deleuze's idiosyncratic appropriation of Kant, we need to turn to his early book on Kant.[36] Kant's philosophical *tour de force* consists in developing an immanent critique of reason (whether speculative or practical), in which reason judges itself, in so far as all of its ideas and representations are generated immanently, and not from experience, or from other instances that would remain external or superior to it. Indeed, and according to Deleuze's faithful assessment of Kant's views:

> In the first place, a representation can be related to the object from the standpoint of its agreement to or conformity with it: this case, the simplest, defines the *faculty of knowledge*. Secondly, the representation may enter into a causal relationship with its object. This is the *faculty of desire*:

'the faculty which, by virtue of its representations, becomes the cause of the reality of the objects of these representations'.[37]

Kant begins by turning to pure reason as a speculative faculty, or a faculty of theoretical knowledge, in his *Critique of Pure Reason*.[38] There, he distinguishes the legitimate and illegitimate uses of theoretical reason, accounts for the presence and genesis of both, and offers ways of avoiding the illegitimate uses, which lead reason astray, and generate 'illusions' or 'paralogisms'.[39] A few years later, he turns to an immanent critique of reason in its practical, or moral, dimension – that is, as a faculty not of knowing, but of desiring and acting.[40] Like theoretical reason, practical reason has the nasty habit of generating its own illusions. Instead of 'symbolising', that is to say, of using the form of the natural law as a 'type' for practical reason, the understanding occasionally seeks a 'schema' that might relate the moral law to a sensible intuition.[41] Furthermore, instead of simply commanding, without allowing our sensible inclinations and empirical interests to interfere with the moral principle, practical reason occasionally allows our desires to compromise our duty. The problem specific to practical reason, then, is one of knowing how to make sure that it remains self-legislating, and not allow any external, empirical and, for that matter, 'impure' interests, to contaminate the purity of the moral law. Contrary to the critique of pure theoretical reason, what is in need of 'critique' in practical reason, and what tends to generate illusions, is not *pure* practical reason, but the impurity (the empirical interests) that finds its way in its midst. The problem of practical reason is one of knowing how to maintain and secure its purity. In that respect, it's the exact opposite of the problem of pure speculative reason, the illusions of which stem from its ability to generate and pursue representations that are disconnected from experience. In both instances, we have a 'natural dialectic' that needs to be held in check by reason's own critical powers.

There is another, more disturbing dialectic, which stems from an illusion internal to practical reason.[42] It is worth mentioning, not only because Deleuze emphasises it in his book on Kant, but also because it influences his own position in *Anti-Oedipus*, and thus his critique of psychoanalysis. Pure practical reason excludes all pleasure or satisfaction as the determining principle of the faculty of desire. That being said, whenever the moral law determines the faculty in question, whenever the faculty of desire is subordinated to duty, and thus corresponds to its legitimate use, it experiences a certain satisfaction, a kind of negative pleasure that reveals our independence from sensible inclinations. It is, Kant says, a purely intellectual contentment that reveals the formal agreement of our understanding with our reason. Now the problem is that we tend to confuse this negative pleasure with a positive sensible feeling, or even with the very motivation of the will. We tend to confuse this active, intellectual satisfaction with something sensible, or experienced. This amounts to an illusion internal to pure practical reason, and one that it can't avoid. The antinomy, therefore, has it source in the immanent satisfaction of practical reason, and the inevitable confusion of that specific form of satisfaction with happiness. It is quite natural, therefore, that we are sometimes led to believe that happiness is itself the cause of, or the motivation for, virtue, and other times that virtue is itself the cause of happiness, when they are in fact entirely separate.

In what sense does Deleuze's own conception of desire relate to Kant's revolution? What are the immanent criteria to which he subjects his own critique? What are the legitimate and illegitimate (or transcendent) uses of the faculty of desire? We need to distinguish between those aspects that Deleuze retains from Kant, and radicalises, and those aspects that he criticises and rejects.

Following Kant's method, it is a matter of developing an immanent critique of the faculty of desire as the practical faculty – a matter, that is, of identifying its syntheses and the illegitimate uses (or *paralogisms*) it generates, most visible in the Oedipal construction of psychoanalysis. If, in a way, *Difference and Repetition* constitutes Deleuze's critique of pure reason, in which the transcendental and the empirical are united in a 'transcendental empiricism', or a 'superior form of empiricism', *Anti-Oedipus* corresponds to his critique of practical reason. The transcendental method is applied to the syntheses of the faculty of desire, which Deleuze identifies with the unconscious. Besides the method, Deleuze retains the following two crucial traits from Kant's analysis: first, and going back to Kant's own definition, the faculty of desire doesn't relate to its own object through 'correspondence', 'conformity', or what phenomenology would call 'intentionality', but through a relation of causality: the representation of the object is the cause of the reality of that object. A fundamental consequence of this view is that the object of desire cannot be said to be missing, or lacking in any way. It can only be produced. The conception of desire as lack, which runs through the entire history of philosophy, Christianity and political economy, is an 'illusion' that stems from a transcendent, illegitimate

Ethics

use of that faculty. Second, Deleuze refuses absolutely to link desire with pleasure, or satisfaction. This sets him apart from Freud and the school of psychoanalysis (every wish or *Wunsch*, Freud claims, is *Wunschbefriedigung*), but also from political economists as different as Bentham and Marx, who associated happiness with the satisfaction of interests and desires. The connection desire–pleasure is a further 'illusion' that requires its own critique. 'Lack' and 'pleasure' will turn out to be the most significant illusions of the faculty of desire.

Where Deleuze differs sharply from Kant, as we'll see, is in his assessment of the moral law, and the way in which desire is ultimately subordinated to duty. Duty, according to Kant, is the ultimate and only legitimate instance of desire. The subordination in question amounts to a resurgence of transcendence; it posits in advance what we *can* do by saying what we *must* do. This is in strict opposition to Spinoza, who writes: 'We do not endeavour, will, seek after or desire because we judge a thing to be good. On the contrary, we judge a thing to be good because we endeavour, will, seek after and desire it.'[43] With Spinoza, then, and against Kant, Deleuze reverses this order, and posits the question of ethics as the question regarding what we *can* do, and the extent to which we can express – through action, thought and creation – the infinite power of substance. For Deleuze, ethics is a matter of power, not duty. Duty, especially in the form of the moral law, is an inhibitor of power. It stems not from an understanding of nature, and our place in it, but from the positing of a law disconnected from nature, and superior to it. In that respect, Deleuze's own enterprise consists of a complete reversal of Kantianism. Naturally, from a Kantian perspective, it can only be seen as a return to dogmatism, and pre-critical thought. But there is little doubt that Deleuze wants to have it both ways: he believes ontology can be developed alongside ethics, and the transcendental, critical method be used as a way of overcoming the very separation that Kant had introduced between the order of knowledge and that of action. In typical fashion, then, Deleuze uses Kant against himself, or makes him pregnant with a child that Kant himself would have not recognised. For the child in question is a cross between Kant and Spinoza, or a transcendental philosopher and a schizophrenic.

Let me now turn to what Deleuze and Guattari call the syntheses of the unconscious, and to the manner in which the analysis of those syntheses frames their critique of psychoanalysis, which I will analyse in the second part of this chapter. I return to the syntheses themselves, and the schizophrenic paradigm, in the final part of the chapter.[44]

In many ways, the pages devoted to the syntheses of the unconscious in the first chapter of *Anti-Oedipus* consist of a reading of Schreber's 'Memoirs of a Nerve Patient' (1903), and one that attempts to rescue Schreber from Freud's own interpretation.[45] From the outset, and by way of clarity, let me emphasise the following two decisive features of the syntheses of the unconscious. First, they are all syntheses of *production*. This means that the unconscious, as the site of desire itself, is only production, and not representation. Desire does not 'express' anything in the ordinary, that is, linguistic-semantic sense: it is not the signifier of a hidden signified, it is not a metaphor or a symbol for something else, withdrawn and unspeakable in itself. It does not 'express' itself in myths, tragedies, or dreams – the essence or meaning of which need to be extracted through a work of interpretation – but in reality itself, which it *produces* immediately as history, society, economics, art, or literature. Far from being disconnected from the socio-economic realm, which, Marxism tells us, is primarily a matter of interest, desire is actually the key to understanding social and historical processes. Far from being a mere effect, or ideological determination, it is the engine that drives history. Far from being limited to the family, and to the Oedipal triangle, it is social, and even cosmic. Such is the reason why, ultimately, Deleuze and Guattari insist we do away with the idealist category of expression,[46] and propose instead that we understand desire in terms of units of production, that is, as a piece of a larger machine, or a factory. Why talk of machines and factories? To emphasise the fact that desire does not represent anything, and especially not something that it lacks, does not express anything in the linguistic-semantic sense, but *does* or *produces* something.[47] Unlike that of expression and dramatisation, which Deleuze privileges in the late 1960s, the vocabulary of industrial production allows him to radicalise his immanent understanding of nature, life and the unconscious. Nature is itself machinic, or productive, and there is no opposition, but only continuity, between nature and the determinations usually opposed to it, especially in psychoanalysis, such as desire, history, or culture in general. In that respect, there is no opposition between man and nature (or God): man is a piece of a larger machine, a particular process of production within a more inclusive production. This fundamental idea commits Deleuze and Guattari to a critique of idealism, especially in its psychoanalytic form, and

Ethics

a strong materialist position (which Deleuze had already initiated in *Difference and Repetition* and in his book on Spinoza).

Second, we need to note that Deleuze and Guattari equate this productive machine with schizophrenia, not as a clinical entity and reality, but as a *process*. Schizophrenia is not a 'case' or a 'person', but 'the universe of productive and reproductive desiring-machines'.[48] It's that universe that the syntheses describe, and psychoanalysis betrays. Ultimately, we need to understand how schizophrenia reveals the full reality of desire. I leave the detailed analysis of this question for the final part of this chapter.

The first synthesis is that of production *per se*, or that of connection. Its law or rule stipulates that all desiring-machines are binary, that is, coupled with another. In other words, the productive synthesis is essentially *connective*. The grammatical law of desiring-machines is first and foremost that of the 'and . . .', 'and then . . .'. A machine always connects itself with another machine, another flow, and can do so in a number of ways: it can combine itself with it, interrupt it, draw off part of it, etc. Naturally, because the machine that is interrupted, or drawn from, is itself connected to another machine, or set of machines, whose flow it interrupts or drains off, the binary series is linear in every direction. It grows and expands in several directions at once, *rhizomatically*. Desire is this assemblage that cuts and flows, and produces what Kleinian psychoanalysts call 'partial objects' in the process.[49] Desiring-machines produce parts, organs and ourselves as organisms. Remarkably, though, and in a way that has massive consequences, Deleuze and Guattari claim that this process, the process of desire, production and organisation, doesn't exhaust the *reality* of desire: 'at the very heart of this production, within the very production of this production, the body suffers from being organized in this way, from not having some other sort of organization, or no organization at all'.[50] Beyond or, better said perhaps, beneath the productive-connective desire, and its libidinal energy, which produces organs and partial objects, there is another type of desire, a purely fluid and free desire, flowing without interruption. Beyond the various connections of desire, and the various machines they produce, there is the longing for an uninterrupted, unorganic flow, which Artaud called 'the body without organs' and expressed in the following terms: '*No mouth/No tongue/No teeth/ No larynx/No esophagus/No stomach/No belly/No anus.*'[51] Deleuze and Guattari identify this singular type of desire with the death drive: 'The full body without organs is the unproductive, the sterile, the unengendered, the unconsumable . . . The death instinct: that is its name . . . .'⁵²

What's remarkable, then, and *seems* to amount to a contradiction, is that, having emphasised production as the one defining feature of desire, Deleuze and Guattari almost immediately go on to identify another type of desire or drive, wholly unproductive, unconnective and unconsumable, and thus escaping the very economy and syntheses of the unconscious. Strictly speaking, then, it is not correct to assert that, for Deleuze and Guattari, desire is pure production; or if it is, it needs to be distinguished from, and yet thought in relation to, a dynamic, force or drive that is itself wholly *unproductive*, if not *counter-productive*. Yet far from following Freud and his idea that at the heart of organic life lies this counter-force that aims to destroy it, and return to inorganic, dead matter, Deleuze and Guattari see it as an altogether different type of body, a different material assemblage, which generates different affects and dispositions (those of the schizophrenic, as we shall see). Between the productive, machinic dimension of desire, and the non-productive, non-organic flow of the body without organs, there isn't so much an opposition, or a struggle, as a particular mode of interaction, which we shall have to analyse in detail, in this chapter as well as the remaining chapter. In the end, the economy of desire as a whole can be reduced to the various ways in which desiring-machines, their drive towards connection, and their libidinal energy, relate to the body without organs, and its aversion for organicity. Whereas the organ-machine operates through connections and interruptions of flows, the body without organs constitutes 'a counterflow of amorphous, undifferentiated fluid'.⁵³

Deleuze and Guattari recognise that the relation in question has the *appearance* of a conflict between the two forces. In fact, every production of a machine seems unbearable to the body without organs. Once again, Artaud is the authors' main source of inspiration: 'The body is the body/it is all by itself/and has no need of organs/the body is never an organism/organisms are the enemies of the body.'⁵⁴ Interestingly, Deleuze and Guattari understand this 'repulsion' *for* and *of* the desiring-machines on the part of the body without organs as the source of what psychoanalysis calls 'primal repression' (*Urverdrängung*), and about which Freud had little to say, other than the fact that its origin remains mysterious, and precedes the birth of the superego. For Deleuze and Guattari, the repulsion in question also accounts for paranoia: since the body without organs experiences those machines as 'an overall persecution apparatus', it repels

Ethics

them.⁵⁵ For Deleuze and Guattari, then, it is a matter of emphasising the manner in which the 'slippery, opaque, taut surface' of the body without organs resists organ-machines and tries to escape their grip. Paranoia is not a primal phenomenon, but 'a result of the relationship between the desiring-machines and the body without organs, and occurs when the latter can no longer tolerate these machines'.⁵⁶

That being said, besides being a counter-force or counter-movement to the power of connection, immediately visible in paranoia, the body without organs is also and at the same time the 'quasi-cause' of the desiring process as a whole. The two operations or modes of production co-exist, precisely in so far as the body without organs is the necessary surface, or the quasi-cause, on which the process of production of desire as a whole is recorded:⁵⁷

> The body without organs, the unproductive, the unconsumable, serves as a surface for the recording of the entire process of production of desire, so that desiring-machines seem to emanate from it in the apparent objective movement that establishes a relationship between the machines and the body without organs.⁵⁸

It is striking to see Deleuze and Guattari have recourse to the notion of emanation, given its central role in *Expressionism in Philosophy: Spinoza*. In Chapter 2, we saw how that notion, which indicates the type of causality that characterises the undifferentiated One in relation to its various hypostases and entities, prepares the way for that of expression as immanent causality. Such is the reason why, ultimately, and in the context of *Anti-Oedipus*, we cannot speak of a *contradiction* between the process of production of desire as a whole and the unproductive, unconsumable surface of the body without organs; yet we have every reason to speak of a tension, or an opposition between them.

The body without organs is the surface that records (*surface d'enregistrement*) the production of desire – in the same way that capital is the surface on which the capitalist, the machines and the agents of production are recorded. The conclusion we need to draw is that production is not *recorded* in the same way that it is *produced*.⁵⁹ In other words, to the law of connection that defines the first synthesis we need to add a second law and a second synthesis, which is one of *distribution*. Connective syntheses were all of the type: 'and then . . .'. Disjunctive syntheses, by contrast, are of the type: '*soit . . . soit*'. A difficulty of translation arises at this point. Ordinarily, '*soit . . . soit*' would mean 'either . . . or'. The problem, however,

125

is that Deleuze and Guattari distinguish very clearly between the 'either . . . or' that marks an alternative, and an incompatibility, between two mutually exclusive terms (either this or that), and the much more open-ended, and ultimately compatible 'either . . . or . . . or' that '*soit . . . soit*' can *also* designate. The translators are therefore entirely correct in rendering '*soit . . . soit*' as 'either . . . or . . . or'. The latter designates the mode of synthesis, combination, assemblage, or desire of the schizophrenic: 'The "either . . . or . . . or" of the schizophrenic takes over from the "and then".'[60] From the point of view of the body without organs (BwO), or the surface on which everything glides, the syntheses between organs or parts – the productive *connections* betweens machines – amount to the same thing. They are entirely compatible, or compossible. They amount to a sliding 'grid' (*quadrillage*) placated on the surface of the BwO.

Furthermore, the appearance of this second synthesis amounts to a shift, or even a transformation, in energy: where the *libido* characterises the connective 'work' of the desiring production, the *Numen* designates the disjunctive energy of inscription and distribution. The allusion to Roman religion, and to the divine power of the emperor in Ancient Rome, shouldn't fool us. It is not a matter of identifying the BwO with God, and the organs with finite creatures (although one could argue that that is precisely the reading Deleuze himself gave of Spinoza). Rather, it is a matter of identifying the energy of the BwO as divine, in so far as it is the surface on which all syntheses and the whole of production is recorded. Such is the reason why schizophrenics, such as Schreber or Nerval, develop such a close connection with God. It is this formidable and literally schizo-phrenic energy which Deleuze and Guattari call 'divine'. Following Freud, they emphasise how, contrary to the hysteric, whose production is one of condensation (*Verdichtung*), the production (or desire) of the psychotic is one of infinite division, distribution, or dissemination.[61] Neurosis combines and connects (and connects everything, ultimately, to Oedipus, who is the point of absolute condensation), paranoia rejects, but the psychotic delirium dis-joins or dis-juncts, cuts across the *social* triangle of neurosis (mummy-daddy-myself), and splinters into a manifold of names, periods and animals. In other words, the schizophrenic or 'miraculating' machine amounts to a different relation between the desiring-machine and the body without organs, a different mode of production, in which the body without organs is a force of *attraction* for the desiring-machine, rather than the latter being an object of *repulsion* for the body without organs. This is particularly visible

Ethics

in Schreber's own account of the miracles (the 'rays') that God performs on Schreber's own body, and which lead to the creation of a new body and a new race.[62]

Deleuze and Guattari insist that the relation between syntheses is not dialectical: the attraction-machine doesn't replace the repulsion-machine, and the third synthesis, to which we shall turn in a moment, doesn't synthesise or reconcile the first two in a third moment or stage. Rather, the three machines co-exist. The body without organs records the *entire* process of production of desire, in no specific (whether chronological or logical-dialectical) order. This anti-dialectical position is not directed at Hegel exclusively. In fact, it is primarily directed at the psychoanalytic, and especially Lacanian, dialectical interpretation of the various stages in the formation of the Oedipus complex. It is introduced as an alternative account of the production of desire as well as an explanation of the oedipalisation or triangularisation of the production in question through socio-economic critique: if the analyst tells us 'that we must necessarily discover Schreber's daddy beneath his superior God',[63] it's because of the existing social order and code, which stipulates that we are our name, our father, our mother. The syntheses of psychoanalysis, its familial dialectic, are an effect or product of a socio-economic order, bourgeois and capitalistic. The exchange of money and family ties constitute its very core.

The final synthesis is that of 'consumption', 'voluptuousness', or 'enjoyment'. Why? Deleuze and Guattari began with the 'opposition' between desiring-machines and the body without organs. We saw how the repulsion of these machines, as found in the paranoiac machine of primary repression, gave way to attraction in the miraculating machine. The appearance of a dialectical progression persists, as a 'genuine reconciliation' of the two seems to involve a third moment and a third machine, which would function as 'the return of the repressed'.[64] Such a reconciliation, and a final synthesis, does indeed exist. Freud himself acknowledges it when he stresses that Schreber's illness reaches a turning point, which eventually leads to the Judge recovering all his faculties, precisely at the moment at which he 'becomes reconciled to becoming-woman'.[65] Quoting as evidence a passage by Schreber himself, in which he speaks of his transvestite tendency, and his willingness to indulge it in private ('when I am *by myself*'), Deleuze and Guattari suggest that this moment of reconciliation, or this final synthesis, be referred to as 'celibate machine'.[66] This 'new alliance' between the desiring-machines and the body without organs signals the birth of 'a new humanity' and a 'glorious organism'. It is a new humanity, because it has undergone the profound transformation of the first two syntheses, and experienced to the end the tension between the two opposed tendencies of the organism and the body without organs, or the forces of organisation and disorganisation. It is now a 'glorious' – as opposed to a 'partial' – organism, in so far as it has undergone the disjunction or the dissemination of the organism in the second synthesis, without reverting to the first. Above all, though, what is glorious about this new organism is the fact that its organs are not the site of an imaginary or symbolic relation to reality, but the experience of reality itself, as pure intensity. It reveals human life as a life of *intensive quantities*. Let me explain.

As the final synthesis, in which the very opposition between the first two is maintained, the synthesis of consumption produces a 'subject' – the subject of desire in the strong and real sense. In a moment of sudden and retrospective illumination, the subject grasps itself as the residuum of the desiring-machine as a whole, and is able to say to himself: 'So *that's what it was* all about! *That's what* was going on.' The final synthesis is one of *conjunction*, and it takes the form of a retrospective recognition ('so that's what . . .'). If Deleuze and Guattari qualify it further as a synthesis of *consumption* and *consummation*, it's because the machine that it designates involves a voluptuous, autoerotic (or 'automatic') energy (*Voluptas*), beyond the energies of repulsion and total attraction; it is the energy of self-recognition and auto-affection. This, once again, is particularly visible in Schreber's account, which speaks of the intense *Seligkeit* that is common to God, who does not have a body, but only 'nerves', and the miraculated body of Schreber himself.[67] A kind of 'sensual pleasure' (*volupté*) accompanies the birth of the subject. As Marx had recognised, no matter how alienated, subjectivity produces a form of *jouissance*, which consists in feeling oneself, or affecting oneself: even suffering is a form of self-enjoyment. The subject is produced through the production of consumption. In their analysis of the third synthesis, and its relation to the first two, Deleuze and Guattari are remarkably close to Levinas' analysis of the economic sphere as the sphere of auto-affection – of production, consumption and enjoyment (*jouissance*) – which he develops in *Totality and Infinity*, and to which he opposes the ethical sphere of desire as the desire for and of a transcendent Other. Deleuze and Guattari, however, do not oppose economy and ethics: desire is entirely economical and social, entirely productive of its object, entirely immanent.

Ethics

What exactly does the celibate machine produce? What that synthesis produces is intensity, or 'intensive quantities'. Once again, it's the figure of the schizophrenic that exemplifies that state of pure intensity, in which a threshold is being crossed, and a new mode of being – a 'becoming' – is *felt*: the '*I feel* that I am becoming a woman', 'that I am becoming a god' of the schizophrenic indicates a raw, primary emotion, beyond or, better said perhaps, beneath the hallucination and the delirium. The feeling itself is absolutely and only real, and not delirious or hallucinatory. The schizophrenic subject is first and foremost, and before anything else, a 'zone of intensity on his body without organs'.[68] In that respect, the body without organs is like an egg: it is characterised by, and 'crisscrossed with axes and thresholds, with latitudes and longitudes and geodesic lines, traversed by *gradients* marking the transitions and the becomings'.[69] In the following, emotional passage, the voice of the philosopher merges with that of the clinician:

> Nothing here is representative; rather, it is all life and lived experience: the actual, lived emotion of having breasts does not resemble breasts, it does not represent them, any more than a predestined zone in the egg resembles the organ that it is going to be stimulated to produce within itself. Nothing but bands of intensity, potentials, thresholds, and gradients. A harrowing, emotionally overwhelming experience, which brings the schizo as close as possible to matter, to a burning, living centre of matter.[70]

The schizo signals the most extreme state of the production of intensive quantities, and the consumption/consummation of matter. S/he is the pure subject, who experiences or lives matter itself, without representation, imitation, or symbolisation. This new and glorious form of subjectivity coincides precisely with the 'transcendental experience of the loss of the Ego'[71] and, one could say, the birth of the Eggo. Ever since *Difference and Repetition*, Deleuze has been referring to the world as an egg, constituted by intensive quantities which signal the point or threshold at which an event occurs, a becoming takes place, a system bifurcates and enters a different state. Naturally, the world of intensities is such that some, if not all, eventually develop into extensities, organs and parts. But not those of the schizophrenic. It is of the utmost importance, then, to understand that the forces of attraction and repulsion, and the intensities which they produce, don't amount to a final synthesis, in which those tensions and oppositions are reduced or tamed; they don't designate the final state of equilibrium of a system. For such a state is precisely that in which all intensities have been extended, and all differences in potential have been reduced. The synthesis of conjunction coincides with the highest state of the system *qua* dynamic, that is, as rife with events, possibilities and unsuspected life forms. Following Simondon, Deleuze and Guattari describe the intensities as a whole as the 'metastable states through which a subject passes'.[72] Metastability designates the state of a system – whether physical, chemical, or biological – that is neither stable nor simply unstable, but far from equilibrium and, as such, open to various actualisations.

3. The Problem: Oedipus in Psychoanalysis

In the remainder of this chapter, I would like to show how the Deleuzian-Guattarian conception of desire (or the unconscious) requires a critical engagement with psychoanalysis, and eventually leads to an alternative theory and practice of the unconscious, which they call 'schizoanalysis'.

A. BEFORE *ANTI-OEDIPUS*

Up until *Anti-Oedipus*, Deleuze had been a keen and astute reader of Freud, as well as an admirer of Lacan. Chapter 2 of *Difference and Repetition* devotes a long section to Freud's pleasure and reality principles, which it interprets in the light of the three syntheses of time introduced earlier on in the chapter, and as entirely compatible with Lacan's conception of the phallus as a 'symbolic' or 'virtual' object. The three syntheses of time are the passive syntheses of the living present in Habitus; the synthesis of Eros and Mnemosyne (or of Freud-Lacan and Bergson), which coincides with the active synthesis of the ego and the passive synthesis of the past, or with the imaginary, real and symbolic objects, on the one hand, and the virtual objects, on the other; and, finally, the synthesis of empty time, which Deleuze identifies precisely with the death instinct. In *Anti-Oedipus*, he goes further and associates the death instinct with the uttermost possibility of desire and life. It designates the regime of life that is precisely not that of the organism, the specific regime which, following Artaud, and his experience of schizophrenia, Deleuze refers to as the body without organs. It is not a question, therefore, and as I have already suggested, of opposing the life instincts and the death instinct, as if they were mutually exclusive. Rather, it is a matter of understanding how they refer to two very different regimes of life, and two extreme poles, namely, a neurotic and a schizophrenic pole, or a primary narcissism, oriented towards sexual goals, and a secondary narcissism, animated by an altogether desexualised, neutral energy. On one level, then, Deleuze's assessment of the Freudian death instinct is entirely positive:

> It is this relation between the narcissistic ego and the death instinct that Freud indicated so profoundly in saying that there is no reflux of the libido on to the ego without it becoming *desexualised* and forming a neutral *displaceable* energy, essentially capable of serving Thanatos.[73]

In secondary narcissism, the libido flows back towards (*reflue sur*) the ego, in what Deleuze characterises as an empty time, without present or memory, and the constitution of a neutral energy:

> Time empty and out of joint, with its rigorous formal and static order, its crushing unity and its irreversible series, is precisely the death instinct ... The correlation between Eros and Mnemosyne is replaced by that between a narcissistic ego without memory, a great amnesiac, and a death instinct desexualised and without love.[74]

In a move that prefigures the more radical stance of *Anti-Oedipus*, and the identification of the death instinct with the BwO, however, Deleuze departs from Freud. Whereas Freud sees the death instinct as indicative of a tendency towards a pre-vital state, and towards a purely inanimate and undifferentiated state of matter, Deleuze sees the death drive as an experience of pure time, or *pure form without matter*, in which the ego does not die as such, but experiences 'the state of free differences when they are no longer subject to the form imposed upon them by an I or an ego, when they assume a shape which excludes my own coherence no less than that of any identity whatsoever'.[75] Far from designating the point at which the ego is attracted towards dead, inanimate matter, the death instinct reveals the life that is not of the ego, and of its identity. Far from signalling a state of regression, dissociation (*Spaltung*), projection, or fantasy, the death instinct reveals desire in its free state. As one astute commentator puts it: 'Fundamentally, the death instinct is indeed the result of a neutralisation of the libido and memory, and the consequence of a desexualisation of the libido. However, it is not with a view to the inanimate, but to the free circulation of the energy of desire.'[76] The mistake, then, consists in identifying life with the ego, and desire with the libido. Deleuze's whole enterprise, in that respect, and from the beginning, consists in opening the ego onto that other, immanent, life, in freeing that energy – the energy of desire – from the demands and constructions of the ego, and the erotic. It is a matter of moving from the connective synthesis, in which the libido is bound, to the disjunctive synthesis, in which the energy of desire is free. In that respect, *Difference and Repetition* prepared the ground for the more openly critical and polemic stance of *Anti-Oedipus*.

B. THE FREUDIAN LEGACY

Far from being entirely negative, Deleuze and Guattari's relation to psychoanalysis, and to Freud in particular, is in fact ambivalent. It is characterised by a mixture of fascination and repulsion, fidelity and rejection. Guattari summarises their attitude by saying that in Freud there is 'an entire element of machinery, of production of desire, of units of production', combined with '*the other element*, namely, a personification of this production apparatus (the Superego, the Ego, the Id), a theatrical production [*mise en scène*] that substitutes mere values of representation for the true productive forces of the unconscious'.[77] And in a footnote of *Anti-Oedipus* itself, Deleuze and Guattari speak of 'Lacan's admirable theory of desire', which appears to 'have two poles: one related to "the object small *a*" as a desiring-machine, which defines desire in terms of a real production, thus going beyond both any idea of need and any idea of fantasy; and the other related to the "great Other" as a signifier, which reintroduces a certain notion of lack'.[78] On one level, then, psychoanalysis is fascinating in that it reveals the unconscious, and the operations of desire, as a machine (a 'desiring machine'[79]), and analyses them as processes of production: the unconscious is a machine that produces its own energy, and creates its own forces. This aspect of Freud's work, which Deleuze and Guattari want to retain, is perhaps best expressed in his 1915 paper 'The Unconscious'.[80] At the same time, however, Freudian psychoanalysis almost immediately subjects those productive and intensive forces to the rule of transcendent, rigid and authoritative structures: the Ego, the Superego, the Id, and, last but not least, the Oedipus complex. In that respect, although the key text is perhaps 'The Ego and the Id' (1923),[81] Freud himself claims that he had 'discovered' the Oedipus complex as early as 1897, in the course of the self-analysis that led to the publication of *The Interpretation of Dreams* (1900–1901).[82] On the one hand, then, Freud's conception of

Ethics

the unconscious reveals the existence of an impersonal, transcendental field of intensive forces, and a raw, productive energy – the very field, and the very energy, which Deleuze and Guattari see embodied in the schizophrenic, and constitutive of the higher forms of life. It is that very field, however, which Freud closes down, inhibiting along the way the liberating force of desire through the introduction of a series of solidifying procedures. He discovers the productive, machinic, essence of desire, but proceeds almost immediately to turn it into a force of representation, centred on the ego and its libido, and played out like a family drama:

> The whole of desiring-*production* is crushed, subjected to the requirements of *representation*, and to the dreary games of what is representative and represented in representation. And there is the essential thing: the reproduction of desire gives way to a simple representation, in the process as well as the theory of the cure. The productive unconscious makes way for an unconscious that knows only how to express itself – express itself in myth, in tragedy, in dream.[83]

In other words, Freud saw something decisive, but failed to go all the way: in the face of the wild, intensive forces he had discovered, he got cold feet and went on to tame and codify them. Potentially liberating, psychoanalysis is ultimately repressive. On the one hand, *Anti-Oedipus* is Deleuze and Guattari's effort to affirm, extend and radicalise the productive, machinic dimension of the Freudian (and Lacanian) unconscious. On the other hand, it is the systematic critique of the way in which Freud eventually subjected this productive, essentially liberating discovery to a series of transcendent, repressive operations, centred on the Oedipus complex. This is what Deleuze and Guattari call the 'idealist' turning of psychoanalysis – a turning that was there from the start – and to which, ultimately, they want to oppose their materialist, immanent conception of desire: 'We were trying to find an immanent conception, an immanent way of working with the syntheses of the unconscious, a productivism or constructivism of the unconscious.'[84]

C. THE LACANIAN LEGACY

The idealist turn of psychoanalysis is radicalised in Lacan's thought, especially in the manner in which it combines the Hegelian – or, better said perhaps, the Kojèvian – *dialectical* conception of desire, as it appears in the 'master–slave' dialectic of the *Phenomenology of Spirit*, with the structural anthropology of Lévi-Strauss and the structural linguistics of Jakobson. In fact, given this radicalisation, and Lacan's influence on the French philosophical scene in the 1960s and 1970s, including on Deleuze and Guattari before they began to collaborate, it is not an exaggeration to say that Lacan is the primary target of *Anti-Oedipus*. In the second main section of the book ('Psychoanalysis and Familialism'), we find the following statement, aimed at Lacan: 'The three errors concerning desire are called lack, law, and signifier. It is one and the same error, an idealism that forms a pious conception of the unconscious.'[85] Such is the reason why, in what follows, I will highlight some of the constitutive features of Lacan's thought, and his interpretation of Oedipus in particular.[86] I will then turn to Deleuze and Guattari's critique of what they call his 'errors', and which would perhaps be best described as the 'illusions', or 'illegitimate uses' of the syntheses already mentioned. They all amount to a tendency to conceive of desire as a moment of rupture, or a break, within the continuum or plane of nature, and as introducing a plane of transcendence by elevating lack to a transcendental or structuring position.

From the very start, Lacan defines the human subject as a subject of *desire*. Yet it is only with the recognition of the unconscious, and of the Freudian legacy, that the theory of desire is completed. Before moving into the specificity of Lacan's interpretation of the unconscious, it is important to emphasise the extent to which he distinguishes desire from need, or instinct, and from animal life in general: according to Lacan's hypothesis – one that has significant consequences – the emergence of desire, especially in its Oedipal sense, is the result of a biological, evolutionary deficiency, visible in the fact that the human infant is born prematurely, and remains dependent for a long time after his or her birth. Lacan's claim, then, is that far from being the result of a particular successful adaptation of the species, the astounding psychic development of the human being, as well as the emergence of language and culture that it made possible, are the result of a biological deficiency, a *lack*, which we try to compensate for, not just in our early childhood, but *throughout our life*.[87] This idea of the human as a biologically inadequate, or disadapted, being is at the heart of Lacan's thought, and already signals a primary level of lack. Desire, in its facticity as well as its individual history, reveals this biological shortcoming, whilst also providing ways of overcoming it. What lacks at the level of biological life is eventually compensated for through a complex cultural and symbolic construction, at the heart of which figures Oedipus. Through a series of processes of alienation, identification and recognition, the child is socialised, and it is only through this symbolic process of socialisation that s/he is eventually able to reproduce and perpetuate the species to which s/he belongs. Lacan believes that re-adaptation, a – never complete – re-direction of man's narcissistic and (self)destructive ego libido towards the genital object (and therefore to the accomplishment of his animal task with respect to the species), is made possible only through the mediation of (the resolution) of the Oedipus complex, which is to say, culturally.

This process, as I have suggested, coincides with the constitution of the unconscious: 'It is desire which achieves the primitive structuration of the human world, desire as unconscious.'[88] In other words, and contrary to what Hegel and Kojève argued, 'it's not as consciousness that the subject recognises himself; there is something else, and beyond'.[89] It is that 'something else', or that 'beyond', which Lacan seeks to understand. In other words, he is concerned to understand the object of the subject's desire as a desire for an elusive object, to which the subject would find itself irreversibly bound, but which it would never *actually* possess, an object that would remain 'other' and 'beyond'. It's desire understood in that way, that is, as that which can never be had, which 'structures' the human as such, not as a biological entity, but as a cultural construction. In that respect, desire can be seen as the condition of possibility – or, better said perhaps, the genetic condition of the existence – of subjectivity: as the transcendental condition of subjectivity, it is not itself an object in any recognisable sense. In fact, Lacan insists that it is always lacking, and it is *qua* lacking object that it can structure and generate the existence of the subject. The subject 'is', 'exists', or comes to be, qua *desiring* subject, only in and through that lack: 'Being comes into existence as an exact function of this lack'.[90] Such is the reason why, still in *Seminar IV*, Lacan claims that the lack of object 'is not a negative, but the very engine [*le ressort*] of the subject's relation to the world'.[91]

The question, however, concerns the ontological status of the lack in question: how can the economy of desire function as the giving and taking of something that is lacking, not accidentally and temporarily, but structurally? How are we to understand this *manque d'objet* that is at the heart of the dialectic of unconscious desire?

This is where Lacan introduces the phallus. Unlike the penis, which is real, the phallus is an imaginary object, with a symbolic value.

Now, according to Lacan, what defines the phallus is that man and woman, child and parent, lack it. But they do so in different ways, and women more than men, in so far as women also lack its real or physiological correlate, namely, the penis. And that is precisely what women want, especially in the child. For the mother, the child is a substitute for the missing phallus. Far from wanting to call Freud's view into question on that point, Lacan takes it for granted (*'C'est là pour nous une donnée'*), and complicates it. What the mother sees in the child is the image of the missing phallus. Thus there is an asymmetrical love, a misunderstanding, as it were: the child believes he is loved for what he is, but is actually loved as a substitute for an original lack. There comes a time, however, when, for the first time and in an incomplete way, the child grasps the difference between the sexes. Yet the child does so on the basis of the penis itself: sexual difference is understood as with or without penis, which means that the vagina is seen only as an absence or lack of penis. That is precisely the point at which the child understands that he is not loved for himself, that it's not he who is loved, but a certain 'image' of him.[92]

The child accedes to the next stage of the Oedipal process when he realises that the mother too is 'deprived', or that she lacks (in the real) the symbolic phallus. The child identifies with that image, but only to realise (unconsciously) that it is the image of a lack, a lack that he sees in himself as well as in his mother: as the ultimate object of desire, the phallus is always lacking, structurally as it were. It is, Lacan claims, 'lacking in its own place'.[93] This is also the point at which the image of the father (the imaginary father) emerges, first, by depriving the mother of the child qua phallus (and so the mother is deprived for a second time, as a result of the father's command), and simultaneously by dispelling the child's mistaken belief that he is the only object of his mother's desire. For both the mother and the child, what is prohibited by the (imaginary) father is their incestuous relationship ('You will not sleep with your mother!' 'You will not reintegrate your product'). The second time is concomitant with the moment at which the 'No!' of the father – i.e. the voice of the Law – resonates for the first time. The imaginary father is not a real person, in so far as the 'no', the Law (the signifier Name-of-the-Father), has already been internalised by the mother, whose role is, from the start, symbolic, and through whom, therefore, the Law is 'mediated'.[94] This time corresponds to the ordinary image that we have of Oedipus: love for the mother, or the parent of the opposite sex, and hatred towards the father, or the parent of the same

Ethics

sex. Paradoxically, the child starts to compete aggressively with his imaginary father in order to be his mother's phallus only after the mother has actually been deprived of him, only, that is, when faced with the commandment at this stage. But, when compared with the phallic *Gestalt*, or image of the father, the child soon realises the utter inadequacy of his own real correlate of the imaginary phallus.

The third and final stage, which defines the resolution of the dialectic, is initiated by the (real) father who shows the child that s/he is the one who has what the mother lacks: the child realises that s/he cannot compete with him. This is the child's castration proper. The Oedipus complex is completely resolved when the child – irrespective of his or her sex – identifies symbolically with the *image* of father and thus internalises the Law. The subject resolves the Oedipus complex by identifying with the *imago* of the father, from which s/he derives his ego-ideal. Following Lévi-Strauss' seminal *The Elementary Structures of Kinship* (1949), Lacan reaffirms the universality of the resolution of the complex in the prohibition of incest, as well as the emergence of the Law, and the possibility of transgressing it, which follows from it.[95] It's through the prohibition of incest, understood as a universal law of culture, that the human distinguishes itself from the rest of the natural real, and that culture is itself granted a universal *structure*.

To conclude this brief exposition of Lacan's conception of the unconscious, and of Oedipus, let me emphasise the role of castration in the resolution of the Oedipus complex, and the problem of desire. In so far as desire is desire of incest, the prohibition of incest, and the fear of castration that is its corollary, marks the point at which the human posits and experiences a realm of transcendence – of law and morality – that is distinct from that of nature. The solution to the problem of desire, then, involves the institution of a symbolic order through which desire is at once recognised and denied, in short, repressed. The only way in which desire is recognised is through the recognition of the law, and the constitution of a moral conscience or a superego. The law of desire, then, is not the law of nature, but the law that negates and exceeds nature. It is the supernatural law, or the order of the father (the 'Name-of-the-Father'). Castration is the *a priori*, or the condition of possibility, of society, and thus of all social desire. It defines the field of desire as such. What is most significant, however, is the way in which the law is no longer something that is imposed from the outside, but an authority, and an instance of punishment, which is internalised. As a result of this process, there is no escape from the superego. As Freud puts it in *Civilisation and its Discontents* (VII), there is no longer any difference between the wrong action and the wrong intention: they are both equally punished by the superego, which is the cruellest of all authorities.[96] Guilt and bad conscience, as the price to be paid for the solution to the aporia of desire, are high, and certainly higher than what Deleuze and Guattari say we ought to be willing to pay.

4. The Solution: Schizoanalysis

A. The destructive task of schizoanalysis

To be sure, Lacan's conception of desire, and of signification, cannot be equated with any straightforward lack (the lack of castration). For the Signifier, as the origin of sense, is what is 'lacking in its own place'. Its value is symbolic, and not real, or even imaginary. It designates an event that never took place ('*place du mort*', '*case vide*'), the constant displacement of which accounts for the logic of desire itself. The lack, in other words, is structural. Structure, we recall from Deleuze's own essay on structuralism, is embodied in realities and images (the real father, for example, or the image of the father) according to series that can be determined. Furthermore, if it generates those realities and images, it never derives from them.[97] At once distinct from the real and the imaginary, the symbolic cannot be defined either by pre-existing realities, to which it would refer (relation of *denotation*), nor by imaginary contents, which it would implicate (relation of implication), and which would grant it a *signification*. The elements of a structure possess neither an extrinsic denotation, nor an intrinsic signification. They do possess a sense, however, which is one of 'position' only, as Lévi-Strauss pointed out.[98] The operation of sense, Deleuze argues, amounts to a topology, that is, to a logic of places or *loci*, and not contents. The position or place comes before that which fills it. It is a transcendental – and not merely formal – logic precisely in so far as it is mapped after a transcendental or structural space, a pure *spatium*. For Lacan, lack is not a straightforward, actual deprivation, but an empty position. The question, however, is one of knowing whether, by shifting the lack from a real, or even imaginary position, to a symbolic, or transcendental one, Lacan doesn't actually reinforce it. Is lack understood in that sense not another form of the negative, and another index of transcendence? In other words, is the

Ethics

decisive difference between an imaginary (Freudian) Oedipus, which focuses on the actual parental figures, and a symbolic, structural, or topological (Lacanian) Oedipus, which focuses on an object that is forever missing, and which structures and governs the play of desire? Or is the real difference

> between Oedipus, structural as well as imaginary, and something else that all the Oedipuses crush and repress: desiring-production (*la production désirante*) – the machines of desire that no longer allow themselves to be reduced to the structure any more than to persons, and that constitute the Real in itself, beyond and beneath the Symbolic as well as the Imaginary?[99]

Fundamentally, the Lacanian operation of displacement, and the new way in which he combines lack, law and signifier, doesn't change anything. If anything, it makes things worse, precisely to the extent that it interprets lack structurally, that is, as an operation for which there is no end, no solution, other than in the recognition of a Law that designates the breaking point with the natural, or real order. This is how, despite its atheism, Lacan's version of psychoanalysis remains religious. To be sure, Lacan turns lack into an empty position and no longer a deprivation, the law into a rule of the game and no longer a commandment, and the signifier into a distributor and no longer an ultimate meaning. But all of that is to no avail, in so far as these notions 'cannot be prevented from dragging their theological cortege behind – insufficiency of being, guilt, signification'.[100] To be sure, Deleuze and Guattari go on to argue,

> the structural interpretation challenges all beliefs, rises above all images, and from the realm of the mother and the father retains only functions, defines *the prohibition and the transgression* as structural operations. But what water will cleanse these concepts of their background, their backworld [*arrière-mondes*] – religiosity?[101]

It is indeed the spectre of transcendence, and even religion, that haunts psychoanalysis. Prohibition, transgression, guilt, castration and signification – these aren't determinations of the unconscious as such, but of the unconscious as seen and interpreted by a priest. Interpretation, which is itself at the heart of the analytic process, 'is our modern way of believing and of being pious'.[102] The analyst is himself, to borrow Montebello's pun, the interpreast,[103] that is, the one under whose supervision the fundamental meaning of the patient's dreams, fantasies and symptoms is revealed. The open-ended, if not interminable cure operates like an endless interpretation of signs, and in that respect can be identified with a paranoid regime. The only point at which such a regime can cease, and the paranoia be overcome, is through the total subjectivation of the patient to the process of transference. At that point, the analyst has become the substitute of the Signifier itself (the Name-of-the-Father). Psychoanalysis, therefore, has a double machine at its disposal:

> On the one hand, there is an *interpretation machine*, whose purpose is to translate whatever the patient says into another language: whatever the patient says is already supposed to mean something else. In this kind of paranoid regime, every sign refers to another sign in an unlimited network of signs, perpetually expanding its scope in a spiral sweep: the sign which has been deemed a signifier refers to a signified, which itself spits back signifiers (the hysteric is meant to ensure this feed-back or echo which perpetuates psychoanalytic discourse *ad infinitum*). On the other hand, there is also a machine of subjectivation, and this represents a whole other regime of signs. In this case, the signifier is no longer grasped in relation to some signified, but in relation to a subject. The point of significance has become the point of subjectivation: the psychoanalyst himself.[104]

According to Lacanian psychoanalysis, the ultimate goal of the talking cure resides in the patient's ability to distance himself from the captive, imaginary relation to the other. This process of symbolisation takes place through the relation of transference to the analyst, who is granted the double function of the imaginary father and the symbolic Law.[105] It is this 'the imperialism of the Signifier' – especially in the form of the Name-of-the-Father qua transcendent signifier, or 'signifier of signifiers' – and the domination of the structuralist paradigm, which Deleuze and Guattari want to destroy, at the theoretical as well as practical level.[106]

If Oedipus does indeed crush and repress the unconscious, if psychoanalysis generates a metaphysics, and instances of transcendence, which smother desire, then schizoanalysis will consist of a relentless struggle against that new religion. In its critical, destructive dimension, schizoanalysis bears little resemblance to the refinement and sophistication of, say, deconstruction – to say nothing of psychoanalysis itself, which, by allowing us to 'work through' guilt, the law, castration, etc., and internalise them, only reinforces them:

> Destroy, destroy. The task of schizoanalysis goes by way of destruction – a whole scouring of the unconscious, a complete curettage. Destroy Oedipus, the illusion of the ego, the puppet [*le fantoche*] of the superego,

Ethics

guilt, the law, castration. It is not a matter of pious destructions, such as those performed by psychoanalysis under the benevolent neutral eye of the analyst. For these are Hegel-style destructions, ways of conserving.[107]

Ultimately, schizoanalysis designates a way out of psychoanalysis, and schizophrenia a way out of neurosis and hysteria.

We have a magnificent example of such a destruction, or curettage of the psychoanalytic unconscious, in Deleuze and Guattari's reading of Kafka. In the chapter of *Kafka: Toward a Minor Literature* entitled 'Immanence and Desire', the authors go to great trouble to show that, despite appearances and many commentaries, the famous Law of *The Trial* is not a formal, transcendent law, with respect to which one finds oneself guilty from the start, but the expression of an immanent *desire*, which generates its own criteria and produces its own machine. To be sure, in *The Trial*, the Law *appears* to have this transcendent status; it appears to be a pure form, a law devoid of object, in short, a practical law to which one would be merely subjected and which, as such, could not be known. And it even seems to suggest that guilt is the prerequisite, or the *a priori*, which corresponds to the transcendent law, and applies to everyone, whether guilty or innocent. Finally, because the law is without an object of knowledge, it is determined only to the extent that it is spoken, and it is spoken only in the act of sentencing. In short, one's guilt would be an effect of the law, expressed in the sentence. Yet this law – at least on Deleuze and Guattari's reading – is precisely the law that *The Trial* presents in order to deconstruct or dismantle it (*la démonter*), especially in the brief and final chapter devoted to K's execution, as well as in the immediately preceding chapter, in which the priest represents the discourse of the law.

The first aspect of this dismantling consists in 'eliminating any idea of guilt from the start', guilt being precisely part of the accusation itself: guilt paralyses, separates one from one's power, and is the greatest obstacle to conducting one's own affairs. In the words of Kafka himself, which Deleuze and Guattari quote: 'Above all, if he were to achieve anything, it was essential that he should banish from his mind once and for all the idea of possible guilt. This legal action was nothing more than a business deal such as he had often concluded to the advantage of the Bank . . . .'[108] Furthermore, K realises that if the law remains unknowable, it is not because it remains withdrawn in its own transcendence, but simply because it is devoid of any interiority: it is always in the office next door, or behind the following door, *ad infinitum*. If it can't be found, it's not because it is transcendent, forever withdrawing, or lacking in its own place, as Lacan would say of Poe's purloined letter, but because it can only be produced: like the concepts of thought, it is not given in advance, in ourselves or in an intelligible world, up above or deep down (there is a transcendence of depth too), but awaiting its own production. Such is the reason why, following Spinoza, Deleuze recognises natural law as the only law, why he equates law with right, and prefers to identify justice with ethics and jurisprudence, rather than morality. Finally, the law is not stated as a result of the need to express its alleged transcendence; it is almost the exact opposite: it is the statement, the enunciation, which constructs the law, in what amounts to a purely immanent process: 'the law is confused with that which the guardian utters, and the writings precede the law, rather than being the necessary and derived expression of it'.[109]

In the end, Kafka reveals a law that is not transcendent, but immanent, does not presuppose guilt, but innocence, is not purely formal, but is the expression of a machine-desire (the bureaucratic machine). Kafka's operation consists in dismantling a certain assemblage, an abstract machine (the transcendence of the Law), and offering another in its place, infinitely more real: desire. Desire is itself an assemblage, a machine, a segment of reality, and not the longing of an isolated subject. '*Where one believed there was the law, there is in fact desire and desire alone. Justice is desire and not law.*'[110] It's not as if desire were desire *of* or *for* justice. Desire is never desire for something, like consciousness is never consciousness of something. Rather, it *is* something. It is not characterised by the lack or absence of its object, but by what it does. Its source is neither objective (the good, the beautiful, the just, the Other) nor subjective (the desiring subject). Object and subject are both instances of transcendence. Rather, desire is an assemblage, part of a machine, to the operation of which it contributes, or which it inhibits. The same goes for desire's relation to power: there is no *désir de pouvoir*, that is, a desire to repress or be repressed, a sadistic or masochistic desire. Power is itself an instance of desire, a form of plenitude, participation, or contribution. The desire for power is only the desire to be part of this or that machine – the bureaucratic, capitalistic, or fascistic machine. This means that there is no such thing as Power, and that a desire for power is never a desire for a transcendent entity. Like the law, power does not stand above, but within. As Foucault was able to demonstrate with respect to a number of fields (such as

Ethics

knowledge, the prison, psychiatry, or sexuality), there are only segments of power: the bureaucratic segment, the psychiatric segment, etc., each with its specific staff, clients, relations. In the same vein, Kafka's 'Letter to his Father' gathers and accentuates all the traits of the Oedipal relation, but to the point of producing its own parody, and thus a way out of Oedipus. Through the writing machine, and by producing a blown up picture, or something like a caricature, of the father–son relation, Kafka is able to trace a line of flight, a different organisation and a different desire, and one that has nothing to do with an operation of sublimation.[111]

This is the point at which Kafka's work reveals its deep affinity with the thought of Spinoza. We recall how Spinoza himself interpreted God's commandment to Adam as emanating not from some moral, transcendent imperative – The Law – but from an immanent law of nature, the knowledge of which alone can reveal what's good and bad for him, and for human beings in general. The law in question – and the extent to which the notion of law is the right one to use in this context is a significant issue – is nothing like a moral imperative, but a necessity that derives from understanding one's nature, or essence, adequately. In other words, from the point of view of God, or nature, all we need to understand is what modes, and the human mode in particular, are capable of, what they can and cannot do, or what their degree of power is. Their power, and the human power *qua* desire, is what, following Hobbes, Spinoza calls 'natural right'. What a body can do (its power) is its right: it is the nature of a given body to take its power to its end, or extreme realisation, and that is what is *good* for it. The question of 'rights', for Spinoza, is first and foremost a question of *natural* rights, a question, that is, of knowing what one's power is, and of asserting it. It precedes duties and prohibitions, which come about only with the social contract, and in a state that is no longer natural. Every man – whether wise or foolish, reasonable or demented, strong or weak – equally seeks to preserve, and persevere in, his existence, and to pursue his desire. Each 'has as much right as he has power'. The fool is as much part of Nature as the wise man, and does not disturb the order of Nature.[112] From the ontological and ethical point of view, there is room for only one law, and that is the law of nature. Such a law 'is never a rule of duty, but the norm of a power, the unity of right, power, and its exercise'.[113] Law, in other words, is identical to right. The moral law, on the other hand, which 'purports to prohibit and command', involves a kind of *mystification*: 'the less we understand the laws of nature, that is, the norms of life, the more we interpret them as orders and prohibitions – to the point that the philosopher must hesitate before using the word "law", so much does it retain a moral aftertaste . . .'.[114] Conversely, the more we understand the laws of nature, and find ways of increasing our power, the less room there is for the moral standpoint. The problem with which Deleuze is confronted from the start, and the challenge he faces, is that of the 'co-extensivity of the human being and nature',[115] which the term *desire* signals.

B. THE CONSTRUCTIVE TASK OF SCHIZOANALYSIS

Ultimately, what's at stake in Deleuze and Guattari's critique of psychoanalysis is precisely the possibility of thinking, and experimenting with, a desire that is only, and fully, real, of experiencing a reality that does not immediately slip into its own negation, and broaches a space of transcendence, in relation to which the real is only ever deficient. At stake in what Deleuze and Guattari call schizoanalysis is a desire that is not the sign of a transcendent law, but of a potency of being (*puissance d'être*), not the indication of a lack, but of a plenitude, not a matter of representation, but of production. In other words, it is a matter of reaching the critical, and indeed *self*-critical, point of psychoanalysis, and Oedipus in particular – the point, that is, at which the very notion of structure, and the lack it presupposes, collapse, dissolve, and open onto reality as the true object of desire:

> What is this point of self-criticism? It is the point where the structure, beyond the images that fill it and the Symbolic that conditions it within representation, reveals its reverse side as a positive principle of non-consistency that dissolves it: where desire is shifted into the order of production, related to its molecular elements, and where it lacks nothing, because it is defined as the natural and sensuous objective being, at the same time as the Real is defined as the objective being of desire. For the unconscious of schizoanalysis is unaware of persons, aggregates, and laws, and of images, structures, and symbols . . . It is not structural, nor is it symbolic, for its reality is that of the Real in its very production, in its very inorganization. It is not representative, but solely machinic, and productive.[116]

Schizoanalysis is the name that Deleuze and Guattari give to this theoretical and practical enterprise. It is the practice aimed at freeing a transcendental unconscious defined by the immanence of its criteria. It is a form of critique, one that is not unlike the Kantian attempt to uncover the criteria immanent to reason itself, on the basis of which its legitimate (or immanent) and illegitimate (or transcendent) uses need to be established. Oedipus is the very figure of transcendence, inasmuch as it introduces a lack, a cruel form of negativity, at the very heart of the unconscious. The goal, then, is to 'disoedipalise' (*désœdipianiser*) the unconscious, or to 'schizoise' it. Once we've wrested desire from lack altogether, and freed it from negativity, whether real or symbolic, we can return to the real itself, but a real without negativity – the very real that, according to Deleuze, Spinoza had sought to thematise. What we are left with is the schizoid body, or the body without organs – a body that is not so much opposed to the organs *per se* as to their organisation in what is called the organism. For Deleuze and Guattari, schizophrenia (or, better said perhaps, a certain becoming-schizophrenic) amounts to the transcendental experience of the loss of the ego (whether understood as ideal-ego or ego-ideal), an experience that Deleuze already understood Sartre and Proust to be seeking, and Artaud to have actually realised.[117] But the transcendental is no longer the symbolic. It now designates the inorganic, or, more precisely, the an-organic: the real, life, or matter.

In the final section of this chapter, and by way of returning to the syntheses of the unconscious introduced earlier on, let me take a closer look at the reason why the desiring-machine is most visible, or visible in its free state, in schizophrenia, or, more adequately, and in so far as Deleuze and Guattari distinguish between schizophrenia as process and schizophrenia as illness, in the *process* of schizophrenia.

We have already established that instead of taking their cue from the neurotic, hysterical type, or even from the paranoid-psychotic, Deleuze and Guattari seek the nature of desire – present in its raw, or pure state – in the schizophrenic. Schizophrenia reveals the true, 'machinic' nature of desire. It's a paradox of sorts, Guattari remarks in the interview with Deleuze already mentioned, that whilst so much of the clinical material of psychoanalysis – from Freud, Bleuler and Jung to Klein and Lacan – comes from psychosis, psychoanalysis insists on reducing the voice of the schizophrenic to that of the neurotic, and to Oedipus especially, and the productive nature of desire to a representational process.[118] Guattari's conviction, which Deleuze shares, is that neurosis needs to be understood on the basis of schizophrenia, and not the other way around. It's not a question, therefore, of celebrating the 'madness' of the schizophrenic, of encouraging their audience to become schizophrenic (as if it were a matter of personal decision: *n'est pas fou qui veut*, as Lacan used to say).[119] It is hard to imagine Guattari minimising the pain and suffering endured by the schizophrenics he used to work with, and harder still to believe that Deleuze and Guattari ever sought to imitate them. Rather, it is a matter of distinguishing between schizophrenia as a process, which Deleuze and Guattari refer to as 'schizophrenisation', and schizophrenia as a clinical condition, which reveals more about the treatment and the mental institution than the actual process itself.[120] As one commentator puts it: 'it is not the disease process but the treatment which is the cause of the catatonic zombies and ranting paranoiacs that haunt the popular imagination'.[121] The question, then, is to know what Deleuze and Guattari 'see' in schizophrenia that enables them to think the very nature of the unconscious, or desire, differently.

First, and by contrast with the neurotic, the problems of the schizophrenic are 'real' problems. This doesn't mean that the problems of the neurotic don't exist. It does mean, however, that they are not *real*. Reality is what's at issue here. If the problems of the neurotic aren't real, it's because they are – as Freud and Lacan have demonstrated convincingly – imaginary, or symbolic. They reveal a relation to reality that is one of mediation and representation, of fantasies, for the analysis and treatment of which Freudian psychoanalysis has developed useful tools. It's normally thought that the schizophrenic suffers from a disconnection with reality, and finds refuge in a world of his own. But the situation is exactly the opposite, and it's only because the world of the neurotic is understood as the real world that the schizophrenic can be understood in that way. Schizophrenia, we recall, is a 'harrowing, emotionally overwhelming experience, which brings the schizo as close as possible to matter, to a burning, living centre of matter'.[122] If anything, then, Deleuze and Guattari insist, the schizophrenic suffers from an excess of reality, from an inability, that is, to not identify *entirely* with the world as a whole, in its geographical, historical, social, biological, etc., vastness, diversity and, above all, *intensity*. If the schizophrenic isn't concerned with the name of the father, it's because, as Nietzsche claimed in a letter to Burckhardt dated 5 January 1889, immediately before collapsing into madness, '*every name of history is I*'.[123] Here, it is not a question of the madman who takes himself for so-and-so, who identifies with this or that historical figure on the theatre of representation: 'there is no ego that identifies with races, peoples and persons in a theatre of representation, but proper names that identify races, peoples, and persons with regions, thresholds, or effects in a production of intensive quantities'.[124] If anything, Artaud's theatre of cruelty, and

Ethics

his writing as a whole, were about the production of such intensive quantities.

The second aspect of schizophrenia, already implied in the first, is that the 'stage' on which schizophrenia is played out is precisely not a stage, especially not that of the family, but the world itself and as a whole, and this includes non-human as well as human life, history, society, etc. For the schizophrenic, nothing is a matter of representation, or fantasy; nothing is imagined, or symbolised; everything is lived, immediately, and with a degree of intensity that is hard to fathom. To understand the discourse and desire of the schizophrenic, it is pointless, therefore, to try to reduce them to narrow Oedipal triangulation:

> It is strange how schizophrenics keep being brought back to problems that are not their own, as is abundantly clear: father, mother, law, signifier, etc. The schizophrenic is elsewhere, and there is no reason to conclude that the schizophrenic lacks something that does not concern him or her. Beckett and Artaud have said all there is to say about it. We must get used to the idea that certain artists or writers have had greater insight into schizophrenia than psychiatrists or psychoanalysts. We make the same mistake when we define schizophrenia in negative terms or in terms of a lack (dissociation, loss of reality, autism, foreclosure) and when we model schizophrenia on a familial structure in which this lack can be located. In fact, the phenomenon of delirium does not reproduce, even in an imaginary way, a family story organised around lack. On the contrary, delirium is an overflowing of history; it is universal history set adrift. Races, civilizations, cultures, continents, kingdoms, powers, wars, classes, and revolutions are all mixed together . . . And there is no reason to believe that what delirium expresses is merely its manifest content. What delirium expresses is the way in which desire invests a whole social field that is historical, and the way in which unconscious desire embraces its irreducible objects.[125]

It is absurd, therefore, to carry on describing the schizophrenic in purely negative terms, to claim, for example, that he lives in denial (*Verleugnung*) of the reality of a constitutive absence, namely, the lack of phallus in the mother and in himself, that he is unable to face and symbolise castration itself, in short, that his actions are defined by a symbolic deficiency, which causes whatever is 'rejected' (*Verwerfung*) or 'foreclosed' (*forclusion*) in the symbolic to reappear in the real, but as a hallucination, when, in fact, he is overflowing with a different kind of reality, one that is historical, social, economical, or racial, and which he experiences with such intensity that it becomes unbearable.[126] The schizophrenic reveals an unconscious that is not lacking in anything, and that does not lend itself to the familiar and familial, or Oedipal, interpretation. To the interpretative machine, it opposes a productive machine: it does not mean anything, but is immediately productive, and immediately real. To the machine of subjectivation (of symbolisation and transference), it opposes a process of desubjectivation, or deterritorialisation:

> Now we see the difference between paranoia and schizophrenia (even those forms of schizophrenia labelled paranoid): the 'I-will-not-leave-you-alone' of the paranoid, and the 'leave-me-alone' of the schizophrenic; the paranoid combination of signs, and the machinic assemblages of schizophrenia; the massive wholes of paranoia, and the tiny multiplicities of schizophrenia; paranoia's vast territories of reactive integration, and schizophrenia's active lines of flight.[127]

The schizophrenic signals the limit of our society, our body politic, and our own body. But, Deleuze says, it is 'an abhorred limit, always suppressed, always cast out'.[128] The only question, then, becomes one of knowing how to prevent the breakthrough that schizophrenia signals from collapsing into a breakdown, how, in other words, to distinguish a *becoming*-schizophrenic from a *being*-schizophrenic. It is a very thin line, as the case of Artaud, amongst others, testifies. It is the line that, in his later work, Deleuze himself sought to tread. This, I believe, is what he meant when he claimed that the transcendental itself could and needed to become an object of experience.

Most exemplary, in that respect, is the case of 'Miss Miller', a young American schizophrenic who wrote the epic of the Indian Chiwantopel. Initially presented by Théodore Flournoy in an article from 1906, her writings achieved notoriety through Jung's lengthy analysis.[129] Despite the fact that Jung's interpretation consists of a systematic reterritorialisation of the geographical, historical and natural delirium of the patient onto a pre-identified (albeit archetypal) family structure, we can still see at work a desire and an unconscious that has from the start exceeded the family boundaries. Miss Miller informs us that she has always been fascinated by the Aztecs and the Incas, and that the figure of Chiwantopel most certainly comes from her early interest in the history of pre-Columbian America. As for the name Chiwantopel, she relates it to one of the volcanoes around Mexico City (the Popocatepetl), as well as to another word or name, A-ha-ma-ra-na, which evokes something Assyrian to her, something close to Assurabama, which, according to her, means 'he who makes cuneiform bricks'. But this latter name evokes another – Ahasverus. Ahasver is the wandering Jew, condemned to err until the end of time. She 'sees' many more characters, a city, a tree and a forest, where the dramatic end of Chiwantopel eventually takes place. As for Chiwantopel, he is on horseback, and his horse is his 'faithful brother'. All of this leads to another delirium, Jung's own interpretative delirium: every character, plant, place, or name is said to 'represent' or 'symbolise' something, and always family 'types'. Together, they constitute the stage on which Miss Miller's own personal, family drama is played out. All of that aspiration to break free, to extend beyond the limits of her own social background and historical situation, all of that desire to *become* something else (a different geography, historical time, race, gender, etc.), is reduced to an unresolved relation with her mother and father, to the construction of a narrative through which she is able to carry out, act out, or represent, what she cannot achieve *in reality*. But the 'names of history' aren't derived from the Name-of-the-Father; races, peoples, cultures and continents aren't substitutes for mummy-daddy. At every stage and in every possible way, the 'delirium' of the schizophrenic escapes the triangulation of Oedipus. It escapes rhizomatically, by growing roots and creating lines of flight in all directions. To the castrating trinity of Oedipus, it opposes the liberating weaving of the spider's web.

Confronted with the reality of the little boy and the horse, or the masochist and the horse (a different horse, yet a single becoming), psychoanalysis wants to know who the horse is, who it *represents*, which subject hides behind the animal. And the answer is inevitable: mummy and daddy, in one configuration or another. 'What's the fantasy?' asks the analyst. But Deleuze and Guattari insist that something quite different is happening, that the little Hans, or the masochist, are caught up in something that has nothing to do with a fantasy, but with their own desubjectivation and the emergence of an assemblage that reveals an altogether different plane. They are not imitating the horse as such, or even believing *that* they are a horse. Rather, they are *becoming* horse (not literally, but virtually, not analogously, or metaphorically, but concretely), thus creating a new mode of substance, a man-horse, which has left both man and horse behind, and is reducible to neither. The same goes for the wolf-child. Of course, in this phenomenon, it is not a question of an actual production, as if the child actually became an animal. But it is not a question of a resemblance either, as if the child imitated animals that had actually raised it. Finally, it is not a question of a symbolic metaphor, as if the autistic child that was abandoned or lost merely became the 'analogue' of the animal. All such characterisations, all such interpretations – interpretation as such, perhaps – function analogically, and perpetuate transcendence. According to René Schérer and Guy Hocquenghem's reading, with which Deleuze and Guattari agree, it is a matter of recognising 'something shared or indiscernible', a proximity 'that makes it impossible to say where the boundary between the human and animal lies', and this not only in the case of autistic children (as, supposedly, is the case with the wolf-children), but of all children.[130] It is as though, Deleuze and Guattari go on to argue, independent of the evolution carrying them towards adulthood, there were room in the child for other becomings, other possibilities that are not regressions, but creative involutions bearing witness to, in the words of Schérer and Hocquenghem, 'an inhumanity immediately experienced in the body as such', unnatural nuptials 'outside the programmed body'. Similarly, I would argue, as adults, in the presence of children, our own or those of others, we find ourselves caught in this becoming-child. It has nothing to do with being childish, with pretending to be a child, nothing, that is, to do with regression. But it has everything to do with the possibility of entering this space that, following the vocabulary of topology, Deleuze and Guattari characterise as a 'zone of vicinity' (*zone de voisinage*), that is, a zone of indetermination, or uncertainty, between forms, where there is just one block of becoming, a single assemblage and reality: the becoming-child. Becomings are always molecular. Deleuze and Guattari make their point somewhat humorously: 'You do not become a barking molar dog, but by barking, if it is done with enough heart, with enough necessity and composition, you emit a molecular dog.'[131] In short, to become is not to reach another form, but to identify the zone of proximity, or indiscernibility, such that we can no longer distinguish ourselves from *a* woman, *an* animal, or *a* molecule. It has to do with this experience of the impersonal, yet an impersonal that is far more vital than my own life; it has to do with Life – not my life as a fixed, organic totality, but as an intensive field of virtual changes or becomings that cannot be anticipated.

At that point, the schizophrenic body is constituted by axes and gradients only, by poles, potentials and thresholds – in short, by purely intensive determinations. We would be mistaken in believing that the true enemy of the body without organs are the organs themselves. The enemy is the organism as such, that is to say, 'any organization which imposes on the organs a regime of totalization, collaboration, synergy, integration, inhibition, and disjunction'.[132] If the body without organs ignores and rejects the organism, it is in the sense of the organisation of the organs in *extension*, which restrict and limit what the body can do. But beneath the organisation of the organs, the body without organs brings about a certain *intensity* of the body; it enters into a relation of intensity with the organs: the body without organs actually mobilises and appropriates the organs, although differently, by allowing them to function in a regime other than that of the organism. Far from being destroyed, annihilated, or virtually dead, the schizophrenic body lives through every intensity of the body, in what turns out to be an almost unbearable state, as Artaud, Nietzsche, or Nerval knew all too well. Suspended between the death instinct that does not kill, but frees life from its own organisation, and the life that engulfs and dissolves the ego, the schizophrenic signals the infinite power of desire.

Whether schizophrenic, paranoid, masochistic, or intoxicated, the body is engaged in experiments of the transcendental, in transformations of the real, and not in fantasies fuelled or structured by lack. The masochist, for example, does not seek pain, and not even pleasure through pain. Rather, s/he seeks a different organisation of the body, another way of living his or her body, a certain intensity of the body, which can take place only through pain. In fact, the process in which it is involved is more akin to a disorganisation of the body, which can be achieved only by populating the body with waves of pain. The masochist uses suffering as a way of constituting a body without organs and bringing forth a certain plane of desire. And there is a joy that is immanent to that process, immanent to desire itself, as though desire were filled by itself and its contemplations, a joy that implies no lack or impossibility and that is certainly not measured by pleasure (or pain for that matter). The schizophrenic goes one (dangerous) step further, radicalises this dis-organisation, renounces all codes, and becomes catatonic. No doubt, there are other, possibly better ways, and other procedures outside masochism, or schizophrenia. Once again, it is not a matter of adopting schizophrenia as a model to be imitated, but as a process in which desire is visible and produced in its raw, free state. It is a matter, then, of discovering and exploring the many ways in which desire can be produced, of connecting the various machines that constitute our own body with other bodies, in what amounts to new and singular assemblages, or becomings: 'Never interpret', 'never fantasise', Deleuze tells Claire

Parnet in *Dialogues*; instead, 'experiment, machine, assemble'.[133] 'Experiment, don't signify and interpret! . . . Semiotize yourself, instead of rooting in your prefab childhood and Western semiology.'[134] Ask yourselves: 'What are your desiring-machines, what do you put into these machines, what is the output, how does it work, what are your non-human sexes?'[135] The question, in other words, is one of finding out how to constitute one's own BwO, how to find one's own regime, lines of flight and deterritorialisation.

Notes

1. Deleuze, www.webdeleuze.com/php/texte.php?cle=190&groupe=Spinoza&langue=2, p. 1.
2. Deleuze, www.webdeleuze.com/php/texte.php?cle=190&groupe=Spinoza&langue=2, p. 3. Let me also note, in passing, and as a question to which I shall return, that morality thus defined is also the basis for the classic theory of natural law, as defined initially by Cicero, who combined Platonic, Aristotelian and Stoic traditions. According to Deleuze, Hobbes and Spinoza break with that tradition, and propose instead an ethical, or immanent, conception of natural rights. It is only when we replace the classical concept of essence – the human being as rational animal – with the concept of power (puissance) that we can replace morality, and the classical conception of natural law which it enables, with ethics, and the modern, specifically Hobbesian and Spinozist, conception of natural law, or right.
3. See *EPS*, 197/217.
4. On the notion of affection, its connection with the body, and the ideas that affections produce in the human mind, see Spinoza, *Ethics*, II, Propositions 16–29.
5. See Nicholas of Cusa, *De Possest* (Latin text as contained in J. Hopkins, *A Concise Introduction to the Philosophy of Nicholas of Cusa* [Minneapolis: Banning, third ed. 1986]) and Gilles Deleuze, *Cours de Vincennes* from 09/12/80, p. 1.
6. Part III of the *Ethics* is entirely devoted to 'The Origin and Nature of the Emotions', of which Spinoza gives the following definition: 'By emotion [*affectus*] I understand the affections of the body by which the body's power of activity is increased or diminished, assisted or checked, together with the ideas of these affections' (III, Preface, definition 2).
7. 'However, nobody as yet has determined the limits of the body's capabilities: that is, nobody as yet has learned from experience what the body can and cannot do, without being determined by mind, solely from the laws of its nature in so far as it is considered as corporeal. For nobody as yet knows the structure of the body so accurately as to

explain all its functions, not to mention that in the animal world we find much that far surpasses human sagacity, and that sleepwalkers do many things in their sleep that they would not dare when awake – clear evidence that the body, solely from the laws of its own nature, can do many things at which its mind is amazed' (*Ethics*, III, Proposition 2, Scholium).

8. See Descartes, *Les passions de l'âme*, I, articles 1 and 2, *Œuvres et lettres*, pp. 695–6.
9. *Ethics*, III, Prop. 2, Scholium and II, Prop. 13, Scholium. See also *EPS*, 198–200/218–20.
10. *Ethics*, I, Appendix, p. 239.
11. *Ethics*, V, Prop. 6, Scholium and V, Prop. 39, Scholium.
12. *Ethics*, V, Prop. 20, Scholium.
13. *Short Treatise*, II, Chapter 26, p. 100.
14. Part IV of the *Ethics* is entitled 'Of Human Bondage'.
15. See *EPS*, Chapter 14 ('What Can a Body Do?'), especially 204–6/224–6.
16. *Ethics*, IV, Prop. 39.
17. *EPS*, 218/239. Deleuze is here referring to *Ethics*, IV, Definition 1; IV, Prop. 31; and most of all IV, Props 38 and 39.
18. *EPS*, 219/240.
19. Spinoza gives the following definition of desire: 'desire is the very essence of man, that is, the conatus whereby man endeavours to persist in his own being' (*Ethics*, IV, Prop. 18, Proof).
20. *EPS*, 220/242.
21. *EPS*, 226/247.
22. *EPS*, 242/263.
23. *EPS*, 222/243 and 252/273.
24. 'The desire that arises from pain is diminished or checked by the very emotion of pain' (*Ethics*, IV, Prop. 18, Proof).
25. See *EPS*, 225/246.
26. Many of the questions and concerns that drive EPS, especially Chapters XV and XVI, were already formulated in *Nietzsche and Philosophy* (especially Chapter II, §1; Chapter III, §13; and the whole of Chapter IV, devoted to *ressentiment* and bad conscience), published six years earlier. The connection is even more explicit in *Spinoza, philosophie pratique* (Paris: Les éditions de minuit, 1981), especially Chapter II.
27. *Ethics*, I, Appendix, 241–3.
28. 'When men became convinced that everything that is created is created on their behalf, they were bound to consider as the most important quality in every individual thing that which was most useful to them, and to regard as of the highest excellence all those things by which they were most benefited. Hence they came to form these abstract notions to

explain the nature of things: Good, Bad, Order, Confusion, Hot, Cold, Beauty, Ugliness; and since they believed that they are free, the following abstract notions came into being: Praise, Blame, Right, Wrong' (*Ethics*, I, Appendix, 241–2).
29. Spinoza, *Ethics*, IV, Prop. 18, Proof.
30. With respect to consciousness, see Deleuze's 'second commentary' on Bergson in *C-1*, 84/56.
31. Ultimately, and despite Deleuze and Guattari's insistence, I prefer to speak of desire in connection with expression, rather than production, not only to preserve the connection with the Spinozist background introduced previously, but also to mark a reservation with production itself as exhausting the process of desire. Whilst it is clear that Deleuze and Guattari see production as an alternative to representation, and to expression as 'an idealist category' (*AO*, 12/6), and the model of the factory as an alternative to that of the stage, I am not convinced that it is the only alternative, or indeed the best. In fact, I would go as far as to claim that by locking desire into a logic of production, Deleuze and Guattari fail to see the extent to which desire also functions aneconomically, unproductively, and that its flows, and processes of deterritorialisation, can also take the form of a radical worklessness, and pure expenditure, thus suspending the machinic framework in which it is meant to operate. That being said, everything happens as if Deleuze and Guattari themselves had anticipated that objection, and the problem it signals, by connecting the production of desire with the unproductive and unconsumable dimension of the 'body without organs'. This problem is addressed in the second synthesis, which I analyse further down.
32. *N*, 198/144–5.
33. *N*, 25/14.
34. See René Girard, 'Delirium as System', trans. Paisley N. Livingston and Tobin Siebers in Gary Genosko (ed.), *Deleuze and Guattari: Critical Assessments of Leading Philosophers* (London: Routledge, 2001), pp. 679–712.
35. *AO*, 89/83.
36. See *KCP*, especially the Introduction and Chapter II.
37. *KCP*, 8/3.
38. Kant, *Critique of Pure Reason*, trans. Werner S. Pluhar (Indianapolis: Hackett, 1999).
39. See Kant, *Critique of Pure Reason*, A 341–405/B 399–432.
40. Kant, *Critique of Practical Reason*, trans. Werner S. Pluhar (Indianapolis: Hackett, 2002).
41. See Kant, *Critique of Practical Reason*, Analytic, 'Of the Typic of Pure Practical Judgement'.
42. See Kant, *Critique of Practical Reason*, Dialectic, 'Critical Solution to the Antinomy'.

Ethics

43. Spinoza, *Ethics*, Part III, Prop. 9, Scholium.
44. For an exhaustive exposition of the syntheses of the unconscious (connective, disjunctive and conjunctive), see Ian Buchanan, *Deleuze and Guattari's* Anti-Oedipus (London: Continuum, 2008), pp. 50–64. See also Pierre Montebello's own account, which focuses on the distinction between connective and disjunctive syntheses, in *Deleuze* (Paris: Vrin, 2008), pp. 177–82. For a systematic and genetic account of the Deleuzian conception of the unconscious, and its Bergsonian, Nietzschean and Jungian roots, see Christian Kerslake, *Deleuze and the Unconscious* (London: Continuum, 2007).
45. See S. Freud, 'Psycho-analytic Notes on an Autobiographical Account of a Case of Paranoia (Dementia Paranoides)', in *The Standard Edition of the Complete Works of Sigmund Freud*, Vol. XII (London: Vintage, 2001), pp. 9–82. Henceforth SE, followed by volume and page numbers.
46. AO, 12/6.
47. That being said, desire can be said to 'express' something in the more technical, Spinozist sense identified in Chapter 2: to desire is to express or realise one's essence, to embody or incorporate one's essence as power.
48. AO, 11/5.
49. According to Laplanche and Pontalis' definition, partial objects are, for the most part, body parts, whether real or fantasised (breast, faeces, penis), and their symbolic equivalents, towards which partial sexual drives direct themselves, without envisaging the person as a whole as their object. A person can identify or be identified with a partial object. See J. Laplanche and J. B. Pontalis, *Vocabulaire de la psychanalyse* (Paris: Presses Universitaires de France, 1967), p. 294.
50. AO, 14/8.
51. Written in November 1947, this text without a title was published in *84*, no. 5–6, 1948. Now in Artaud, *Œuvres* (Paris: Gallimard, 2004), p. 1581.
52. AO, 14/8–9.
53. AO, 15/10.
54. The text from which this passage was extracted was also published in *84*, no. 5–6, 1948. Now published in Artaud, *Œuvres complètes* (Paris: Gallimard, 1974), Vol. 13, p. 104.
55. AO, 15/10.
56. AO, 15/10.
57. AO, 17/12.
58. AO, 17/12.
59. AO, 18/13.
60. AO, 18/13.
61. 'Paranoia decomposes just as hysteria condenses' (Freud, SE, XII, 49).

62. See Freud, *SE*, XII, 17–21.
63. *AO*, 20/15.
64. *AO*, 23/18.
65. *AO*, 24/18.
66. See Michel Carrouges, *Les machines célibataires* (Paris: Arcanes, 1954). Deleuze and Guattari justify their choice of the word, and their tribute to Carrouges, in *AO*, 24–5/19. For a lengthier discussion of Carrouges and his 'celibate machines', see Ronald Bogue, *Deleuze on Literature* (London: Routledge, 2003), pp. 69–78.
67. See Freud, *SE*, XII, 29.
68. *AO*, 26/21.
69. *AO*, 26/21.
70. *AO*, 26/21.
71. *AO*, 100/93.
72. *AO*, 26/20.
73. *DR*, 147/111.
74. *DR*, 147/111.
75. *DR*, 149/113.
76. Montebello, *Deleuze*, p. 181.
77. Guattari said this in an interview – in which Deleuze also took part – with the magazine *L'Arc*, Vol. 49, 1980, p. 49. Reprinted in *N*, 28/16.
78. *AO*, 34/28.
79. The expression *'machine désirante'*, Deleuze tells us, is one that Guattari was already using when he first met with Deleuze in 1968. At the time, however, it was still thought within the confines of Lacanian orthodoxy – 'structures, signifiers, the phallus, and so on' – and needed 'some schizophrenic help' to be freed from such limitations (*N*, 24–5/13–14)
80. Freud, 'The Unconscious', *SE*, XIV, 159–215.
81. Freud, 'The Ego and the Id', *SE*, XIX, 1–66.
82. Freud, *The Interpretation of Dreams*, *SE*, IV and V.
83. *AO*, 63–4/61.
84. *N*, 197/144.
85. *AO*, 132/121.
86. Much of the account that follows is indebted to Lorenzo Chiesa's remarkably instructive and lucid *Subjectivity and Otherness: A Philosophical Reading of Lacan* (Cambridge, MA: The MIT Press, 2007), especially Chapters 1 and 2.
87. See Lacan, *Écrits*, 96/4.
88. Lacan, *Seminar II*, 307/224.
89. Lacan, *Seminar IV*, 17.
90. Lacan, *Seminar II*, 306/223.
91. Lacan, *Seminar IV*, 36.

Ethics

92. Lacan, *Seminar IV*, 71.
93. Lacan, *Seminar IV*, 81–2, 176.
94. Lacan, *Seminar IV*, 194.
95. This identification of the symbolic and the Law is crucial, in that it implies an ethics of psychoanalysis, which Lacan eventually developed in *Seminar VII*. As early as 1950, however, Lacan expressed succinctly the three interconnected tenets of his future ethics: a) following St Paul, Lacan affirms that 'it is the law that creates sin'; b) consequently, against Lombroso's criminology, he argues that 'criminal instincts do not exist'; c) finally, and following Freud's *Totem and Taboo*, he affirms that the Law is based on a primordial crime. See Lacan, 'Introduction théorique aux fonctions de la psychanalyse en criminology', *Écrits*, 125–49, and especially 126, 130, 146.
96. See Freud, *Civilisation and its Discontents*, SE, XXI, 57–145.
97. See 'How Do We Recognize Structuralism?', DI, 241/172.
98. C. Lévi-Strauss, 'Réponses à quelques questions', *Esprit*, 33/11 (1963), p. 67.
99. AO, 61/59.
100. AO, 132/121.
101. AO, 132/121–2. Translation modified.
102. AO, 202/187.
103. Montebello, *Deleuze*, p. 141.
104. 'Four Proposition on Psychoanalysis', TRM, 77/85–6.
105. See Lacan, *Seminar I*, which is entirely devoted to the nature of the relation between the analysed and the analyst. See also *Seminar XI*, Chapters 10–15 and 19.
106. What's remarkable is that this criticism seems to apply to Deleuze's own, previous work, and to *Proust and Signs* in particular, which analyses the universe of *In Search of Lost Time* as constituted by various sets of signs – social, erotic, aesthetic – which the narrator learns to interpret and decode. We could go as far as to say that, on one level, the world of Proust is the world of paranoia *par excellence* – a paranoia that is most visible in matters of love and desire, driven almost entirely by jealousy and extreme narcissism, whether that of Swann in relation to Odette, Marcel in relation to Albertine, or Charlus in relation to Morel (or even Marcel himself). There isn't a single gesture, word, or feeling, which they take at face value, without assuming that it betrays a thought, a desire, or an emotion of a different kind on the part of their lover. And yet, at the same time, the *Recherche* introduces an altogether different plane, and even a different image of desire. Such is the reason why the chapter ('Anti-Logos') that Deleuze added to the first edition of *Proust and Signs* in 1972, and a number of pages from the two volumes of *Capitalism and Schizophrenia*, are so remarkably different from the chapters of the first edition, why they are no longer concerned to emphasise the signs,

compulsions and paranoia of the novel, but its becomings, its lines of flight, whether in relation to the characters and the situations they find themselves in, or the style of the novel. (See, for example, *AO*, 380/350). I return to Deleuze's reading(s) of Proust in Chapter 6.
107. *AO*, 371/342.
108. F. Kafka, *The Trial*, trans. Will and Edwin Muir (New York: Schocken Books, 1956), p. 127.
109. *K*, 82/45.
110. *K*, 90/49.
111. See *K*, Chapter 2 ('An Exaggerated Oedipus').
112. *EPS*, 237/258.
113. *EPS*, 237/258.
114. *EPS*, 247/268.
115. *AO*, 68/65. For some reason, those words were omitted in the English translation.
116. *AO*, 370–1/342.
117. See Deleuze's comments on Sartre's 'La Transcendance de l'Ego' (first published in *Recherches philosophiques*, 1936–37) in *Logic of Sense*, fourteenth Series ('On The Double Causality'). On Proust, see *PS*.
118. *N*, 27/15
119. Guattari does claim, however, to be 'in love with' schizophrenics, and to feel 'attracted' by them (*N*, 26/14)
120. See *AO*, 134/123, 336/310; *N*, 38/23.
121. Buchanan, *Deleuze and Guattari's* Anti-Oedipus, p. 40.
122. *AO*, 26/21.
123. Nietzsche, *Selected Letters of Friedrich Nietzsche*, trans. Christopher Middleton (Chicago: University of Chicago Press, 1969), p. 347. Three days before, in a letter to Cosima Wagner, Nietzsche writes of all the historical figures he had been: Buddha, Dionysus, Alexander the Great, Caesar, Voltaire, Napoleon . . .
124. *AO*, 103/95.
125. *TRM*, 25–6/25–6.
126. From Pankow to Maldiney, Tosquelles and Oury, schizophrenia is associated with a lack of unity and a failure in identification, with a form of dissociation (*Spaltung*) and a fragmentation (*morcellement*, in Oury's words), in short, with the symbolising function of the image of the body, whether this image be conceived as specular, in the case of Pankow, or as *Leib*, in the case of Maldiney and Oury. In the words of Tosquelles, it amounts to 'a collapse of transcendence', or of the Symbolic in Lacan's sense (cited by Oury in 'Hysterical Psychosis: An intervention by Dr. Jean Oury', Paris, 30 November 2003; trans. David Reggio, www.goldsmiths.ac.uk/history/news-events/hysterical. php).
127. *TRM*, 27/27–8.

128. *TRM*, 27/28.
129. C. G. Jung, *Symbole der Wandlung. Analyse des Vorspiels zu einer Schizophrenie* (Zurich: Rascher, 1952); trans. R. F. C. Hull, *Symbols of Transformation: An Analysis of a Prelude to a Case of Schizophrenia* (Princeton, NJ: Princeton University Press, 1956).
130. René Scherer and Guy Hocquenghem, 'Co-ire', *Recherches*, no. 22 (1976), pp. 76–82. In that text, they criticise Bettelheim's thesis, which considers the becoming-animal of the child merely as an autistic symbolism that expresses the anxiety of the parents more than any reality of the child. See Bruno Bettelheim, *The Empty Fortress* (New York: Free Press, 1967).
131. *ATP*, 337/275.
132. 'Schizophrenia and Society', in *TRM*, 20/20.
133. *Dialogues*, 60/45.
134. *ATP*, 173/139.
135. *AO*, 384/354.

6

Aesthetics

Taking the examples of Proust and Bacon, I now wish to illustrate the affinity between philosophy and art, or between concepts, affects and percepts, and the manner in which the two planes I've identified in Chapter 3 necessarily co-exist in the work of art. More specifically, I want to show the extent to which art – and here I will be referring to literature and painting only – is involved in the same process as the one described in Chapter 5 in relation to schizophrenia. Like the schizophrenic, the artist (and the reader or the viewer in his or her wake) is involved in an experience of, and an experiment with, the pure intensities of the body without organs. Art too consists of a glorious dissolution and overcoming of the ego in favour of the purely intensive state of the body without organs.

1. Proust

In a famous passage from *Finding Time Again*, Marcel compares his book with a dress, and a cathedral.[1] We know that Proust's concern with cathedrals goes back to the years when he was planning and writing *Jean Santeuil*, and so precedes his translation of Ruskin's *The Bible of Amiens* by a few years.[2] We may even want to agree with a commentator's claim that

> for the writer, the study of cathedrals is a way of conjuring the failure of *Jean Santeuil*, which occurred as an excess of dispersion and fragmentation. The cathedral embodies stability, concentration, continuity also, and is opposed to the perpetual risk of incompletion.[3]

In what follows, however, and by way of illustrating Deleuze's own reading of Proust, I should like to show that dispersion, fragmentation and discontinuity are in fact defining and *constitutive* features of *À la Recherche* itself. In other words, Proust's great novel is also a work that integrates the very excess that led him to abandon his first novel: it assumes the risk of incompletion fully, and even affirms it as such. If the image of the dress, as well as that of the cathedral,

Aesthetics

characterises indeed a certain level of unity of the *Recherche*, and accounts for a certain plane on which the novel unfolds, it exhausts neither its nature nor its architecture. Juxtaposed to the first plane, or perhaps cutting across it, lies a second plane, less apparent, and less controlled, almost by definition. This second plane reveals a distinct coherence, as well as a unity, which challenges the classical conception of the novel, if not the classical concepts of philosophy itself – those very concepts and values which Fraisse claims Proust saw in cathedrals: continuity, stability and concentration. By contrast with the unity of the cathedral, or that of the dress, Deleuze compares the unity of the second plane with that of the patchwork. Let me stress from the start, however, that the singularity of Proust's novel, whether at the level of its architecture or of its characters, lies perhaps in its ability to gather those two planes in a kind of productive tension, one that elevates each plane to a superior degree of expression. This tension reaches its climax in Marcel's first kiss to Albertine, which I'll analyse in some detail. Ultimately, we shall see that two very different kinds of plane – a plane of organisation and a plane of fragmentation, or immanence – co-exist and interact in the novel. It will be a matter, then, of emphasising the manner in which the structure, outline and organic unity of the work find themselves confronted with an excess they cannot integrate, a fracture they cannot reduce. It will be a matter, therefore, of analysing the manner in which Proust's novel opens itself to an excess that once threatened to annihilate it, but which it is now in a position to integrate and recognise in its ontological dimension and its artistic potential.

In the second part of *Proust and Signs*, written for the second edition, Deleuze raises quite explicitly the question of the unity of the *Recherche*.[4] Specifically, he raises the question of what I would call the *other* unity of the *Recherche*, thus taking up the challenge that Proust's novel poses for philosophical thought, and to which I was just alluding. This unity, he suggests, is not the one that Proust had in mind initially. It is not even, I would claim, the type of unity that one discovers only retrospectively, almost despite oneself. Such a unity is precisely the one that Proust evokes in *The Prisoner*, in a passage where he discusses Wagner and nineteenth-century literature:

> Wagner, as he took from his desk a delicious fragment to introduce, as a *retrospectively* necessary theme, into a work of which he had not yet dreamed, when he was composing it, and when, having written one mythological opera, then a second, then more, he realized he had composed a Ring Cycle, must have known something of the same intoxication Balzac

felt when, casting over his novels the eyes of both a stranger and a father, and seeing in one the purity of a Raphael and in another the simplicity of the Gospel, he suddenly saw, *with the light of hindsight* [*une illumination rétrospective*] that they would be even more beautiful if brought together in a cycle in which the same characters would recur, and added to his work the final brushstroke, the most sublime of all. This unity was an *afterthought*, but not artificial.[5]

However remarkable, this unity revealed only in the end, this 'retrospective illumination', which discovers a necessity all the more effective in that it does not abolish chance, is not the unity with which Deleuze is concerned. For such a unity still partakes of an ideal of organicity, where beginning and end, however distant, finally meet up, where every piece fits in, every part refers to the whole, and where the work as a whole follows a thread, however hidden. This ideal governed the construction of cathedrals, as well as that of the *Recherche* itself, up to a point. The French word *plan*, which Deleuze turns into a concept, summarises it rather nicely. The *plan* can refer to an architectural plan, a battle plan, or the structure and outline of a book. In each case, it carries a sense of purpose and goal. At school, children are told never to even begin a piece of writing before having a clear *plan*, that is, without knowing exactly where they are going, what their final goal is, and how their writing is going to be organised. Oriented to and by its own end, the *plan* is essentially teleological. In that respect, the *plan* also refers to the unity or coherence of the piece in question. Inevitably, it contains a number of parts – most often an introduction, a central part and a conclusion – which all work together to achieve a common end. It constitutes an organic totality, each part reflecting the whole and containing it virtually. It is both linear (it has a beginning, a middle and an end) and circular (the end justifies and gathers the beginning).

The unity I'm interested in highlighting, however, is of a different kind. It belongs to another logic, and another conception of the work, perhaps less rooted in the nineteenth century. It reveals another kind of *plan*, a plane that is altogether different from the plane of organicity I've just alluded to. In what follows, I'd like to analyse it from a twofold perspective: that of the structure of the novel as a whole, and that of some of its characters and episodes.

Whilst complex and intricate, the structure and unity of the *Recherche* are well known. We know that, from the start, Proust knew how his novel was going to end. Initially, the novel was to comprise two volumes only, *Time Lost* and *Time Regained*. The end was

Aesthetics

planned from the beginning, with the beginning. This means that, from the arche-teleological point of view, the novel did not evolve much from the moment it was first conceived. Its unity, outline and circular structure were firmly in place from the start. What was missing, however, was the middle. And it is from the middle, precisely, that the novel grew, almost out of proportion, from two to seven volumes, between the publication of the first volume in 1913 and that of *Time Regained* in 1922. It grew in part thanks to a technique of pasting and folding which Céleste Albaret, then Proust's housekeeper, *confidante* and secretary, came up with when, having already filled the margins and the space between the lines of a given page of his manuscript, Proust was distraught at the thought of not being able to introduce further corrections and additions.[6] To be sure, there were contingent reasons for such considerable additions: soon after the publication of *The Way by Swann*, the war broke out, Grasset (Proust's publisher) was drafted in 1916 and the publishing house had to close down temporarily, thus finally allowing Gallimard to convince Proust to change publishers and giving him the chance to revise and expand his novel continuously. This is how the character of Albertine was born, and how the second half of *In the Shadow of Young Girls in Flower*, *The Prisoner* and *The Fugitive* were written. But, we may wonder, since when does a delay in publication translate automatically into developments of that magnitude? It is rather as if the novel were animated by a logic of growth of its own – an unexpected, unplanned and yet irrepressible need to outgrow its initial dimensions, not by extending its life beyond its planned end, not, that is, by adding segments at the end of the book, but by growing from the middle. Specifically, the novel grew by a process of swelling, thus revealing a remarkable elasticity, which must have been there from the start, virtually as it were, and which materialised by chance and with the help of the contingencies of time. As for the time of the novel itself, it was forced to slow down, at times almost infinitely, and reveal a different quality. As readers, we find ourselves trapped, bogged down almost, in an infinitely elastic and uncanny duration. The sense of duration that emerges from the novel is the result not of a time that keeps pressing ahead along a straight line, but of a time that halts, moves downward, and drags us into unsuspected depths. The *Recherche* is not (only) what the French call *a roman fleuve*, that is, an endless, river-like novel; it is (also) what we could call a *roman marais*, or *a roman delta*, that is, something resembling a swamp, or a delta. In addition, when Proust receives the proofs of his book, he keeps rewriting the novel, writing new pages, inserting relative and conjunctive propositions in between principal clauses: the Proustian sentence also swells up, grows and expands from the middle, exceeding and deforming the classical sentence, disorienting the reader, literally losing him in its meanders. Proust's sentence ceases to be a line, and becomes a rhizome. Ultimately, it resembles the swollen face of Rembrandt in the self-portrait briefly mentioned in *Finding Time Again*: there is something deformed, almost monstrous, about it.[7] It is subjected to an excess that makes us feel dizzy. Similarly, doubling Proust's novel as it were, Marcel's book grows anarchically, cancerously, like an organism gone mad, hovering between organisation and disorganisation, between order and chaos:

> Because I often had to glue one piece on to another, the papers that Françoise called my manuscribbles [*paperoles*] kept getting torn. But wouldn't Françoise be able to help me mend them, just as she would put patches on the worn-out parts of her dresses or, while she was waiting for the glazier, as I was for the printer, she would stick a piece of newspaper over a broken pane in the kitchen window? Françoise would say to me, pointing to my note-books, eaten away like wood that insects have got into: 'It's all moth-eaten, look, that's a pity, there's a page here that looks like lace', and examining closely like a tailor: 'I don't think I can mend this, it's too far gone. It's a shame, those might have been your best ideas . . .'[8]

Something decisive takes place in that space, *between* beginning and end, and in that process that the arche-teleo-logic (the structure and unity) of the novel could neither anticipate nor master. Besides the logic of organisation, besides the genesis and planned structure of the novel, or submerging them from within, an unanticipated and somewhat unmasterable logic of deformation and disarticulation unfolds – one that is very similar to Bacon's own technique in painting. Besides the circular unity of the novel, then – the unity that was there from the start and organised the novel as a whole – there is another unity, one that is not the principle or the cause of the novel, but its *effect*.

In addition, and more significantly still, there is a level or plane internal to the novel itself, involving local characters or situations. This is the plane that draws Deleuze's attention. On the one hand, he claims, the unity of the characters of the novel is one of envelopment, implication or encasing (*emboîtement*): every character, name or thing is like a box containing an infinite number of other boxes. The voice of M. de Charlus, 'that motley character, pot-bellied and closed, like some box of exotic and suspect origin', contains, in the words of Deleuze, 'broods of young girls and tutelary feminine souls'.[9] Similarly, 'the name Guermantes is also like one of those tiny balloons in which oxygen or some other gas has been stored' or else like one of those 'little tubes' from which we 'squeeze' the right colour.[10] And the taste of the madeleine, of course, envelops the essence of Combray. The Proustian image that best characterises this type of unity is that of the Japanese papers which, when thrown in water, open up and reveal an unexpected variety of shapes and colours. It is the incessant curiosity of the narrator that, above all, allows the characters, names and places to reveal their hidden reality. With respect to this first figure of encasing, or envelopment, the role of the narrator is, quite literally, to ex-plicate or develop a content that is incommensurable with its container. The explication in question must be understood quite literally: the narrator explicates what is implicated, makes explicit what is only implicit, or develops what is initially enveloped. In so doing, he reveals what was initially hidden, much like a developer in photography.

The second type of unity is that of *complication*. We already came across this concept in Chapter 2, and in connection with Spinoza's relation to Neoplatonism. Neoplatonic in origin, and particularly developed in the Renaissance, it takes on a distinctive meaning in Deleuze's thought. This is a concept that testifies to a new and decisive stage with respect to Deleuze's earlier thought, and to the problematic of implication and explication he develops in the first part of *Proust and Signs*, and in the fourth chapter in particular.[11] Between the plane of explication and that of complication, between the first and the second edition of *Proust and Signs*, Deleuze's thought matured. With the unity of complication, we are no longer dealing with open boxes but with separate and mutually exclusive worlds, with closed vessels that do not communicate amongst themselves (or at least not according to the classical conception of communication). These vessels cannot be brought under the unity of a higher or more general instance, or be seen as the expression of a more or less manifest totality. And yet, if we're going to speak of a unity of the novel in that respect, the closed vessels must communicate in one way or another. At a certain level, they need to be compatible or, better said perhaps, compossible. Their unity, Deleuze insists, is not one of inclusion or encasing, but of juxtaposition. Their relation is no longer one of contained and container, but of transversality. In that respect, they are more like fragments than parts of a whole. However, they are not fragments in the Greek sense, that is, fragments of an obscure, hidden totality, or pieces of a puzzle that can be assembled, or reassembled. A fragment, Deleuze claims, can be understood in two ways at least:

> When a part is valid for itself, when a fragment speaks in itself, when a sign appears, it may be in two very different fashions: either because it permits us to divine the whole from which it is taken, to reconstitute the organism or the statue to which it belongs, and to seek out the other part that belongs to it – or else, on the contrary, because there is no other part that corresponds to it, no totality into which it can enter, no unity from which it is torn and to which it can be restored.[12]

A fragment can be a part that reveals the whole; it can be the microcosm of a macrocosm. But it can also signal a reality of its own, juxtaposed in relation to another, but not leading to a higher unity: a multiplicity of differences, or a set of relations, rather than a gathering of identities, or an organisation of units.[13] We need only think of the little phrase of the Vinteuil sonata ('Why do you need the rest? Just that is *our* piece [*morceau*]', Odette says to Swann): it is a fragment that somehow escapes and exceeds the sonata, and doesn't belong to a lost unity. It does not present or schematise the sonata as a whole, much like 'the little patch of yellow wall' from Vermeer's *View of Delft*, which Proust compares to 'a precious work of Chinese art, of an entirely self-sufficient beauty',[14] does not symbolise the painting as a whole. In this instance, Proust is not interested in the painting or the sonata as a whole, and thus not in the relation between the particular piece and the whole: he is only interested in the fragment and its ability to draw within itself people, places and affects that are essentially heterogeneous. The unity in question, then, will have to be a unity of fragmentation, a unity of the multiple itself.

As a result, we can begin to understand why Deleuze claims that those 'parts', whilst *décousues*, do not carry any negative connotations. A narrative (whether real or fictitious, literary or cinematographic) that is *décousu* (literally, unstitched or unsown, but let us say, disjointed) is normally understood to be lacking in unity and direction, planning and coherence. A well-structured thought, a well-assembled narrative, we are told, must avoid this condition at all cost. By not being sufficiently or tightly woven, an argument, like a narrative, threatens to fall apart. By contrast, the French speak of the *trame narrative* (the woof of the narrative), thereby reinforcing the connection between text and weft, a connection that is there in the word *textus* itself, which, after all, refers precisely to something woven.[15] In Italian, for example (and unsurprisingly), the common origin between text (*testo*) and fabric (*tessuto*) is most obvious. And yet, in this instance, it is a matter of affirming the reality and the positive nature of this disjointed plane, and of exploiting the stylistic and narrative resources of this unity of juxtaposition. In saying that – in one respect at least – the Proustian novel is *décousu*, Deleuze is not claiming that it lacks in unity or coherence. On the contrary: he is affirming that the unity – or at least one of the two senses of unity it reveals – is precisely one of disjointedness. In saying that, he is not denying that the Proustian text is a woven fabric of some kind, but only that the manner in which it is woven or put together does not conform to the usual methods and techniques. If the more classical conception of weaving, especially in relation to writing and thinking (one might think of Plato here), privileges an intricate and continuous fabric, such as a carpet or garment, with its recurrent patterns and coordinated colours, the Proustian text resembles (at least in part) something like a patchwork, that is, an assemblage of disparate and heterogeneous parts, roughly stitched together. Whilst voicing his taste for classical dress-making, and for Fortuny's couture in particular, Proust also innovates in that department: he invents or creates a way of stitching together not just the pages of his book – his famous *paperoles* – but also his characters, the names they bear and their attributes. The vessels, fragments or pieces of cloth that constitute the fabric are not sewn together in a manner that would give a sense of continuity and homogeneity. They are loosely connected with one another, and do not constitute a synthetic totality. They coexist in a kind of spatial and temporal proximity, but without dialectical exchange. Their juxtaposition is not the prelude to their reunification. Their point of contact – their seam – emphasises their difference and their separation, more than their common qualities. It is *either* the way by Swann, *or* the Guermantes way; it is *either* the Verdurin clique, *or* the Guermantes clan.[16] Each world has its language, its code and its rites. They are mutually incompatible, and exclude one another (in fact, Madame Verdurin is a priest of sorts who does not hesitate to excommunicate those who betray the trust of the 'family', by venturing into another world, for example). As a result, one finds oneself having to choose between them, often at great cost, as Swann's affair with Odette, followed by their marriage, reveals most clearly. And yet, as we can gather from the end of *The Way by Swann*, and that of the novel as a whole, worlds that first appeared to be mutually exclusive eventually converge, and even merge. There is always a point at which a piece or a part breaks free from the set to which it belonged and, more or less directly, drifts into another set. There are passages, bridges, or tunnels, therefore, which some of Proust's characters use, or even represent: the violinist Morel, discovered by the Verdurins, is pursued by Charlus; Gilberte Swann marries Saint-Loup; Odette, formerly 'Miss Sacripan' and wife of Swann, rejected by the Guermantes clan, becomes the mistress of the duc de Guermantes; and the old Verdurin widow ends up marrying a 'bore', the prince de Guermantes.

At a more local level, this phenomenon is particularly visible when, after a long and frustrating wait, Albertine finally allows Marcel to kiss her. The reality of the kiss fails to measure up to Marcel's hopes: far from conforming to the ideal of unity and totality Marcel had – quite understandably – projected into such a moment, the actual kiss amounts to its (rather traumatic) shattering. At the very moment at which Albertine is finally in reach of Marcel's lips, she escapes him, her face breaking into a series of disparate and disconnected snapshots, or profiles. The promise of a final and total possession, which that kiss represented for Marcel, vanishes. Moreover, the fragmentation of Albertine's physical appearance, and the experience of (also comical) discomfort it creates, is not followed by a moment of reunification. It is a fragmentation beyond synthesis. The passage is remarkable in that it illustrates the tension that is the result of the co-existence of the two senses of multiplicity in one and the same system (the Albertine system): the multiplicity of synthesis, and that of dispersion, or fragmentation. Albertine is indeed a box, which contains Balbec, and the beach, and her little gang, as well as the secrets of an existence that escapes the grasp of the narrator. But she is also a multiplicity of closed vessels, of fragments.

Before turning to the passage in question, let me simply recall that Marcel had previously recorded his passion for Albertine's cheeks, 'as one can have for a variety of flower',[17] a passion that evolved into an obsession:

> Her cheeks often looked pale; but seen from the side, as I could see them now, they were suffused and brightened by blood which gave them the glow of those brisk winter mornings when, out for a walk, we see stone touched and ruddied by the sun, looking like pink granite and filling us with joy.[18]

At the sight of Albertine's cheeks, Marcel's desire is not for a walk, however, but for a kiss, the very kiss he hopes to give her when invited

Aesthetics

to visit her in bed that evening. At that point, 'the sight of her naked throat and her excessively pink cheeks had so intoxicated [him]'[19] that he leans over to kiss Albertine, who responds by 'pulling the bell for all she was worth'.[20] There is considerable anticipation built up, then, as well as frustration, which all crystallise on the cheek. On one level, the cheek's function is metonymical: it is the part that signals the whole, the part in which the whole – not just the whole of Albertine's body, but the whole of her life, everything that she contains and envelops, and which is the real object of Marcel's desire – is gathered and reflected:

> What a difference there is between possessing a woman with one's body alone, because she is no more than a piece of flesh, and possessing the girl one used to see on the beach with her friends on certain days, without even knowing why it was on those days and not on others, so that one trembled to think one might not see her again.[21]

The cheek is the very promise of an absolute that Marcel hopes to reach, the bodily part on which his love has crystallised. Yet it is this absolute that crumbles before Marcel's eyes. Beyond the desire to possess Albertine, and even to possess what she possesses, namely, a vantage point, a window onto the world, different from his own, what Marcel truly desires is the world as such and as a whole. All desire is desire of the Whole, or the Absolute. But the illusion is to believe that such a desire can be realised in love, since the object of one's love – the desire of the Other – always escapes us. This is what Swann, and subsequently Marcel, learn, at the cost of considerable suffering. From that point of view, the scene of the first kiss signals the impossibility of a total union, and the shattering of that ideal.[22] By kissing that cheek, Marcel hopes to possess an entire life, a life that far exceeds Albertine herself. Kissing her will be like 'kissing the whole Balbec sea-shore'.[23] Could we think of a better image of unity and fusion? By kissing the cheek of the beloved, Marcel hopes to be able to grasp her entire essence, much in the way that, later on in the novel, he will grasp the essence of Combray by biting into the madeleine (with the following, crucial difference, however, that the essence of Combray is discovered involuntarily, in a reminiscence, whereas it is denied to erotic desire). It is precisely this hope that is crushed, however, this ambition that is frustrated, some 400 pages after having been expressed for the first time – not, as had happened previously, as a result of Albertine's refusal to let herself be kissed, but as a result of her acquiescence. The much-awaited kiss tolls the bell of the organic totality. The cheek is no longer the metonymical organ it once was, and in which the whole of Albertine was gathered; it has now become a differentiating factor that brings about a new and fragmented reality. There is no longer one Albertine, but ten Albertines, all unknown and uncanny. Marcel finds himself transported from one plane to another – from Albertine as a box to Albertine as a multiplicity of vessels, from Albertine as an organised body to a body without organs. The narrator's organs themselves, far from working together towards a clear and distinct perception, break down and betray him, leaving him lost and utterly disappointed:

> [A]s my mouth began to move towards the cheeks my eyes had led it to want to kiss, my eyes changed position and saw different cheeks; the neck, observed at closer range and as if through a magnifying glass, became coarse-grained and showed a sturdiness which altered the character of the face . . . now what I saw, in the brief trajectory of my lips towards her cheek, was ten Albertines; because this one girl was like a many-headed goddess, the head I had seen last, when I tried to draw near, gave way to another. As long as I had not touched it, I could at least see this head, and a faint perfume came to me from it. But alas – for when we kiss our nostrils and eyes are as ill-placed as our lips are ill-made – suddenly, my eyes ceased to see, and my nose in turn, crushed against her cheek, no longer smelled anything, so, without my efforts bringing me any clearer notion of the taste of the rose I desired, I discovered, from these abominable signs, that I was finally in the process of kissing Albertine's cheek.[24]

The scene of the first kiss marks the end of a certain ideal – the ideal of organicity and totality.[25] Yet it does not signal the death of unity as such. Rather, it signals the appearance of a different kind of unity: the fragmentary unity.

And if, as far as literature is concerned, metonymy is the trope that designates the organic plane, it is, I believe, metaphor, which corresponds to the fragment, and to the way in which it communicates and resonates with other fragments. Doesn't Proust equate it with style itself, not just in literature, but in painting as well?[26] Like the sea in Elstir's painting, which cannot be distinguished from earth, like the sound of the knife against the plate in the hôtel de Guermantes, like the cheek of Albertine or the patch of yellow wall, metaphor transposes us into another reality. It is the trope through which closed vessels and fragments enter into resonance, the trope of transposition and transference. Its force lies in its ability to displace and gather through differentiation. Whereas metonymy gathers by concentrating the whole into one of its parts, metaphor gathers by extracting heterogeneous parts from their totality, and allowing them to enter into a kind of resonance. Turning to Charlus once again, we could say that he is the Guermantes *par excellence*, the finest example of their blood, wit, disdain and depravity. In that sense, he is their emblem, or, to use a Kantian concept, their schema. At the same time, however, by virtue of his infatuation with Morel, he is the bridge or the tunnel through which the Guermantes clan communicates and resonates with the Verdurin clique, the mole in the Guermantes fortress, and the cause of his own downfall. But these are not exceptions: in the end, every closed system, every vessel turns out to be perforated. There is no pure closure. The vessels can't be opened by the narrator, or synthesised, of course. That is because the mode of openness and disclosure of those systems is not one of unfolding, but of transversal and subterranean communication, linking or stringing fragments together, not in an organic totality, but a motley necklace, or a patchwork.

There is, therefore, a double unity of the *Recherche* – that of the cathedral, or the dress, and that of the patchwork. The novel as a whole oscillates between the classical ideal of organicity, for which a work is a totality in which every part fits, or a body not lacking any organ, and the fragmentation and disorganisation of such a body. On the one hand, Proust perpetuates the ideal of the work as organic; on the other hand, he introduces a plane of fragmentation and unmasterable excess, a BwO. Generalising this double structure, we could say that the quest for organicity, and the development of organs, will always have to reckon with a force of disorganisation, with an anorganic and anarchic principle. Every totality, every organic unity, in the moment in which it is constituted, is swept away by a power of fragmentation and dissemination; every organic unity is traversed by a body without organs. As such, Proust's novel can be seen to oscillate between reason – or rather *logos*, as a power of gathering and a faculty of intellectual synthesis – and anti-*logos*, as a force of dissemination and fragmentation. Stylistically, the novel hovers between metonymy and metaphor. But the two forces are irreducibly bound together, creating a reality between order and chaos, between reason and madness, or *logos* and *mania*. In its own way, the Proustian novel testifies to this eternal *polemos* and this conflicting harmony, this irreducible intertwining that is chaosmos: it reveals a macro-plan and an organic unity, but one that is overcome from the middle, by a rhizomatic and truly monstrous expansion (and it is not an overstatement to say that Proust died of this exhausting swelling, that the life of the novel took over his own); it reveals macro-assemblages, highly structured and rigid sets, but which crumble in the face of mere fragments. Bodies – whether physical, social, or artistic – fall apart, and give birth to new assemblages. In the end, every major character, every name and every place turns out to be on both sides of the divide. Beneath this living metonymy, Charlus, who represents the Guermantes in their mannerisms, their wit, their history, there is, Deleuze insists, this undercurrent of madness, that is, this force pulling him in the opposite direction, towards the abyss. In thus hovering between the classical ideal of organicity and the more contemporary experience of madness in literature, Proust draws a century to an end, and opens up another.

2. Bacon

There is always a figure visible on Bacon's canvas. It is, however, barely recognisable. Elongated, flattened, contracted or compressed, Bacon's figures project an image of extreme violence and produce a sense of unease. It is as if they were subjected to a formidable force threatening to tear them apart. At the same time, however, this violent force seems to belong to them (and us) most intimately. We all have the feeling that under the pressure of certain forces, our bodies could break, snap, or disintegrate. Yet, we also have the feeling that, configured differently, our bodies could bend, fold and enter with those forces into some kind of assemblage, such as the one we evoked in connection with Spinoza and modern ethology. Bacon's bodies belong in the latter category. Subjected to such forces, they do not vanish (or disintegrate) into abstraction. Nor do they retain their usual, organic form. As such, they seem to oscillate between the figurative and the abstract, or between the organic and the inorganic. Yet this oscillation is not born of Bacon's inability to decide between the two paths of figuration and abstraction. Speaking to David Sylvester of a head he's just been painting, Bacon says: 'This image is a tightrope between what is called figurative painting and abstraction. It will go right out from abstraction but will have nothing to do with it.'[27] Bacon's position, it seems, is born of a deliberate search for a way – one that can only be characterised as a 'tightrope' – between the figurative and the abstract. Where figurative painting depicts the life of forms and the organised body, abstract art (at least that of artists such as Pollock, Tapiès, or Burri) renders the chaos of pure intensive forces. As a result, the figures in Bacon's paintings always fall short of a complete dissolution. They move or hover between the striated space of recognisable forms and the smooth space of intensive material flows, thus also holding the two spaces together and opening up yet another – the space of what, following Lyotard, Deleuze calls the figural.[28]

In that respect, everything happens as if Bacon shared the concern and the warning that Deleuze and Guattari formulate, and which I quote here for the second time:

> *How could unformed matter, anorganic life, nonhuman becoming be anything but chaos pure and simple?* Every undertaking of destratification (for example, going beyond the organism, plunging into a becoming) must therefore observe concrete rules of extreme caution: *a too-sudden destratification may be suicidal, or turn cancerous*. In other words, it will sometimes end in chaos, the void and destruction, and sometimes lock us back into the strata, which become more rigid still, losing their degrees of diversity, differentiation, and mobility.[29]

Applied to art, and to Bacon's painting in particular, this word of caution becomes the following: 'The violent methods must not be given free reign, and the necessary catastrophe must not submerge the whole . . . Not all the figurative givens have to disappear; and above all, a new figuration, that of the Figure, must emerge . . . [and make the sensation clear and precise].'[30] Like Cézanne, Bacon aims to extract the flows and intensities, the forces and energies hidden within things by wresting the Figure from the figurative, by allowing the line to follow a different course, without dissolving into formlessness. The mere dissolution of form, as evidenced in the fluid chaos of traits, the explosion of stains and patches, the proliferation of lines that no longer delimit anything, the appearance of lumps, smears or blisters, which much of contemporary art has privileged, is an altogether too brutal plunge into chaos, into pure matter, and the manifestation of an anarchic, unstable life. In a way, a residual and minimal form can be a safeguard against the threat of total chaos, and one that stops the line of becoming from turning into a line of death. It is not brute, amorphous matter that Bacon aims to depict. Nor is it simply organic life:

> I never look at a painting, hardly. If I go to the National Gallery and I look at one of the great paintings that excite me there, it's not so much the painting that excites me as that the painting unlocks all kinds of valves of sensation within me which return me to life more violently.[31]

In the previous chapter, we saw how the space that Deleuze characterises as smooth – and of which Bacon's paintings would be an example – is filled with events or haecceities, and not forms, substances, or properties. What one perceives (or rather *feels*) in a smooth space, we said, are intensities: sonorous and tactile qualities, such as the sound of the wind in the steppe, the creaking of the ice and the song of the sand in the desert. Smooth space is a space of affects (or, to use Bacon's own word, *sensations*), and not representations. Such would be the fundamental aim of art, then – at least that proposed by Bacon and endorsed by Deleuze: to return us, artist and viewers alike, to the life contained and somehow solidified in the world of forms, to free the vital forces and flows contained in the most familiar and (apparently) most inanimate things. Only if art brings us closer to life, only if the life to which we return as a result of art has gained in intensity, is such a detour worthwhile. But the life that art brings us back to is not the organic life of *perception*, the life of what we call lived experience, *Erlebnis*, or *vécu*. Rather, the life that is set free in painting is the life that is trapped and covered up in the organised body; it is the anorganic or dis-organised life of *sensation*. In formulating this demand that art return us to life *more violently*, Bacon achieves in painting the task that Rimbaud – and Artaud after him – had ascribed to poetry, namely, 'to arrive at the unknown through the disjunction of all the senses' (*le dérèglement de tous les sens*).[32] In a very similar spirit, Artaud prefers to speak of 'a kind of constant loss [*déperdition*] of the normal level of reality'.[33]

Let me now turn to some considerations regarding the history of art and aesthetics. These will turn out to be necessary in order to contrast Bacon's 'figural' art with figurative as well as abstract art, and to appreciate further Deleuze's relation to Bacon. By providing this background, I hope to give a better sense of the singularity of Bacon's intervention and Deleuze's interest in it.

The connection between anorganic life and the figural, which we have so far only sketched, needs to be contrasted with another connection, most clearly formulated by the early twentieth century art theorist and psychologist Wilhelm Worringer, whose work Deleuze draws on quite extensively. The connection in question is that between *figurative* art and *organic* life. In drawing it, Worringer is actually following Theodor Lipps' views, which offer a combination of post-Kantian idealism and late nineteenth-century vitalism.[34] To enjoy aesthetically, Lipps claims, means to enjoy myself in a sensuous object different from myself, to empathise myself into it. Aesthetic pleasure is, to use Lipps' formulation, 'objectified self-enjoyment'. There are, Worringer claims, two basic artistic impulses or drives, two fundamental modes in which – to use Riegl's expression – the artistic volition (*Kunstwollen*) is expressed: empathy (*Einfühlung*) and abstraction (*Abstraktion*). What I empathise into, writes Lipps, is quite generally *life*, understood as an activity, a motion, a striving. The feeling of pleasure that I derive from an object is always a feeling of free self-activation. A thing is recognised as beautiful as a result of this empathy. Beauty is this ideal freedom with which I live myself out in the form of an object. Form, in this instance, is neither the 'I' nor the object, but something in between, their common limit as it were, from which we derive a certain pleasure. The value of a line, of a form, consists for us in the value of the life that it holds for us.[35] Conversely, form is ugly when we feel unfree or constrained by the form of the object, when our will to live and act is inhibited.[36]

'Naturalism' is the product of this first type of *Kunstwollen*. Naturalism, Worringer is quick to emphasise, has nothing to do with imitation, inasmuch as it consists in the *projection* of our organic will to live and act into specific forms and lines. It is not a matter, therefore, of an anthropomorphic projection, through which the illusion of life would be reproduced in the representation of the object. Rather, it is a matter of allowing a certain impulse and urge to be recognised and satisfied in the organic form of the object itself.[37] Ornament in the Renaissance, for instance, was not born of a desire to copy the things of the outer world or to render their appearance, but of the urge to project the lines and forms of the organic, which in turn enhance our own sense of life. At stake was not so much the concordance of the artistic representation with the object itself as the need to experience felicitation through the mysterious power of organic form, in which one could feel one's own organism more intensely. In fact, this pleasure is one that we experience every time we trace a free-flowing line:

> If we trace a line in beautiful, flowing curves, our inner feelings unconsciously accompany the movements of our wrist. We feel with a certain pleasant sensation how the line as it were grows out of the spontaneous play of the wrist. The movement we perform is of unrestrained facility: the impulse for movement once given is continued without effort. This feeling of pleasure, this freedom of formation, is now unconsciously transferred to the line itself, and what we have felt in executing it, we ascribe to it as expression. In this case, then, we see in the line the expression of an organic beauty because the execution of the line was in conformity with

our organic feelings. If we meet such a line in another composition, we experience the same impression as if we ourselves had drawn it.[38]

The true object of the projection, in which the 'I' externalises and realises itself, is precisely neither an object – whether a worldly object, such as a thing or a living being – nor the image of an object as it is represented in the work, but the life value that this or that line or form holds for us. It derives its beauty from the feeling of life that we project into it. Drawn by the organic-aesthetic forms, in which we ourselves take part as living beings, we experience our own being as immanent to the universal *élan vital* that is the heart of nature, understood precisely as *phusis*, that is, as growth and flourishing. The Quattrocento, Worringer claims, epitomises this 'delight in organic form'.

But not all *Kunstwollen* is for empathy. Besides the drive to organicity, there is the drive to abstraction. Here again, the explanation that Worringer provides is essentially metaphysical as well as psychological. It's not the explanation as such that Deleuze will retain, but aspects of the description. The drive to abstraction, Worringer claims, is born of our sense of dread and our great inner unrest in the face of the state of flux in which we encounter most phenomena. Eastern civilisations especially sought from art a happiness that did not consist in the possibility of projecting themselves into the forms of nature, of enjoying themselves in them, but in an urge to free themselves from their contingency as human beings and the seeming arbitrariness of organic existence in general. Their need for tranquillity and stability in the face of the universal flux of living nature was achieved in the contemplation of a necessary and unshakable object, an abstract form of 'crystalline' regularity and high order, most manifest in the Egyptian pyramid. 'Their most powerful urge [*Drang*] was, so to speak, to wrest the object of the external world out of its natural context, out of the unending flux of being, to purify it of all its dependence upon life, that is, of everything about it that was arbitrary.'[39] What those people called beauty was a refuge from the vital and the organic, an escape from the temporal into the eternal.

Unlike empathy, which, when applied to the work of art, became naturalism, abstraction translated into what, following Aloïs Riegl, Worringer calls 'style'. The longing for a stable and tranquil form leads to an abstract beauty, dominated by the geometrical style, and constructed according to the supreme laws of symmetry and rhythm. The abstract line tends to be regular and geometrical; it

Aesthetics

provides the greatest possibility of aesthetic satisfaction for someone seeking refuge from the instability and flux of phenomena: 'For here the last trace of connection with, and dependence on, life has been effaced, here the highest absolute form, the purest abstraction has been achieved; here is law, here is necessity, while everywhere else the caprice of the organic prevails.'[40] Form is no longer the expression of life, but of essence. Space, and depth especially, in so far as it is an essential dimension of perception, and thus of life, becomes an obstacle to the realisation of abstraction. As such, it needs to be reduced to the minimum, if not altogether eliminated (as contemporary abstraction has shown). This is how relations of depth and perception were transformed into relations of plane and intellection, how the abstract space was restricted to verticality and horizontality alone, thus allowing form and background to appear on a single, essentially superficial plane. In abstraction, both are equally close to the vision of the spectator, and delimited only by a highly regular line, which is an outline. The outline isolates the form as essence, that is, as a closed unity protected from accidents, change, deformation and corruption.

Nowhere, Worringer claims after Riegl, is this phenomenon more visible than in the distorted drawings of Egyptian art – until, should we add, the advent of abstraction in contemporary art. These drawings display a considerable effort to wrest vision from the unclear factors of perception, which grants the external world its relativity. We observe in them a tendency to extract a universal value from a natural object, one capable of forming a self-contained totality for the imagination and of providing the spectator with the tranquillising spectacle of that object in the irrefragable necessity of its closed material individuality. Such an ambition could be realised in the plane alone, where the tactile means of representation, and the 'haptic' quality of the vision, could be most strictly preserved.[41] Aside from space, and especially depth, the other dimension to be repressed in abstraction is temporality. The abstraction of a pure form from the natural world amounts to a negation of its becoming and the possibility of elevating it to the status of universal truth. Not only did the Egyptians translate depth relations into surface relations, they also gave the outline, which expressed the uninterrupted material unity and flowing vitality of the object, a particular additional modification, one that was only exacerbated in contemporary abstract art. As Riegl notes, wherever possible, the line was drawn absolutely straight, in response to a marked tendency towards maximum regularity in the composition. Where deviations from the straight were unavoidable, they were incorporated in a curve that was as regular as possible.

Riegl and Worringer, whose writings on abstraction were written at the end of the nineteenth and the very beginning of the twentieth century, did not yet know the abstract art of a Malevich, a Kandinsky, or a Mondrian. Yet aren't those painters abstract in the very sense we've just sketched? Were they not themselves in search of a world of essences, of perfect regularity and crystalline beauty? Could they not be seen as the Egyptians of modern times? We could consider them, and Mondrian especially, as having transposed in painting the purely crystalline and abstract ideal of the Egyptian pyramid. As Maldiney emphasises, twentieth century abstraction dared to do what classical abstraction – including cubism – had never dared, or dreamed, to do, that is, produce works that presupposed the prior negation or destruction of the world as a whole.[42] Hitherto, abstraction had wanted to safeguard the individuality of things and living beings, albeit minimally. 'Pure' abstraction, on the other hand, pushes the Egyptian artistic drive to the limit, and renders it literally ab-solute, that is, devoid of any links with the external world. There is no longer anything for it to integrate outside the work. It is no longer rooted in the phenomenal world; it no longer refers to anything worldly. In a sense, there is no longer anything to be abstracted, nor any place to do this abstraction from. The world that a movement such as *De Stijl* creates is simply outside nature. It no longer relies on any natural hypothesis. It is its own point of departure. It has eliminated naturalism entirely. To the world of nature, it opposes a purely ideal world, which it creates and inhabits. In many respects, it is closer to the world of mathematics than to that of artistic representation. As such, it is the realisation in art, and thus in the realm of the sensible, of a coherence that Plato could envisage solely in the mathematical and philosophical realm. Its world is inhabited by forms in the sense of idealities and essences. The abstract line is not just inorganic; it is also no longer an outline delimiting an object, however regular. The primary aim of this new abstraction, Mondrian claims in *Die Neue Gestaltung*, is to express the universal in and through the individual, understood here as *pure* form (and not outline). Every style in history, Mondrian claims, has an a-temporal content and a temporal manifestation. The atemporal content is what he calls the *universal* in style, and the temporal manifestation the *individual* in style. The time, the manifesto stipulates, has now come for painting to allow style itself to become manifest and become the object of painting.

For style as such cannot be made visible in the representation of an object. It is now a question of manifesting the universal in style in and through the individual in style.[43] Abstraction has always sought to express the absolute. But pure abstraction alone seeks to express it absolutely, through the generation of forms.

In addition to the drives and tendencies of abstraction, radicalised in the twentieth century, and those of empathy, present in organic art throughout history, the last century witnessed the emergence of an altogether different type of artistic volition, one that exceeds Riegl and Worringer's classification. If the artistic tendency in question can be described as abstract, inasmuch as it isn't figurative, it is not as a result of an urge to find in art a refuge from the flux of the natural world. On the contrary: its resistance to figuration and representation is actually born of an urge to engage with a level of reality and experience that can find its adequate expression neither in the organic, harmonious line, nor in the stable and regular form of abstraction, but in a specific arrangement of matter, colour and lines. In its move away from the organic as well as the abstract form, this type of informal art radicalises and absolutises our intimation of a reality in flux and constant becoming, by revealing the material forces and the intensive flows beneath the organic, which even the ordered constructions of abstraction cannot escape. It is abstract, yet not geometrical. It is material, yet not organic. It signals the presence of brute matter before the emergence of life, the insistence of chaos before the emergence of order. It is a world in which all forms have dissolved in favour of a fluid chaos of wild traits and a manifold of material components. All it wants to do, it seems, is give matter a chance, reverse the classical subordination of matter to form, free the flows and forces controlled and repressed in the classical pictorial architectonic. Where the line has been retained, it is a line that no longer delimits anything, whether an organic or geometrical form; in fact, it can hardly be seen as a line, such is its power of disorganisation and dissolution. The composite textures and stains of Dubuffet, Pollock's drips and Sam Francis' splashings of colour, the art of Tapiès or Burri all testify to this urge or drive to expose painting to the brute forces of formless matter.

Bacon's work is irreducible to the various artistic tendencies we have sketched thus far. It is neither organic nor inorganic, neither figurative nor abstract, neither purely material nor ideal. It occupies an intermediate position, between organic life and lifeless abstraction. In that, however, he is not without predecessors. Interestingly enough,

Worringer identifies a type of non-organic vitality in art, especially in northern European medieval art. Early northern ornament reveals a line of a singular nature, different from both the organic 'classical' line and the abstract 'Egyptian' line. This is a line that, at times, breaks and changes directions abruptly, and at other times returns to itself in a peripheral and swirly movement. As such, it announces the Baroque line, and that of Borromini especially, the undulation of the façade, the spiralling of the cupola or the column. Whilst devoid of organic expression, it is of the utmost vitality: Worringer marvels at 'the restless life contained in this tangle of lines'.[44] There is a life there, he claims, a vigorous, urgent life, which compels us to follow its movements. Yet because this life is not the organic life that draws us gently into its movement, because it is not the life of classical Greece and Rome, which signalled a harmony between man and nature, it is not a joyous life. In the classical edifice, and in the Ionic temple in particular, the organic and empathy were entirely co-extensive: 'When contemplating Classical ornament in its organic purity and moderation we feel as if it sprang naturally from our own sense of vitality. It has no expression but the one we give it.'[45]

It is not harmony, however, but disharmony, born of an experience of a repellent and hostile nature, which presides over the production of Barbarian, Northern European art, and its culmination in the Gothic style. With the Gothic cathedral, Worringer claims, we feel a strong appeal for our capacity for empathy, and yet its inner constitution isn't exactly organic. We, as humans, are not the measure of northern ornament. Rather, 'we are met by a vitality that appears to be independent of us and challenges us, forcing upon us an activity to which we submit only against our will'.[46] In short, the Northern line does not get its life from any impress that we willingly give it, but appears to have an *expression of its own*, which is stronger than our life. It is this vitality greater than our own, this life that exceeds organicity, which Deleuze sees in Bacon. There is one essential difference between Bacon and Gothic art, however. The vitality and force that we recognise in the Gothic is that of divine transcendence. There is no such upward movement, no such verticality in Bacon: unlike the Gothic line, Bacon's line is not drawn towards the heights of transcendence; it does not use the 'tumult of sensations' that characterises the Northern experience to 'lift itself out of itself' and into 'a world above the actual, above the sensuous'. It does not seek to experience the 'thrill of eternity' in a form of intoxicated ecstasy.[47] His paintings are not constructed like a Gothic cathedral. It is not transcendence

Aesthetics

in stone that Bacon seeks to accomplish, but immanence in painting: the forces and the flows that he opens the body to are the material forces of nature, not the spiritual forces of God. The 'logic' that presides over his painting is neither one of (organic) perception, nor one of (intellectual) abstraction, but one of *sensation*. It is by remaining at the level of sensation, by depriving painting of the resources of narrativity, organicity and formality that Bacon is able to achieve immanence in painting.

Let me now return to Bacon's paintings, and to the bodies they depict. Like Albertine in the moment at which Marcel is about to kiss her, the vast majority of Bacon's bodies seem to undergo a radical transformation of their ordinary shape and situation. Specifically, they give the impression of being in the process of disorganising themselves entirely, that is, of emptying themselves of their own organicity: in a scream or a smile, in excrementing, vomiting or spilling blood, through the mouth or the arse, through the erasing of the eyes or a general fluidification of the body, they seem to be undergoing something like an escape from organicity. How could there not be a violence attached to that movement? How could it not appear as monstrous to our own perception? The body that's painted no longer has any organs, that is, parts that work together in order to guarantee the day-to-day functioning of the body. All it has are levels and thresholds. Like an egg, it has axes and vectors, zones, movements and dynamic tendencies, with respect to which forms – those very forms, the Theory of Form tells us, which life needs in its day-to-day dealings with the world – are only contingent or accessory. Organs are now fragments, which Bacon isolates and allows to communicate with something else altogether, to produce a hitherto unimaginable assemblage and reveal the presence of another, virtual life that cuts across the life of the organised body. Not analogically, that is, as a result of some resemblance, or even some mental association, but as a result of a line of life, an intensive flow that does not follow the lines and bifurcations of the organised body, but that of the body without organs. 'Bacon and Artaud meet on many points: the Figure is the Body without organs (dismantle the organism in favour of the body, the face in favour of the head) . . .'.[48] The violence that we find in Bacon's paintings is also akin to the cruelty Artaud advocated for the theatre. It is not, as Deleuze insists, linked to 'the representation of something horrible', but to 'the action of forces upon the body' or the 'intensive fact of the body'. It is the violence of a body returned to the forces and tensions that its own organisation and organic life have managed to tame and control.[49]

There is no doubt that Bacon's figures retain some degree of resemblance with their model. At the same time, however, resemblance is clearly not what Bacon's paintings are about. The logic of sensation is not predicated on resemblance, that is, on the possibility of recognising a model – a form – in the copy. It is a misunderstanding to believe that art aims to reproduce the outline or the familiar appearance of its 'model', and to believe, therefore, in the presence of something like a model, if by model we understand that which needs to be reproduced identically. Far from being something self-evident, the model is a question and a problem for the painter, an enigma, even, and one that he sets out to solve by painting it, one that can be addressed by way of painting only. Speaking again of his portraits, and of those of Michel Leiris in particular, Bacon says: 'I really wanted these portraits of Michel to look like him: there's no point in doing a portrait of somebody if you're not going to make it look like him.'[50] Painting must record the world it depicts. It aspires to be 'real' or 'factual'. And yet,

> of those two paintings of Michel Leiris, the one I did which is less literally like him is in fact more poignantly like him. What is curious about that particular one of Michel is that it does look more like him and yet, if you think about Michel's head, it's rather globular, in fact, and this is long and narrow. So that one doesn't know what makes one thing seem more real than another.[51]

Bacon is expressing a paradox and a mystery. A paradox: by looking less (objectively) like Michel Leiris the portrait manages to look more like him (without referring to the manner in which the subject – the painter – perceives him). A mystery: what is it that allows us to recognise more reality (I would say more truth) in the painting than in the original? The solution to both problems, I believe, lies in the process and reality of deformation, analogous to what I called metaphor in relation to Proust, in so far as it too involves a displacement and a transposition. In order to look like Michel Leiris, or like any model, the painting must deform them: 'I'm always hoping to deform people into appearance; I can't paint them literally.'[52] Or again: 'What I want to do is to distort the thing far beyond the appearance, but in the distortion to bring it back to a recording of appearance.'[53] It is as if, by choosing to deform his subjects, rather than reproduce their familiar traits and contours, Bacon were able to bring out a quality or state of the subject that is not immediately apparent, yet truer or more essential to him or her. What is deformed in the painting is the habitual, familiar outline of the model. But this is the outline that art is precisely seeking to move beyond. Why? Because it is the line of ordinary perception, the form that emerges from our practical, everyday dealings with the world, and which the Theory of Form designates as the *good form*. It is a misunderstanding to act as if the painting were a recording of a *perception* of the model. In 'recording' the model, the artist aims to bypass perception. For we perceive objects and forms which, far from being the reality and truth of that object, only indicate what we normally retain from it, out of need and habit. And it is perception thus understood that creates all the clichés and ready-made images that art must overcome in order to arrive at a pure *sensation* of its subject. By deforming his subjects, Bacon tells us very clearly that he isn't interested in representing them, that is, in reproducing the *form* of their appearance. It's precisely the form in which the subject normally appears that's the problem. He who sets out to paint grass, a wave, or a peach, for example, will be overwhelmed from the very start by the forms of the peach: a peach is something soft, like a baby's skin, sweet and juicy, like the summer itself, etc. The painter will have to move beyond those clichés and avoid those forms in order to arrive at the genuine force and intensity of the peach, in order to paint the peach as if for the first time. The operation of de-formation is precisely this twisting free of form, this distortion through which something else – the plane of sensation – is liberated.

Deformation is the dislocation of form, that is, the transition from the plane of form to another plane of reality (and not into another form), one that is not dominated by perception and habitual recognition, but by sensation and recognition of a different kind, as I already suggested in connection with Albertine's cheek. This is the reason why, having said that his art aims to *record* reality, Bacon also claims that art aspires to be 'deeply suggestive or deeply unlocking of areas of sensation other than simple illustration of the object that you set out to do'.[54] Speaking of the head I was alluding to a moment ago, Bacon tells David Sylvester that it amounts to 'an attempt to bring the figurative thing up onto the nervous system more violently and more poignantly'.[55] The violent shock that we experience in the face of Bacon's paintings is at bottom a function of their ability to provoke our nervous system directly, to deal with affects and sensations in their raw state, without the mediation of a stable form, of perception, imagination, or intellection. Elsewhere, prompted to define the difference between an illustrational and a non-illustrational form, he says:

'Well, I think that the difference is that an illustrational form tells you through the intelligence immediately what the form is about, whereas a non-illustrational form works first upon sensation and then slowly leaks back into the fact.'[56] This – the plane of sensation – is where art takes place for Bacon. To a large extent, then, form is in the way of what Bacon tries to capture and record in his paintings, that is, a raw state of being that affects us, a set of sensations that simmer beneath the superficial nature of form. It is as if, by wanting to see beyond the form, Bacon wanted to bring us down to another level of reality, truer than that of organised life, in which everything has its place and every point of view is an overview. Sensation, Bacon insists, is what takes place in the passage from one 'order' or 'level' to another. Such is the reason why sensation requires deformations. It is precisely in so far as abstract as well as figurative painting remain on the same level – the level of form and of the brain – that they cannot isolate a figure and get to the level of sensation. To be sure, they can produce transformations, that is, modifications of form, or the passage from one form to another, assuming all along that form is the only true aim of art. But they cannot arrive at a deformation of the body. All transformations take place on a single plane, that of form, whereas deformation marks the passage from one plane to another, from the final, organised body to the a-formal and intensive world of intensive forces.

As a pictorial strategy, deformation is an invitation to *see*, but to see *differently*. It's all a question of what is meant by *seeing*. Following Worringer and Riegl, Deleuze distinguishes between an optical and an haptic vision, that is, between a vision of distance and one of proximity. If Bacon's canvas can be said to call for an haptic vision, it also represents a radicalisation of that vision, in so far as it wants to translate vision immediately into sensation, without any detour of narrative, interpretation, imagination or intellection. It is a vision without perception. Consequently, it becomes a matter of 'seeing' the raw meat or the carcass in a crucifixion, the scream or the smile as such in the mouth, etc. It is not pain that the scream suggests, but the scream itself; not the self-contentment that the smile reveals, but the pure smile. Bacon does not aim to paint the face, its history, its past and present, and the narrative that every face tells, but the head, this chunk of meat in which the body is gathered – a fragment, in the sense we have already come across in connection with Albertine's cheek. The face, Deleuze writes, 'is a structured, spatial organisation that conceals [*recouvre*] the head, whereas the head is dependent upon the body'.[57] The head is a striated space, a set of coordinates, which we read all too easily – an invitation to recognise, understand and interpret. Remarkably, in Bacon's portraits, and by contrast with traditional portraiture, our gaze is not directed towards the gaze of the subject, to which we naturally turn as to the clue that will reveal its most intimate secrets, its inner life, its story. In his paintings of figures or portraits, the eyes are often closed (as in *Study for portrait II* and *III*, after the life mask of William Blake), as if forbidding this privileged way into the life of the subject, the life of the soul – the very life that Marcel thought he would find and possess by kissing Albertine. Sometimes, the eyes are erased (as in some of the portraits of George Dyer), or in the process of being erased (as in *Three studies for portrait of Lucian Freud*, 1966). At other times, they are distorted to the point of monstrosity (*Pope no. II*, 1960, for example, is cross-eyed), as if suggesting a total lack of something like an inner life: there is nothing to be retrieved, interpreted or read, no story to extract, no depth. Bacon's Figures do not want to tell a story. They have nothing to say, quite literally:

> I mean people can interpret things as they want. I don't even interpret very much what I do. By saying that, don't think that I think that I'm inspired, but I work and what I do I may like the look of, but I don't try to interpret it. After all, I'm not really trying to *say* anything, I'm trying to *do* something.[58]

What those paintings want to do, however, is liberate the forces of life that representation – illustration and narration – always leave to one side, the very forces of life that do not indicate the particular life of this or that subject, the lived content which this or that visible form expresses, and which the art of portraiture has traditionally taken upon itself to represent, but the impersonal and pre-individual forces and facts that are enveloped in the form: the carcass in the crucifixion, the scream in the pope's face, etc. It is perhaps no coincidence that Bacon chooses the most iconic, immediately recognisable images and narratives to extract from them something that is entirely surprising and unfamiliar, and which we can nonetheless recognise – according to an operation of recognition that is quite distinct from that based on mere resemblance – as somehow there from the start, at once enveloped in them and exceeding them. Thus, the familiar scene of the crucifixion becomes the scene of something else altogether, as opposed to yet another representation of the same narrative. The reproduction of Velasquez' representation of Pope Innocent X is no longer a representation of representation, nor a picture in praise and recognition of a great master, but the presentation of a vital potential contained in the original, and now set free, liberated from its familiar, recognisable form. It is no longer a question of representing the world, of juxtaposing forms and weaving narratives, nor even of introducing a variation in a classical theme, but of extracting and presenting the flows that operate beneath the surface of things, of tearing subjects and objects apart, allowing their content to spill out and adopt a different material configuration. There is only surface, and transversal movement. There is no longer a form emerging from a background, no longer a foreground and a background, a surface and a depth. The great fields of colour surrounding Bacon's figures rarely suggest something like an environment, a background that would allow us to reconstruct something like a coherent narrative, a 'scene', whether already familiar or to be filled in by our imagination. What there is, though, is a force of becoming, visible in the head itself (and not in the face, which is already coded, mapped, *known*). There is a becoming animal, a becoming ape, for example (as in *Study of nude with figure in a mirror*, 1969), in the same way that there is a becoming human of the baboon (as in *Study of a baboon*, 1953), the mouth of which we find again in two different studies after Velasquez' portrait of Innocent X from 1949 and 1953. It would be a grave mistake, therefore, to think of the process of deformation, and of the lines of becoming, in terms of a transformation. For the movement of deformation is not from one form to another, but from the organised, stable body to the disorganised, fragmented body (or the Figure). It is a movement that signals a shift from imagination and intellection to sensation. To the idealism of transformation (and perception), Deleuze opposes the realism of deformation (and sensation).

With Bacon, painting can no longer be envisaged as an organic totality; it has become a collection of fragments. If it retains a unity – as I believe it does – it is in the sense I defined in relation to Proust, that is, as a patchwork. As a result of this type of unity – one we are not accustomed to – Bacon's paintings can seem somewhat artificial. But, paradoxically, it is precisely this artificiality that Bacon claims for painting, if it is to break with habits and clichés, and produce the sensation he is after:

> For instance, in a painting I'm trying to do of a beach and a wave breaking on it, I feel that the only possibility of doing it will be to put the beach and the wave on a kind of structure which will show them so that you

Aesthetics

> take them out of their position, as it were, and re-make the wave and a piece of the beach in a very artificial structure . . . I just hope that this painting, no matter how artificial it is, will be like a wave breaking on a seashore.[59]

Only in this 'oblique' manner can it hope to achieve the desired effect. Otherwise, it's 'just one more picture of a sea and a seashore'.[60] What will make it something different?

> Only if I can take it far enough away from being another picture, if I can elevate, as it were, the shore and the wave – almost cut it out as a fragment and elevate it within the whole picture so that it looks so artificial and yet so much more real than if it were a painting of the sea breaking on the shore.[61]

By being elevated to the position of a fragment, by being extracted from its organic totality, its ordinary environment, the wave attains a level of intensity and a reality otherwise unsuspected. It is now a pure wave, a pure sensation, like the small patch of yellow wall from Vermeer's painting or the 'piece' from Vinteuil's sonata in Proust's novel, like the contact of fresh grass on Rimbaud's feet in the poem *Sensation*, or like the patch of grass in another painting called 'landscape 1978'. It's just a bit of grass, Bacon claims, but with remarkable movement, and looking like fur, encased in the typical glass cube, and from which Bacon is able to extract a pure sensation. The production of this sensation, the realisation of this intensity is entirely a function of its seemingly artificial creation. Proust claimed that if God had created things by naming them, the artist recreates them by naming them *differently*. Every creation is a re-creation, and this is the reason why realism in art is of no value. Bacon formulates this idea in his own words:

> In one of his letters Van Gogh speaks of the need to makes changes in reality, which become lies that are truer than the literal truth. This is the only possible way the painter can bring back the *intensity* of the reality which he is trying to capture. I believe that reality in art is profoundly artificial and that it has to be *re-created*.[62]

More remarkably, and in a manner once again reminiscent of Proust, Bacon insists that in painting those fragments (grass, water, faces or rather bits of them, like Albertine's cheek, etc.) he is trying to capture their 'essence' or their 'energy'.[63] Essence is nothing spiritual, but a material force or an energy emanating from a thing or a person. It is this 'abbreviation into intensity'[64] that Bacon has sought – and managed – to produce.

Notes

1. 'I should construct my book, I don't dare say, ambitiously, as if it were a cathedral, but simply as if it were a dress I was making'. Marcel Proust, *Le temps retrouvé*, *À la recherche du temps perdu*, Jean-Yves Tadié, General Editor (Paris: Gallimard, 1989), Volume IV, p. 610; translated as *Finding Time Again*, *In Search of Lost Time*, Christopher Prendergast, General Editor (London: Penguin, 2002), Volume 6, p. 343. Throughout, I shall refer to the English edition, followed by volume and page numbers in the French edition.
2. See Luc Fraisse, *L'Œuvre cathédrale. Proust et l'architecture médiévale* (Paris: Librairie José Corti, 1990).
3. Fraisse, *L'Œuvre cathédrale*, p. 79.
4. Deleuze, *PS*. My analysis will focus on the chapter entitled 'Cells and Vessels'.
5. Proust, *The Prisoner*, 144/III, 666–7. My emphasis.
6. Those bits of paper pasted onto the manuscript were known to the printers as '*béquets*', and are referred to in the novel as 'manuscribbles [*paperoles*]'
7. Proust, *Finding Time Again*, 215/IV, 485.
8. Proust, *Finding Time Again*, 344/IV, 611.
9. Cited in *PS*, 141/116.
10. Cited in *PS*, 141/116.
11. The chapter in question is entitled 'Essences and The Signs of Art'; the fact that Deleuze mentions 'complication' in that chapter shouldn't fool us, for it is used interchangeably with 'implication'.
12. *PS*, 136/112.
13. In that sense, the fragments that are here in question resemble the fragments of German Romanticism, and of Friedrich Schlegel in particular, for whom the total or absolute work, the fragment, reveals an incompletion that is universal and essential. See Friedrich Schlegel, *Philosophical Fragments* (Minneapolis: Minnesota University Press, 1991); trans. Peter Firchow, with a Foreword by Rodolphe Gasché. See also M. Blanchot, 'L'Athenaeum', in *L'entretien infini* (Paris: Gallimard, 1969), pp. 515–27; J.-L. Nancy and Ph. Lacoue-Labarthe, *L'absolu littéraire* (Paris: Éditions du Seuil, 1978), pp. 57–80 in particular ('L'exigence fragmentaire'). It is this very 'fragmentary exigency' that Blanchot takes up again and develops in *L'écriture du désastre* (Paris: Gallimard), pp. 96–102 in particular), which he connects with the notions of '*désastre*' and '*désœuvrement*'. One could argue that, in his own way, Proust himself responds to this exigency.
14. Proust, *The Prisoner*, 169/III, 692.
15. All of this, of course, takes us back to Homer's *Odyssey*, and to the paradigmatic image of Penelope's woof. Like Penelope, Proust undoes

Aesthetics

     with one hand what he has done with the other, or adds onto the tight fabric of the novel a looser one.
16. If the conjunction that characterises the cell or the box is the coordination 'and' (Albertine is youth itself *and* the little gang *and* Balbec *and* the waterfront *and* an infinity of other boxes, which Marcel's jealous curiosity seeks – in vain – to discover in their entirety), that of the closed vessels is the disjunctive 'or'.
17. Proust, *In the Shadow of Young Girls in Flower*, 466/II, 242.
18. Proust, *In the Shadow of Young Girls in Flower*, 507/II, 283.
19. Proust, *In the Shadow of Young Girls in Flower*, 509/II, 285.
20. Proust, *In the Shadow of Young Girls in Flower*, 510/II, 286.
21. Proust, *The Guermantes Way*, 360/II, 657.
22. The absolute that the narrator eventually reaches is of a different kind, namely, of the kind that's been used to characterise the ambition of German Romanticism – a *literary* absolute, which makes room and integrates the reality of the fragment. The literary absolute, therefore, is not synonymous with the dialectical absolute, or with a self-differentiated totality, inasmuch as it affirms the unsurpassable reality of the fragment.
23. Proust, *The Guermantes Way*, 361/II, 658.
24. Proust, *The Guermantes Way*, 362-3/II, 660-1.
25. Cinema could be shown to have undergone a similar transformation. Let us take an example from Orson Welles' *The Lady of Shanghai* – certainly a favourite of Deleuze's. At the very end of the film, the rich and wretched lawyer and his no less deceiving wife find themselves trapped in an octagonal room made of mirrors. Multiplied as it were *ad infinitum* by those mirrors around them, consumed by hatred, they shoot at one another furiously, without being able to know whether they are shooting at their spouse or only at their reflection, each image splintering into infinity. In that scene, it is the organic ideal of cinema itself that is shattered, in what amounts to a spectacular farewell. To this *organic* image, Deleuze tells us, we should oppose the *crystal*-image (see C-2, Chapter 4).
26. Proust, *Finding Time Again*, IV, 467/4, 198.
27. David Sylvester, *Interviews with Francis Bacon* (London: Thames & Hudson, revised edition 1980), p. 12. Henceforth *Interviews*, followed by page number.
28. J.-F. Lyotard, *Discours, Figure* (Paris: Klincksieck, 1971). The figural is clearly and methodically distinguished from the figurative, which introduces issues of representation and imitation that Lyotard wants to avoid.
29. *ATP*, 628/503. My emphasis.
30. *FB*, 71/110.
31. *Interviews*, 141.

32. The famous letter to Paul Demeny from 15 May 1871 (*Lettres de la vie littéraire d'Arthur Rimbaud* [Paris: L'imaginaire Gallimard, 1990], p. 45), known as the *lettre du voyant*, can never be quoted enough. It is the purest expression of the artistic life, that is, of the life that calls on (and for) another organisation of the senses, of the body and the world. It is matter of seeing, but of seeing differently, from the disorganisation of the senses. The body without organs – at least the organs in so far as they work together in perception, with a view to a practical goal and according to an organic necessity – alone can 'see' in that way. The artistic life is no longer bound to life by action: 'Poetry will no longer lend its rhythm to action, it *will be in advance* [*La Poésie ne rythmera plus l'action: elle* sera en avant]' (p. 49). In that respect, the seeing of the Poet is also a *foreseeing*, a seeing beyond the confines of ordinary perception. Two days prior to his letter to Demeny, Rimbaud had sent a letter to Georges Izambard, in which he first formulated his manifesto. It is from this first version that I quoted: 'I want to be a poet, and I am working to make myself a *seer* . . .' (p. 38). And what are we to say of the short poem entitled 'Sensation' (in *Œuvres poétiques* [Paris: Garnier Flammarion, 1964], p. 28) other than that it echoes in words the ambition that Bacon set for painting?

33. Artaud, 'Le pèse-nerfs', *Œuvres* (Paris: Quarto Gallimard, 2004), p. 161.

34. Wilhelm Worringer, *Abstraktion und Einfühlung* (1908) (Munich: R. Piper & Co. Verlag, 1921); trans. Michael Bullock, *Abstraction and Empathy* (London: Routledge & Kegan Paul, 1958). Theodor Lipps, *Ästhetik. Psychologie des Schönens und der Kunst* (Hamburg & Leipzig, 1903–1906).

35. Worringer, *Empathy and Abstraction*, pp. 17–18/14.

36. Lipps, *Ästhetik*, p. 247.

37. Worringer, *Empathy and Abstraction*, pp. 37/27–8.

38. Worringer, *Formprobleme der Gothik* (Munich: R. Piper & Co. Verlag, 1927), p. 32; trans. with an Introduction by Herbert Read, *Form in Gothic* (London: G. P. Putnam's Sons, 1927), p. 43.

39. Worringer, *Empathy and Abstraction*, pp. 21–2/16–17.

40. Worringer, *Empathy and Abstraction*, pp. 26/20.

41. The opposition between 'optical' and 'haptic' vision was first formulated by Aloïs Riegl in *Die spätrömische Kunstindustrie nach den Funden in Österreich-Ungarn* (Vienna, 1901); trans. R. Winkes, *Late Roman Art Industry* (Rome: Giorgio Bretschneider, 1985). It is taken up by Worringer and, more recently, by Maldiney and Deleuze. Whereas the haptic plane demands that we see the object up close, as if touching it (*apto* in Greek means to touch), the optical plane involves a certain distance from the object, and so the possibility of optical illusion and delusion. If Egyptian art, and the bas-relief in particular,

exemplify the haptic plane, classical art represents the emergence of the optical vision. Greek art introduced a distinction between planes and invented a perspective, allowing light and shade, hollows and relief, to play off one another. The classical representation amounted to the conquest of an optical space and a vision from afar: form and background are no longer on the same plane, as in Egyptian art. The planes now separate between background and foreground; the outline ceases to be the limit separating and joining together form and background on the same plane, and becomes the self-limitation of form, or the primacy of the foreground. The outline is no longer geometrical; it is now organic. As such, it doesn't simply break with touch, but involves it as part of the organic activity of the human. Optical vision does not amount to an overview. The distance and depth it introduces is that of life itself, that is, that of a gaze immersed in a world of depth and contrast, of light and darkness.

42. H. Maldiney, *Art et Existence* (Paris: Klincksieck, 1985/2003), p. 101.
43. P. Mondrian, 'Die neue Gestaltung in der Malerei', in Hans L. C. Jaffé (ed.), *Mondrian und De Stijl* (Köln: Dumont, 1967), p. 41.
44. Worringer, *Empathy and Abstraction*, p. 139/107.
45. Worringer, *Form in Gothic*, p. 31/42.
46. Worringer, *Form in Gothic*, p. 31/42.
47. Worringer, *Form in Gothic*, p. 50/73.
48. *FB*, 33/45.
49. *FB*, 34/45–6
50. *Interviews*, 146.
51. *Interviews*, 146.
52. *Interviews*, 146.
53. *Interviews*, 40.
54. *Interviews*, 56.
55. *Interviews*, 12.
56. *Interviews*, 56.
57. *FB*, 19/20.
58. *Interviews*, 198.
59. *Interviews*, 148.
60. *Interviews*, 148.
61. *Interviews*, 148.
62. *Interviews*, 172.
63. *Interviews*, 168 and 175, respectively.
64. *Interviews*, 176.

Conclusion

I have tried to unravel the thread of immanence as signalling the consistency of Deleuzian thought. I've pointed to this evasive quasi-concept as revealing the unthought of Deleuze's philosophy, and of philosophy as such. Throughout, immanence turned out to be something like a goal, and an ambition, which would set philosophy apart from onto-theology. Of thought, we can say that it exists on the basis of a horizon, or a presupposition, it cannot quite think, and the concept of which it cannot quite produce. Immanence is itself not a concept, but an image – an image without image – or a plane that is the condition of thought. There is, then, an unthinkable horizon of thought, something that thought inherits, as a task forever to be completed. Immanence is perhaps not what thought thinks, transitively as it were. It is perhaps not the object of thought, but its provenance. Philosophy does not so much think immanence as it thinks within it, and from it: *immanently*. Thought is referred back to immanence as to its own origin, as to this origin that it cannot ground, and in which it is ungrounded. At the same time, however, immanence turned out to be more than a goal or a horizon for philosophy, more, that is, than a regulative ideal. This is because immanence is itself real, or reality itself. It is nothing other than reality in the making. But this reality is not reducible to actuality: what is actual may be rational, as Hegel claimed, but reality is also virtual, and it is with virtual singularities that philosophy is concerned. As a result, to think immanently is to render thought immanent to reality, to its chaotic becoming, its variations, and its vibrations. It amounts to constructing an image of thought that is not posited in advance, independently of the real itself, and orienting it from the start, but that grows from within the real, or Being. Throughout, immanence designated the method as well as the content of thought, the manner in which thought must unfold as well as the matter from which it unfolds. It is this new 'image' which the concepts of structure, genesis, difference, expression, production, becoming, and body without organs, aimed to produce. At every stage, though, Deleuze felt the need to return his work to the loom, in what seemed like an endless effort. This is because immanence seemed to concede ground to transcendence as it was advancing, thus resembling Penelope's woof, which is undone as it is being woven. We realised that there is something like a natural inclination of thought towards transcendence, which Kant had already highlighted. Rather spontaneously, thought tends to reintroduce instances of transcendence, without which it believes it cannot operate: every field – ontology as such, logic, aesthetics, etc. – falls prey to transcendence. And we saw how, as it evolved, Deleuze's thought itself identified such tendencies in some of its own concepts and problematics, thus calling for further developments. *Difference and Repetition* and *Logic of Sense* may have marked an initial stage on the way to the conquest of immanence, and the uncovering of the world of anonymous, pre-individual and impersonal singularities. Ultimately, though, these singularities were only the sufficient reason of subjects and forms, of individuated substances and actual relations. The virtual remained caught within the logic of reason and ground, and so within the ground plan, the *Grundriss*, the design, and not the pure plane of immanence. Following Kant, let us call these residues of transcendence 'illusions'. Once more, we need to be cautious and precise, and emphasise that, contrary to what Kant believed, the ultimate source of this inclination is not thought itself, or reason, which Kant saw as separated from reality. Having posited that thought emerges from the real itself, it is the real as such that produces its own effects of transcendence, which are akin to surface or optical effects. The illusions of transcendence are physical, material illusions. Because they are real, and indeed actual, it is easy to understand why they can so easily be mistaken for the causes. As such, the task of overturning onto-theology amounts to relating the effects of transcendence back to their immanent cause, and not, as the metaphysics of representation and the ontology of analogy believe, to subordinate immanence to some instance of transcendence. Thinking with immanence, then, or thinking immanently, does not mean to eliminate all traces of transcendence. Like couch grass amongst flowers, transcendence grows rather spontaneously, on the back of immanence. There is a tendency of the real, which could be characterised as entropic, to develop intensities into extensities: concepts into opinions (or common sense), images into clichés, sensations into perception, etc. Everywhere immanence produces its effects of transcendence. We needn't worry too much, however, so long as we don't allow transcendence to overgrow and choke immanence. There always will be instances of transcendence, onto-theological or molar tendencies – mirages, if you prefer, in the double sense of illusions and temptations. What matters is that we don't allow philosophy to grow on them. It's a matter of probity. In the end, then, what matters is that the plane of transcendence is itself always traversed and deterritorialised by blocks of becoming, by indiscernible, molecular assemblages that compose an altogether different, heterogeneous reality, and which amount to inexhaustible opportunities for thought. It is with the idea of becoming, really – an idea already formulated in *Logic of Sense*, but taken to its full conclusion in *A Thousand Plateaus* – that thought finally connects with the plane of immanence. But even then, as we saw, transcendence doesn't disappear altogether. Ultimately, the plane of immanence, characterised by processes of involution, or pure becomings, can unfold only by presupposing a plane of organisation, ruled by functions and forms, and from which transcendence may grow. Similarly, the plane of transcendence, or analogy, however secure it may seem, is itself always shot through with processes it cannot control.

We are always, and simultaneously, then, on two planes at once – the plane of being and that of beings; the plane of free, untamed and raw matter, where free and mad particles assemble and separate almost immediately, and the plane of matter, which is organised, structured and fixated in rigid strata, molar entities and heavy assemblages. And yet, at every moment, the ballet of mad, submolecular particles goes on: they gravitate around, and traverse, the entire molar assemblage, opening it onto a line of flight, or an unsuspected becoming. We are always on two planes at once – or rather, in the Fold where the two meet. This is where genuine thought, whether philosophical, scientific, or artistic, resides. We never escape the ontological difference, and when we try to, it is in one of two ways: either through total destratification, deterritorialisation and absolute fluidity, or through absolute fixation, stratification and territorialisation. Thought needs to navigate between the Charybdis of pure becoming and the Scylla of solid being, between schizophrenia and paranoia, or fascism. This is where the life that we call human takes place: in the space between immanence and transcendence. This is where it creates its own concepts, affects, percepts and intensities of various kinds. A *single* life will never achieve immanence completely, and eradicate transcendence once and for all – not even that of Deleuze. Only *a* life, though, impersonal and anonymous, can achieve immanence, that is, plunge into the world of pure singularities and events,

Conclusion

expand and reinvent itself in the process. *My* life, or the life of those we refer to with proper names, are all instances of transcendence. The names we have encountered in the course of this book – Spinoza, Nietzsche, Artaud, Proust, Bacon – do not indicate a site and source of representation, however novel and imaginative, and rooted in the life they could call their own. Rather, they indicate the point at which *their* life becomes *a* life, and the illusion of transcendence dissolves into pure immanence. 'Immanence: *a* life' is Deleuze's last word on life, and his final celebration of it. In his wake, we need to find other ways of living immanence, of creating our own concepts and zones of intensity.

Bibliography

Works on Deleuze

Abou-Rihan, Fadi, *Deleuze and Guattari* (London & New York: Continuum, 2009).

Agamben, Giorgio, 'L'Immanence absolue', in Éric Alliez (ed.), *Gilles Deleuze. Une vie philosophique* (Le Plessis-Robinson: Institut Synthélabo, 1998).

Alliez, Éric, *La signature du monde* (Paris: Les éditions du Cerf, 1993).

Bachelard, Suzanne, *A Study of Husserl's Formal and Transcendental Logic*; translated by Lester E. Embree (Evanston: Northwestern University Press, 1968).

Badiou, Alain, *Deleuze. 'La clameur de l'être'* (Paris: Hachette, 1997).

de Beistegui, Miguel, *Truth and Genesis: Philosophy as Differential Ontology* (Bloomington & Indianapolis: Indiana University Press, 2004).

Bell, Jeffrey, *Philosophy at the Edge of Chaos: Gilles Deleuze and the Philosophy of Difference* (Toronto: Toronto University Press, 2006).

Bogue, Ronald, *Deleuze on Literature* (London: Routledge, 2003).

Bonta, Mark and Protevi, John, *Deleuze and Geophilosophy* (Edinburgh: Edinburgh University Press, 2004).

Bouaniche, Arnaud, *Gilles Deleuze, une introduction* (Paris: Pocket, 2007).

Boundas, Constantin (ed.), *Deleuze and Philosophy* (Edinburgh: Edinburgh University Press, 2006).

Bryant, Levi R., *Difference and Givenness: Deleuze's Transcendental Empiricism and the Ontology of Immanence* (Evanston: Northwestern University Press, 2008).

Buchanan, Ian, *Deleuze and Guattari's* Anti-Oedipus (London: Continuum, 2008).

Colebrook, Claire, *Deleuze: A Guide for the Perplexed* (London: Continuum, 2006).

DeLanda, Manuel, *Intensive Science and Virtual Philosophy* (London: Continuum, 2002).

—— 'Immanence and Transcendence in the Genesis of Form', in Ian Buchanan (ed.), *A Deleuzian Century* (Durham & London: Duke University Press, 1999), pp. 119–34.

Bibliography

Dosse, François, *Gilles Deleuze et Félix Guattari, bibliographie croisée* (Paris: Éditions La Découverte, 2007).
Due, Reidar Andres, *Deleuze* (Cambridge: Polity, 2007).
Hallward, Peter, *Out of this World: Deleuze and the Philosophy of Creation* (London: Verso, 2006).
Hardt, Michael, *Gilles Deleuze: An Apprenticeship in Philosophy* (Minneapolis: University of Minnesota Press, 1993).
Kerslake, Christian, *Deleuze and the Unconscious* (London: Continuum, 2007).
Lambert, Gregg, *Who's Afraid of Deleuze and Guattari* (London & New York: Continuum, 2006).
Montebello, Pierre, *Deleuze* (Paris: Vrin, 2008).
Prado, Bento Jr, 'Sur le "plan d'immanence"', in Éric Alliez (ed.), *Gilles Deleuze. Une vie philosophique* (Le Plessis-Robinson, Institut Synthélabo, 1998).
Toscano, Alberto, *The Theatre of Production: Philosophy and Individuation between Kant and Deleuze* (Basingstoke: Palgrave Macmillan, 2006).
Williams, James, *Gilles Deleuze's Difference and Repetition: A Critical Introduction* (Edinburgh: Edinburgh University Press, 2003).
—— *Gilles Deleuze's* Logic of Sense. *A Critical Introduction and Guide* (Edinburgh: Edinburgh University Press, 2008).

Other works

Artaud, Antonin, *Œuvres complètes* (Paris: Gallimard, 1974).
Bettelheim, Bruno, *The Empty Fortress* (New York: Free Press, 1967).
Blanchot, Maurice, *L'entretien infini* (Paris: Gallimard, 1969).
Blumberg, Albert E. and Feigl, Herbert Feigl, 'Logical Positivism. A New Movement in European Philosophy', *The Journal of Philosophy*, vol. XXVIII, no. 11, 21 May 1931, pp. 281–96.
Boethius, *The Consolation of Philosophy*, translated, with an introduction, by Victor Watts (London: Penguin, 1999).
Bloom, Allan, *The Republic of Plato* (New York: Basic Books, 1968).
Bréhier, Émile, *La Théorie des incorporels dans l'ancien stoïcisme* (Paris: Vrin, 1997).
Carnap, Rudolf, *The Logical Syntax of Language* (Vienna: Julius Springer, 1934).
Carrouges, Michel, *Les machines célibataires* (Paris: Arcanes, 1954).
Chiesa, Lorenzo, *Subjectivity and Otherness: A Philosophical Reading of Lacan* (Cambridge, MA: The MIT Press, 2007).
Cusanus, Nicolas, *Of Learned Ignorance*, translated by G. Heron (New Haven: Yale University Press, 1954).
—— *De Possest*, Latin text as contained in J. Hopkins, *A Concise*

Introduction to the Philosophy of Nicholas of Cusa (Minneapolis: Banning, third edition, 1986).
Descartes, René, *Œuvres et lettres* (Paris: Gallimard 'Bibliothèque de la Pléiade', 1953).
Diogenes Laertius, *Lives of Eminent Philosophers*, VII (Cambridge, MA: Harvard University Press, 1925). Greek text facing an English translation by Robert Drew Hicks. Reprint with an introduction by Herbert Strainge Long, 1972.
Foucault, Michel, *Les mots et les choses* (Paris: Gallimard, 1966).
Fraisse, Luc. *L'Œuvre cathédrale. Proust et l'architecture médiévale* (Paris: Librairie José Corti, 1990).
Frege, Gottlob, 'Logik [1897]', in *Nachgelassene Schriften*, edited by H. Hermes, F. Kambartel and F. Kaulbach (Hamburg: Felix Meiner, 1970); translated by P. Lang and R. White, 'Logic', in *Posthumous Writings* (Chicago: Chicago University Press, 1979).
—— 'Über Sinn und Bedeutung', in *Kleine Schriften*, edited by Ignacio Angelelli (Hildesheim: G. Olms, 1967); translated by Max Black et al. and edited by Brian McGuinness, 'On Sense and Meaning', in *Collected Papers on Mathematics, Logic, and Philosophy* (Oxford: Blackwell, 1984).
Freud, Sigmund, 'Psycho-analytic Notes on an Autobiographical Account of a Case of Paranoia (Dementia Paranoides)', *The Standard Edition of the Complete Works of Sigmund Freud*, Volume 12 (London: Vintage, 2001), pp. 9–82
—— 'The Unconscious', *Standard Edition*, 14, pp. 159–215.
—— 'The Ego and the Id', *Standard Edition*, 19, pp. 1–66.
—— *The Interpretation of Dreams*, *Standard Edition*, 4 and 5.
—— *Civilisation and its Discontents*, *Standard Edition*, 21, pp. 57–145.
de Gandillac, Maurice, *La Philosophie de Nicolas de Cues* (Paris: Aubier, 1942).
Gilson, Etienne, *L'Être et l'essence* (Paris: Vrin, 1948).
Girard, René, 'Delirium as System', translated by Paisley N. Livingston and Tobin Siebers in Gary Genosko (ed.), *Deleuze and Guattari: Critical Assessments of Leading Philosophers* (London: Routledge, 2001), pp. 679–712.
Hegel, Georg Wilhelm Friedrich, *Werke* (Frankfurt am Main: Suhrkamp Verlag, 1986).
Hocquenghem, Guy and Scherer, René, 'Co-ire', *Recherches*, no. 22 (1976), pp. 76–82.
Husserl, Edmund, *Formale und transzendentale Logik*, *Husserliana XVII* (The Hague: Nijhoff, 1974); translated by Dorion Cairns, *Formal and Transcendental Logic* (The Hague: Nijhoff, 1974).
—— *Ideen zu einer reinen Phänomenologie und phänomenologischen Philosophie, I. Buch: Allgemeine Einführung in die reine Phänomenologie,*

Bibliography

Husserliana III, edited by Karl Schuhmann (The Hague: Martnus Nijhoff, 1976); translated by F. Kersten, *Ideas Pertaining to a Pure Phenomenology and to a Phenomenological Philosophy, First Book, General Introduction to a Pure Phenomenology* (Dordrecht/Boston/London: Kluwer Academic Publishers, 1983).

—— *Erfahrung und Urteil*, edited by Ludwig Landgrebe (Hamburg: Claassen, 1954); translated by James S. Churchill and Karl Americks, *Experience and Judgement* (Evanston: Northwestern University Press, 1973).

Hyppolite, Jean, *Genèse et structure de la phénoménologie de l'esprit de Hegel* (Paris: Aubier, 1947); translated by Samuel Cherniak and John Heckman, *Genesis and Structure in Hegel's 'Phenomenology of Spirit'* (Evanston: Northwestern University Press, 1974).

—— *Logique et existence: Essai sur la logique de Hegel* (Paris: Aubier, 1952); translated by Leonard Lawlor and Amit Sen, *Logic and Existence* (Albany: SUNY Press, 1997).

Jung, Carl Gustav, *Symbole der Wandlung. Analyse des Vorspiels zu einer Schizophrenie* (Zurich: Rascher, 1952); translated by R. F. C. Hull, *Symbols of Transformation: An Analysis of a Prelude to a Case of Schizophrenia* (Princeton, NJ: Princeton University Press, 1956).

Kafka, Franz, *The Trial*, translated by Will and Edwin Muir (New York: Schocken Books, 1956).

Kant, Immanuel, *Critique of Pure Reason*, translated by Werner S. Pluhar (Indianapolis: Hackett, 1999).

—— *Critique of Practical Reason*, translated by Werner S. Pluhar (Indianapolis: Hackett, 2002).

Koyré, Alexandre, *Mystiques, spirituels, alchimistes du XVIème siècle allemand* (Paris: Armand Colin, 1947).

Lacoue-Labarthe, Philippe and Nancy, Jean-Luc, *L'absolu littéraire* (Paris: Éditions du Seuil, 1978).

Laplanche, Jean and Pontalis, Jean-Baptiste, *Vocabulaire de la psychanalyse* (Paris: Presses Universitaires de France, 1967).

Lévi-Strauss, Claude, 'Réponses à quelques questions', *Esprit*, 33:11 (1963).

Lipps, Theodor, *Ästhetik. Psychologie des Schönen und der Kunst* (Hamburg and Leipzig, 1903–1906).

Lyotard, Jean-François, *Discours, Figure* (Paris: Klincksieck, 1971).

Maldiney, Henri, *Art et Existence* (Paris: Klincksieck, 1985/2003).

Mandelbrot, Benoît, *Les objects fractals* (Paris: Flammarion, 1975).

Mondrian, Piet, 'Die neue Gestaltung in der Malerei', in Hans L. C. Jaffé (ed.), *Mondrian und De Stijl* (Köln: Dumont, 1967).

Negri, Antonio, *The Savage Anomaly: The Power of Spinoza's Metaphysics and Politics* (Minneapolis: University of Minnesota Press, 1991).

Nietzsche, Friedrich, *Selected Letters of Friedrich Nietzsche*, translated by Christopher Middleton (Chicago: University of Chicago Press, 1969).

Plato, *The Collected Dialogues*, edited by Edith Hamilton and Huntington Cairns (Princeton: Princeton University Press, 1961).
Plotinus, *Enneads*, translated by A. H. Armstrong (Cambridge, MA: Harvard University Press, Loeb Classical Library, 1984).
Proclus, *The Elements of Theology: A Revised Text with Translation, Introduction, and Commentary* by E. R. Dodds (Oxford: Clarendon Paperbacks, 1992).
Proust, Marcel, *À la recherche du temps perdu*, Jean-Yves Tadié, General Editor (Paris: Gallimard, 1989); *In Search of Lost Time*, Christopher Prendergast, General Editor (London: Penguin, 2002).
Quine, Willard van Orman, 'On What There Is', *The Review of Metaphysics*, II (1948).
—— *From a Logical Point of View* (Cambridge, MA: Harvard University Press, 1953).
Riegl, Aloïs, *Die spätrömische Kunstindustrie nach den Funden in Österreich-Ungarn* (Vienna, 1901); translated by R. Winkes, *Late Roman Art Industry* (Rome: Giorgio Bretschneider, 1985).
Rimbaud, Arthur, *Lettres de la vie littéraire d'Arthur Rimbaud* (Paris: L'imaginaire Gallimard, 1990).
—— *Œuvres poétiques* (Paris: Garnier Flammarion, 1964).
Russell, Bertrand, *Our Knowledge of the External World as a Field for Scientific Method in Philosophy* (London: George Allen & Unwin, 1914).
—— *An Inquiry into Meaning and Truth* (London: George Allen & Unwin, 1940).
Sartre, Jean-Paul, 'La Transcendance de l'Ego', in *Recherches philosophiques*, 1936–37, translated by F. Williams and R. Kirkpatrick, *The Transcendence of the Ego* (New York: Noonday Press, 1957).
Schilpp, Paul Arthur (ed.), *The Philosophy of Rudolf Carnap* (La Salle, IL: Open Court, 1963).
Schlegel, Friedrich, *Philosophical Fragments*, translated by Peter Firchow, with a Foreword by Rodolphe Gasché (Minneapolis: Minnesota University Press, 1991).
Schlick, Moritz, 'Die Wende der Philosophie', *Erkenntnis*, 1 (1930).
Sextus Empiricus, *Adversus mathematicos*, VIII, translated by R. G. Bury, *Against the Logicians* (Cambridge, MA: Harvard University Press, 1997).
Spinoza, *Complete Works*, edited, with introduction and notes, by Michael L. Morgan, translated by Samuel Shirley (Indianapolis & Cambridge: Hackett, 2002).
Stewart, Matthew, *The Courtier and the Heretic: Leibniz, Spinoza and the Fate of God in the Modern World* (New Haven & London: Yale University Press, 2005).
Sylvester, David, *Interviews with Francis Bacon* (London: Thames & Hudson, revised edition 1980).

Bibliography

Vernant, Jean-Pierre, *Les origines de la pensée grecque* (Paris: Quadrige/ PUF, 1995).

Wittgenstein, Ludwig, 'Logisch-philosophische Abhandlung', *Annalen der Naturphilosophie*, 1922, no. 14, pp. 185–62; translated by C. K. Ogden, *Tractatus Logico-Philosophicus* (London: Kegan Paul Trench Trubner, 1922).

Worringer, Wilhelm, *Abstraktion und Einfühlung* (Munich: R. Piper & Co. Verlag, 1921); translated by Michael Bullock, *Abstraction and Empathy* (London: Routledge & Kegan Paul, 1958).

—— *Formprobleme der Gothik* (Munich: R. Piper & Co. Verlag, 1927); translated, with an Introduction, by Herbert Read, *Form in Gothic* (London: G. P. Putnam's Sons, 1927).

Index

absurd, 88f
actual, actualisation, 26, 36, 41, 48, 50ff, 60, 62, 63, 72n, 73n, 88, 94, 96, 97, 107, 113, 130, 192, 193
affects, 8, 55, 61, 63, 64, 68, 71, 99, 100, 106ff, 124, 160, 174, 183, 194
Agamben, Giorgio, 14
Althusser, Louis, 59
analogy, 20, 34, 35, 39, 42, 49, 53, 64, 66, 75n, 150, 181, 193, 194; *see also* resemblance
Anaximander, 19
Anaximenes, 19
anorganic, 64, 69, 171, 173, 174
appearance, 26, 40, 52; and art, 182, 183
Aquinas, Thomas, 34
arborescent, arborescence, versus rhizomatic, 67
Aristotle, 42, 64, 83, 93, 94; Aristotelian, Aristotelianism, 8, 30, 31, 34, 64, 91, 92, 93, 152n
Arnauld, Antoine, 45n
art, artistic, ix, 1, 38, 48, 54, 58f, 65, 71f, 73n, 75n, 122, 147, 160–85, 190n, 191n, 194; figurative, 174ff; abstract, 172, 174ff, 184
Artaud, Antonin, 97, 99, 100, 115, 116, 123, 124, 130, 145ff, 174, 181, 195
attributes, 34ff, 46n; and sense, 92ff

Bacon, Francis, 73n, 115, 160, 164, 172–85, 190n, 195
Badiou, Alain, 53, 72n
bad will (*mauvaise volonté*), 8, 10
Beckett, Samuel, 147
becoming(s), ix, x, 3, 25, 42, 48, 49, 59, 60, 69ff, 93, 94, 95, 129, 131, 145, 148, 149, 150, 151, 156n, 157n, 173, 177, 179, 186, 192, 194
being, ix, 9, 15, 16, 19, 25, 28ff, 40ff, 45n, 47ff, 60, 66, 70, 72n, 92, 93, 94, 103n, 105, 106, 129, 135, 144, 176, 192, 194
Bentham, Jeremy, 121
Bergson, Henri, 6, 42, 46n, 48, 53, 70, 72n, 130, 152n; Bergsonism, 63, 153n
Bettelheim, Bruno, 157n
biology, biological, 53f, 63ff, 73n, 74n, 130, 134, 135, 146
Blanchot, Maurice, 188n
Bleuler, Eugen, 145
Blumberg, Albert, 79, 104n
body, bodies, 24, 58, 61, 64f, 90, 92, 94, 98–100, 107ff, 123, 124, 127, 128, 143, 148, 150, 151, 153n, 156n, 169, 170ff, 181, 184ff, 190n; of the earth, 56
body without organs (BwO), 55, 56, 58ff, 68ff, 97, 99, 123ff, 145, 150, 151, 152n, 160, 170, 171, 181, 190n, 192
Boethius, 37

203

Borromini, Francesco, 180
Bréhier, Émile, 92
Bruno, 37f
Burri, Alberto, 172, 179

capital, capitalist, 68, 116, 125, 127, 142
Capitalism and Schizophrenia, 1, 116, 117, 156
Carnap, Rudolf, 79, 86, 102n
Carroll, Lewis, 89, 90, 91, 97f, 100, 116
Carrouges, Michel, 154n
castration, 115, 137ff, 147, 149
categories, 6, 25, 72, 83, 93
causality, 28, 30, 32f, 35ff, 92, 98, 107, 108, 110f, 113, 118f, 120, 125, 193; immanent, 28, 30, 33, 35ff, 39, 125, 193
celibate machine, 127, 129, 154n
Cézanne, Paul, 173
chaos, 62, 69ff, 164, 171, 172, 179; chaosmos, 171
Cicero, 152n
cinema, 1, 72n, 115, 166, 189n
cogito, 9, 10, 15, 22n, 24
common notions, 111, 113
communication, theory of, 7
complication, 37–9, 59, 165, 188n
conatus, 47, 106, 109ff; desire as, 114
concealment (*Verborgenheit*), 52
concept(s), 3, 5ff, 16ff, 22n, 24, 25, 27ff, 42, 47, 48, 55, 70, 71, 73n, 80, 83, 87, 94, 103n, 142, 160, 161, 192ff; *see also* philosophy
conceptual character(s), 7, 8, 56
conjunction, *see* consumption
connection, 50, 51, 64, 70; connective synthesis, 123ff, 132, 151, 153n
consciousness, 14, 15, 24, 72n, 84, 86, 87, 94, 96, 107, 114, 118, 135, 142, 152n

consumption, synthesis of, 127, 128, 129
contemplation, theories of, 7
Cuvier, Georges, 63

Damascius, 37
death drive, instinct, 70, 123, 124, 130, 131, 151
deconstruction, 140
deformation, 164, 177, 182, 183, 184, 186
DeLanda, Manuel, 57f, 73n
democracy, and philosophy, 7, 18f
denotation, 79ff, 87, 88, 92, 98, 138
Derrida, Jacques, 1, 26, 43n, 52
Descartes, René, 9, 10, 13, 15, 17, 21n, 22n, 30, 35, 45n, 79, 107
desire, 47, 60, 66, 72, 88, 108, 110, 111, 113–53, 153n, 168–70
desiring-machines, 123ff, 132, 145, 152
desiring-production, 133, 139
De Stijl, 178
destratification, 49, 56, 59, 67, 69, 70, 173, 194
deterritorialisation, 56, 67, 97, 148, 152, 152n, 194
dialectic, dialectical, 25, 26f, 43n, 53, 54, 119, 127, 133, 135, 137, 167, 189n
difference, ix, 26f, 40–3, 43n, 47, 50ff, 60, 87, 88, 90, 96, 130, 131, 166, 192; and differentiation, 26, 37, 40, 50, 53, 54, 69, 94, 170, 173; and differenciation, 26, 41, 53, 54, 60; and different/ciation, 40, 41, 43, 61, 63
differential, 26, 27, 41, 50, 51, 54, 59, 87, 88, 90
Diogenes Laertius, 91, 92
Dionysian, versus Apollonian, 96
disjointed, disjointedness (*décousu*), 166f

Index

disjunctive synthesis, 125, 126, 132, 153n
disorganisation, 55, 59, 73n, 128, 151, 164, 171, 179, 181, 186, 190n
doxa, 7, 16, 86
dramatisation, 40, 122
Dubuffet, Jean, 179
duration, 70, 163

earth, 19, 55, 56, 60, 62
ego, 86, 129ff, 135, 137, 140, 145, 146, 151, 160
élan vital, 176
emanation, 30–4, 35, 37, 38, 39, 107, 125, 187
eminence, 34, 35, 36, 39, 45n, 53, 107
emotions, 106, 108, 109, 111, 129, 152n; *see also* affects
empathy, and art, 174, 175, 176, 179, 180
empirical, 6, 14, 29, 30, 50, 78, 82, 84, 88, 92, 96, 119, 120
empiricism, 6, 13, 14, 15, 55, 96, 120; *see* logical empiricism; transcendental empiricism
ethics, 1, 46n, 48, 55, 60, 105–50, 155n
ethology, 64, 105, 107, 172
event(s), 2, 3, 5, 6, 16, 18, 20, 21n, 51, 52, 63, 64, 67, 71, 75, 87, 93ff, 104n, 129, 130, 138, 174, 194
evolution, 49, 57f, 63; in Lacan, 134
exogenesis, exogenetic, 13, 16
experience, ix, 2, 6, 14f, 20n, 29, 30, 47, 48, 54, 55, 69, 72, 78, 82, 85, 86, 97, 98, 104n, 106, 111ff, 118ff, 128, 129, 131, 137, 144, 145, 147f, 148, 150, 160, 174, 175, 176, 179, 180

explication, 34, 37–9, 50, 59, 106, 165
expression, 30, 33ff, 40ff, 55, 60, 61, 62, 69, 105, 106, 114, 115, 122, 125, 141, 142, 152n, 165, 175, 180, 192; and the operation of sense, 77, 81, 86, 87, 94, 97, 98, 102n, 116
extension, 54; as attribute in Spinoza, 37
extensity, extensities, 27, 54, 61, 114, 129, 193

fantasy, fantasies, 60, 114, 131, 132, 139, 146, 147, 149, 151, 153n
Feigl, Herbert, 79, 101n, 104n
figure(s), figural, in painting, 173, 174, 181, 185, 186, 189n; versus the figurative, figuration, 172, 173, 174, 179, 183, 184, 189n
floating signifier, 89, 90
Flournoy, Théodore, 148
flow(s), 42, 49, 56, 60, 62, 117, 123, 124, 131, 152n, 173, 174, 179, 181, 186
fold, folding, 58, 59, 69, 96, 194
Foucault, Michel, 43n, 59, 88, 91, 142f
fractal(s), 63, 74n
Francis, Sam, 179
Frege, Gottlob, 78, 79, 80, 91, 92, 100n
Freud, Sigmund, 98, 115, 121, 122, 124, 126, 127, 130ff, 145, 146, 155n
friend, friendship, 7, 8, 18, 19, 21n

genesis, ix, x, 15, 26, 32, 40, 42, 43n, 47ff, 59ff, 73n, 75n, 81, 86, 87, 88, 102n, 192; *see also* exogenesis; ontogenesis

Geoffroy Saint-Hilaire, Étienne, 63, 64, 75n
German Romanticism, 188n, 189n
Gilson, Étienne, 45 n 28
God, 15, 24, 28, 30, 34ff, 45n, 48, 55, 56, 65, 69f, 77, 94, 106, 108, 110, 111, 122, 126, 127, 128, 143, 181, 187
Greek philosophy, 7, 8, 18–20
Guattari, Félix, 5, 8, 10, 12, 18, 20, 48, 56, 57, 58, 60, 62, 63, 64, 67, 68, 70, 71, 73n, 74n, 113–18, 121–8, 130, 132–4, 138–41, 144–6, 149, 150, 152n, 154n, 156n, 173
guilt, 111, 112, 114, 138ff

Habermas, Jürgen, 7
haecceities, 55, 67, 68, 174
haptic plane, 177, 184, 190n
Hegel, G. W. F., 9, 13, 22n, 24ff, 43n, 44n, 127, 135, 141, 192; Hegelian, Hegelianism, 13, 25, 43n, 59, 103n, 133
Heidegger, Martin, ix, 42, 52
Hobbes, Thomas, 143, 152n
Hocquenghem, Guy, 150, 157n
Hölderlin, Friedrich, 20
Homer, 188n
Hume, David, 85
Husserl, Edmund, 14, 15, 77, 81–7
Hyppolite, Jean, 25, 43n, 59

idealism, ix, 6, 13, 14, 16, 51, 55, 96, 115, 122, 133, 134, 152n, 174, 186
ideas, 6, 7, 13, 50, 51, 63, 108, 111, 113, 118, 152n
identity, 14, 25, 26, 41, 42, 54, 83, 86, 96, 131
illusions, 10, 20, 24–7, 112, 119, 120, 121, 134, 140, 175, 190, 193, 194, 195

image(s), 2, 7, 8–20, 21n, 22n, 24, 50, 70, 72n, 81, 86, 87, 88, 114, 136ff, 144, 156n, 172, 176, 183, 189n, 192, 193
immanent, immanence, x, 5, 7, 12ff, 20n, 22n, 24ff, 33, 35ff, 46, 48ff, 59, 60, 64, 66, 69, 70, 71, 74n, 77, 82, 87, 94ff, 105, 107, 110ff, 128, 132, 133, 141ff, 151, 176, 181, 192ff; causality, 28, 30, 33ff, 125, 193; *see also* plane of immanence
implication, 37–9, 80, 138, 164, 165, 188n
individuation, 14, 26, 40ff, 50, 52, 54, 60, 64, 71, 73n, 74n, 87, 95, 96, 113, 193
intensity, intensities, 27, 41, 48, 50, 54ff, 60ff, 67ff, 114, 128ff, 146ff, 160, 172ff, 179, 181, 183, 184, 187, 193ff
intentionality, 84ff, 102n, 120
intuition, x, 3, 6, 9, 11, 40, 119
involution, 39, 47, 49, 63, 98, 150, 194

Jakobson, Roman, 134
joy, 107, 109ff, 151, 168, 180
Judeo-Christianity, 20, 120
Jung, Carl, 145, 148, 149, 153n
justice, 142

Kafka, Franz, 115, 141ff
Kandinsky, Wassily, 178
Kant, Immanuel, 6, 7, 14, 15, 21n, 24, 29, 30, 48, 107, 118ff, 193; Kantian, 24, 40, 102n, 121, 144, 171, 174
Klein, Melanie, 145; Kleinian, 123
Kojève, Alexandre, 43n, 135; Kojèvian, 133
Koyré, Alexandre, 37

Index

Lacan, Jacques, 52, 59, 89, 99, 116, 130, 132ff, 155n, 156n; Lacanian, 115, 127, 133, 139, 140, 154n
lack, and desire, 60, 114, 120, 121, 122, 132, 134ff, 142, 144, 145, 147, 148, 151, 156n
Laplanche, Jean, 153n
Lautman, Albert, 74n
law, 114, 115, 134, 136ff, 147, 155n
Leibniz, G. W., 94
Levinas, Emmanuel, 106, 128
Lévi-Strauss, Claude, 59, 89, 134, 137, 138
libido, libidinal, 65, 123, 124, 126, 131ff
life, 24, 31, 54ff, 62, 63, 65, 71, 73n, 86, 87, 96, 112ff, 122, 124, 128ff, 144, 145, 150, 151, 173ff, 184, 185, 190n, 191n, 194f; *see also* anorganic
life-world, 86
lines of flight, 67, 143, 148, 149, 152, 156n, 1
linguistic turn, 78
Lipps, Theodor, 174f
literature, ix, 1, 59, 114, 122, 160, 161, 170, 172
logical empiricism, 77, 78, 79, 82, 84, 95; *see also* logical positivism
logical positivism, 78–82, 86, 95, 101n, 104n; *see also* logical empiricism
love, as affect, 8, 111, 131
Lyotard, Jean-François, 173, 189n

madness, 69, 71, 100, 145, 146, 171, 172
Maldiney, Henri, 156n, 178, 190n
Malevich, Kazimir, 178
Mandelbrot, Benoît, 74n
manifestation, 52, 53, 80ff, 87, 98

Marx, Karl, 121, 128; Marxism, 122
masochism, masochistic, 61, 142, 149, 151,
materialism, ix, 51, 64, 65, 73n, 115, 118, 123, 133
mathematics, mathematical, 53f, 63, 78, 82f, 87, 178
matter, ix, 19, 42, 55, 56, 59, 60, 62, 64, 69, 124, 129, 131, 145, 146, 173, 179, 192, 194
May '68, 116f
memory, 65, 131,
Merleau-Ponty, Maurice, 85
metaphor, 53, 122, 149, 150; and metonymy in Proust, 170f, 182
metaphysics, 11, 34, 78, 105, 107, 118, 140, 193
metonymy, 169–72
miraculation, miraculating machines, 126, 127, 128
mode(s), 28, 29, 34ff, 41, 105ff, 143, 149
Mondrian, Piet, 178
monism, 16, 25
morality, distinct from ethics, 105ff
moral law, 105, 119, 121, 143
morphogenesis, 74n
multiplicity, 26, 50, 51, 55, 63, 67, 74n, 75n, 93, 166, 168, 170; virtual, 50
music, 54, 58f, 114

naturalism, 64; in art, 175, 176, 178
natural law, 105, 110, 112, 119, 137, 142, 143, 144, 152n
nature, ix, 19, 27, 30, 36, 41, 47ff, 55, 59, 60, 61, 65, 66, 67, 108, 110, 114, 115, 121, 122, 134, 137, 143, 144, 176ff
negative theology, 35, 39
negativity, 25, 26, 27, 34, 60, 103n, 135, 138, 145, 147; *see also* lack

207

Nerval, Gérard de, 126, 151
Neurath, Otto, 100n
neurosis, neurotic, 55, 115, 126, 131, 141, 145, 146
Nicholas of Cusa, 37f, 106
Nietzsche, Friedrich, 13, 17, 21n, 42, 54, 77, 106, 112, 146, 151, 156n, 195; Nietzschean, 22n, 106, 112, 153n
nomad, nomadic, 56, 60, 96; neonomadism, 67
non-being, 26, 103n
nonsense, *see* sense
Numen, 126

Oedipus, 115, 118, 126, 127, 132ff, 139, 140, 143, 144, 145, 149; Oedipal triangle, 122
One, the, 27, 31ff, 45n, 105
ontogenesis, ix, 40, 42, 48, 55, 59, 60, 74n, 102n, 113
ontological difference, ix, 194
ontology, ix, 1, 16, 20, 29, 30, 33, 34, 35, 40, 41, 42, 43n, 47ff, 55, 59, 60, 61, 83, 95, 96, 102n, 193; and ethics, 105–17, 121, 143
onto-theology, 20, 34, 77, 94, 105, 107, 192ff; *see also* emanation
organicity, 124, 162, 170, 171, 172, 176, 180, 181
organisation, organised, 49ff, 55, 56, 59ff, 69, 70, 113, 123, 128, 143, 145, 151, 161, 164, 166, 170, 172, 174, 181, 184, 186, 190n, 194; *see also* plane of organisation and development
organism(s), 53, 57, 58, 61ff, 69, 70, 73n, 74n, 75n, 99, 123, 124, 128, 130, 145, 150f, 164, 166, 173, 175, 181
Oury, Jean, 156n

painting, 11, 114, 160, 164, 170, 172ff, 190n

Pankow, Gisela, 156n
pantheism, 35, 39
paranoia, 115, 124ff, 140, 145, 146, 148, 151, 155n, 194
Parmenides, 41; Plato's, 31, 33
partial objects, 123, 153n
passion(s), 90, 98, 99; and ethics, 107ff
perception, percepts, 55, 71, 72, 85, 113, 115, 160, 170, 174, 177, 181, 183, 184, 186, 190n, 193, 194
phallus, 130, 135ff, 147, 154n
phenomenology, 14, 24, 84, 87, 120
philosophy, as the creation of concepts, 5–12, 17, 18, 24, 47; task of, 17, 24, 59, 78; Greek, 7ff, 18–20; philosophers, 7, 8, 9, 10, 18, 19, 21n, 28, 39, 47, 117, 121, 129
plane (*plan*), 3, 8–12, 48f, 162; of immanence, consistency, x, 10, 12, 14, 16ff, 22n, 24, 25, 28, 29, 47, 48, 49, 53, 55, 58ff, 71, 72n, 74n, 75n, 113, 161, 193, 194; of organisation and development, 49–59, 62, 66, 67, 68, 73n, 75n, 161, 194; of transcendence, 10, 19, 53, 75n, 115, 134, 194; *see also* immanence; transcendence
Plato, 21n, 31, 44n, 167, 178; Platonism, 6, 31, 33, 34, 92, 94, 152n; Neoplatonism, 30, 31, 32, 33, 36, 37, 38, 39, 46n, 165
pleasure, 119, 120, 121, 128, 130, 151, 175
Plotinus, 7, 31, 32, 33, 45n
Poe, Edgar Allan, 89, 142
Pollock, Jackson, 172, 179
Pontalis, Jean-Bertrand, 153n
Popper, Karl, 101n

Index

portmanteau words, 89, 97, 98
power, 32, 36, 37, 64f, 69, 92, 105ff, 114, 115, 118, 121, 141–4, 151, 152n, 153n, 171
problems, as events, 51–5
Proclus, 32, 45n
production, 2, 32, 37, 43, 47, 53, 95, 114, 115, 122ff, 132, 133, 139, 142, 144ff, 148, 149, 152n, 192
Proust, Marcel, 1, 8, 13, 17, 21n, 49, 54, 59, 65, 73n, 75n, 115, 145, 155n, 160–72, 182, 186, 187, 188n, 195; Proustian world, 38, 39
psychoanalysis, 115ff, 127, 130ff, 139ff, 155n
psychosis, psychotic, 126, 145

Quine, W. V. O., 103n

real, the, 13, 14, 15, 20n, 22n, 26, 27, 29, 50, 51, 52, 53, 55, 59, 64, 82, 96, 112, 114, 116, 139, 144, 145, 151, 192, 193; reality, 13, 26, 27, 28, 29, 69, 78ff, 95, 96, 108, 114, 115, 116, 122, 128, 142, 144, 146, 147, 150, 166, 170, 171, 174, 179, 182, 183, 184, 187, 192, 194
realism, 186, 187
reason, 111, 112, 113, 118, 119, 120, 144, 171, 193
recording, 125ff, 182ff
religion, 19, 20, 139, 140
Renaissance philosophy, 37, 39, 165
representation, 16, 25, 40, 68, 70, 91, 115, 118ff, 129, 132, 133, 144ff, 152n, 174, 175, 177, 178, 179, 181, 185, 186, 189n, 191n, 193, 195
resemblance, 14, 15, 29, 39, 51, 149, 181, 182, 185; *see also* analogy
resentment, *ressentiment*, 112, 114
reterritorialisation, 68, 148

rhizome(s), 67, 164; rhizomatic, 123, 149, 171
Riegl, Aloïs, 175ff, 184, 190n
Rimbaud, Arthur, 174, 187, 190n
Rorty, Richard, 7
Russell, Bertrand, 78, 81

Sacher-Masoch, Leopold von, 115
sadness, 110ff; and hate, 111
Sartre, Jean-Paul, 14, 15, 87, 145
Saussure, Ferdinand de, 91
Schérer, René, 150, 157n
schizoanalysis, 55, 115, 118, 130, 138–50
schizophrenia, schizophrenic, 55, 61, 69, 97ff, 115ff, 141, 145ff, 154n, 156n, 160, 194
Schlegel, Friedrich, 188n
Schlick, Moritz, 100n
science, ix, 1, 11, 34, 71, 73n, 78, 79, 82, 83, 84, 86, 88, 100n, 102n
Scotus, John Duns, 35, 45n
sedimentation, 56–8
sensation, 173, 174, 175, 180ff, 193; plane of, 183, 184
sense, 21n, 25, 47, 59, 77–100, 101n, 102n, 116, 138; common sense, 10, 16, 86, 193; good sense, 10, 16, 86, 96; nonsense, 78, 88, 89, 90, 91, 95, 97, 98, 99, 100, 103n
sensible, 6, 13, 31, 32, 38, 39, 53, 119, 120, 178; provokes thought, 59
Sextus Empiricus, 91
signification, 55, 70, 87ff; logical, 80ff, 98, 101n, 102n; Lacanian, 138, 139
Signifier (Name-of-the-Father), 136, 137, 140, 149
Simondon, Gilbert, 73n, 74n, 130
singularities, 26, 41, 47, 48, 50, 53, 55, 56, 60, 62, 65, 74n, 87, 94ff, 192–4

209

smooth space, 62, 67, 68, 75n, 173, 174
Socrates, 44n, 45n, 96
Spinoza, Baruch, 1, 27ff, 40ff, 44n, 47, 54, 60, 61, 63, 64, 95, 105ff, 114, 117, 121, 123, 126, 142, 143, 145, 152n, 165, 172, 195; Spinozist, Spinozism, 27, 35, 36, 55, 61, 64, 115, 116, 152, 152n, 153
Stockhausen, Karlheinz, 59
Stoics, Stoicism, 91ff, 103n, 152n
strata, 56, 59, 62, 67, 68, 69, 70, 73n, 173, 194; stratification, 49, 55ff, 62, 69, 70, 73, 194
striated space, 67, 68, 74n, 173, 185
structuralism, 59, 87, 88, 97, 98, 116, 138, 140
substance, 16, 27, 28, 29, 31, 34ff, 41, 42, 47, 61, 62, 65, 77, 86, 94, 95, 105ff, 114, 121, 149
sufficient reason, 39, 49, 50, 53, 54, 193
superego, 124, 132, 137, 138, 140
symbolic object, 52, 114, 130
syntheses, of desire or the unconscious, 118–30, 132, 152n

Tapiès, Antoni, 172, 179
territoriality, territorialisation, 56, 194
Thales, 19
time, 38, 42, 51, 54, 92, 93f, 130, 131, 163; time-space, 27
topology, 63, 74n, 88, 138, 139, 150
Tosquelles, François, 156n
transcendence, 6, 14, 15, 17, 19, 20, 24, 25, 27, 28, 33, 34, 39, 47, 48, 51, 52, 53, 58, 66, 77, 94, 106, 111, 112, 113, 121, 137, 138ff, 144, 145, 150, 156n, 180, 193, 194, 195; *see also* plane of transcendence

transcendental, transcendentalism, 6, 14, 15, 24, 27, 29, 30, 42, 43, 47, 48, 50, 82ff, 88, 96, 97, 102n, 115, 118, 120, 121, 129, 134, 138, 145, 148, 151; consciousness, subjectivity, 24, 84, 135; empiricism, 6, 14, 15, 20n, 25, 29, 48, 55, 77, 113, 120; field, ix, 14, 15, 29, 47, 50, 53, 86, 87, 102n, 113, 133; logic, 77, 82–7, 138; unconscious, 118, 144
trans-descendence, 52
truth, ix, 7, 8, 9, 13, 16, 19, 21n, 22n, 26, 78–2, 97, 100, 177, 182, 183, 187

Uexküll, Jakob von, 64
unconscious, 66, 86f, 96, 114ff, 118–30, 132–52, 153n
univocal, univocity, 1, 20, 27ff, 40ff, 49, 59, 62, 64, 66, 94, 95, 116
unthought, 3, 10, 18, 24, 86, 192

Van Gogh, Vincent, 187
Velasquez, Diego, 185, 186
Vermeer, Johannes, 166, 187
Vernant, Jean-Pierre, 19
Vienna Circle, 78–2
virtual, 3, 26, 27, 41, 42, 43n, 48, 50ff, 59, 60, 62, 64, 65, 72n, 73n, 75n, 87, 88, 89, 91, 96, 97, 113, 130, 149, 150, 162, 163, 181, 192, 193
vitalism, 174

Welles, Orson, 189n
Wittgenstein, Ludwig, 78, 79, 80, 95, 100n, 104n
Worringer, Wilhelm, 174ff, 184, 190n

zone of vicinity, proximity, 150

IMMANENCE – DELEUZE AND PHILOSOPHY
is part of
PLATEAUS – NEW DIRECTIONS IN DELEUZE STUDIES

Other Titles from this Series

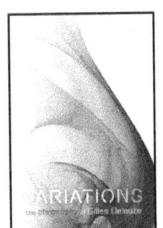

VARIATIONS: THE PHILOSOPHY OF GILLES DELEUZE
By Jean-Clet Martin
Translated by Constantin V. Boundas & Susan Dyrkton
Publication: April 2010, ISBN: 978 0 7486 3882 6

An insightful reading of Deleuze, from a fellow philosopher with whom Deleuze himself corresponded about his work.

POSTCOLONIAL AGENCY: CRITIQUE AND CONSTRUCTIVISM
By Simone Bignall
Publication: May 2010, ISBN: 978 0 7486 3943 4

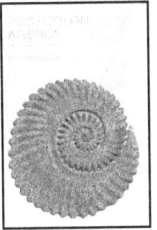

Uses Deleuzian thought to come to a significantly new understanding of the struggles faced by many societies in the aftermath of empire.

DELEUZIAN FABULATION AND THE SCARS OF HISTORY
By Ronald Bogue
Publication: July 2010, ISBN: 978 0 7486 4131 4

Proposes a newly formulated theory of fabulation as the guiding principle of a Deleuzian approach to literary narrative.

BADIOU AND DELEUZE READ LITERATURE
By Jean-Jacques Lecercle
Publication: July 2010, ISBN: 978 0 7486 3800 0

Assesses and contrasts the reading styles of two major French philosophers, Alain Badiou and Gilles Deleuze.

SEE THE FULL SERIES AT WWW.EUPPUBLISHING.COM/SERIES/PLAT

EUP JOURNALS ONLINE
Deleuze Studies

Now three issues per year

Editor
Ian Buchanan, *Cardiff University*
Executive Editor
David Savat, *University of Western Australia*
Reviews Editor
John Marks, *University of Nottingham*
Co-editors
Claire Colebrook, Penn State
Tom Conley, Harvard University
Gary Genosko, Lakehead University
Christian Kerslake, Middlesex University
Gregg Lambert, Syracuse University

Deleuze Studies is the first paper based journal to focus exclusively on the work of Gilles Deleuze. Published triannually, and edited by a team of highly respected Deleuze scholars, *Deleuze Studies* is a forum for new work on the writings of Gilles Deleuze.

Deleuze Studies is a bold journal that challenges orthodoxies, encourages debate, invites controversy, seeks new applications, proposes new interpretations, and above all make new connections between scholars and ideas in the field. The journal publishes a wide variety of scholarly work on Gilles Deleuze, including articles that focus directly on his work, but also critical reviews of the field, as well as new translations and annotated bibliographies. It does not limit itself to any one field: it is neither a philosophy journal, nor a literature journal, nor a cultural studies journal, but all three and more.

A 2010 subscription will include a free supplementary issue of the journal, *Deleuze and Political Activism*, guest-edited by Marcelo Svirsky.

ISSN 1750-2241   eISSN 1755-1684   Three issues per year

Register to receive Table of Contents Alerts at www.eupjournals.com

EU representative:
Easy Access System Europe
Mustamäe tee 50, 10621 Tallinn, Estonia
Gpsr.requests@easproject.com

www.ingramcontent.com/pod-product-compliance
Lightning Source LLC
Chambersburg PA
CBHW061713300426
44115CB00014B/2671